Transdisciplinary Perspectives on Risk Management and Cyber Intelligence

Luisa Dall'Acqua
University of Bologna, Italy & LS TCO, Italy

Irene Maria Gironacci
Swinburne University of Technology, Australia

A volume in the Advances in
Information Security, Privacy, and
Ethics (AISPE) Book Series

Published in the United States of America by
    IGI Global
    Information Science Reference (an imprint of IGI Global)
    701 E. Chocolate Avenue
    Hershey PA, USA 17033
    Tel: 717-533-8845
    Fax: 717-533-8661
    E-mail: cust@igi-global.com
    Web site: http://www.igi-global.com

Library of Congress Cataloging-in-Publication Data

Names: Dall'Acqua, Luisa, 1962- editor. | Gironacci, Irene M., 1988-
  editor.
Title: Transdisciplinary perspectives on risk management and cyber
  intelligence / Luisa Dall'Acqua and Irene Maria Gironacci, editors.
Description: Hershey, PA : Information Science Reference, an imprint of IGI
  Global, [2021] | Includes bibliographical references and index. |
  Summary: "This book explores perspectives and approaches to the
  intelligence analysis and risk management"-- Provided by publisher.
Identifiers: LCCN 2020006980 (print) | LCCN 2020006981 (ebook) | ISBN
  9781799843399 (hardcover) | ISBN 9781799854876 (paperback) | ISBN
  9781799843405 (ebook)
Subjects: LCSH: Cyber intelligence (Computer security) | Risk management. |
  Cyberterrorism.
Classification: LCC QA76.9.A25 T727 2021 (print) | LCC QA76.9.A25 (ebook)
  | DDC 005.8--dc23
LC record available at https://lccn.loc.gov/2020006980
LC ebook record available at https://lccn.loc.gov/2020006981

This book is published in the IGI Global book series Advances in Information Security and Privacy (AISP) (ISSN: pending; eISSN: pending)

British Cataloguing in Publication Data
A Cataloguing in Publication record for this book is available from the British Library.

All work contributed to this book is new, previously-unpublished material.
The views expressed in this book are those of the authors, but not necessarily of the publisher.

For electronic access to this publication, please contact: eresources@igi-global.com.

Advances in Information Security, Privacy, and Ethics (AISPE) Book Series

ISSN:1948-9730
EISSN:1948-9749

Editor-in-Chief: Manish Gupta, State University of New York, USA

MISSION

As digital technologies become more pervasive in everyday life and the Internet is utilized in ever increasing ways by both private and public entities, concern over digital threats becomes more prevalent.

The **Advances in Information Security, Privacy, & Ethics (AISPE) Book Series** provides cutting-edge research on the protection and misuse of information and technology across various industries and settings. Comprised of scholarly research on topics such as identity management, cryptography, system security, authentication, and data protection, this book series is ideal for reference by IT professionals, academicians, and upper-level students.

COVERAGE

- Global Privacy Concerns
- Internet Governance
- Tracking Cookies
- Device Fingerprinting
- Cyberethics
- Privacy Issues of Social Networking
- CIA Triad of Information Security
- Security Classifications
- Data Storage of Minors
- Access Control

IGI Global is currently accepting manuscripts for publication within this series. To submit a proposal for a volume in this series, please contact our Acquisition Editors at Acquisitions@igi-global.com or visit: http://www.igi-global.com/publish/.

Titles in this Series

For a list of additional titles in this series, please visit:
https://www.igi-global.com/book-series/advances-information-security-privacy-ethics/37157

Privacy Concerns Surrounding Personal Information Sharing on Health and Fitness Mobile Apps
Devjani Sen (Algonquin College, Canada) and Rukhsana Ahmed (University at Albany, SUNY, USA)
Information Science Reference • © 2021 • 300pp • H/C (ISBN: 9781799834878) • US $215.00

Establishing Cyber Security Programs Through the Community Cyber Security Maturity Model (CCSMM)
Gregory B. White (CIAS, The University of Texas at San Antonio, USA) and Natalie Sjelin (CIAS, The University of Texas at San Antonio, USA)
Information Science Reference • © 2021 • 221pp • H/C (ISBN: 9781799844716) • US $195.00

Applied Approach to Privacy and Security for the Internet of Things
Parag Chatterjee (National Technological University, Argentina & University of the Republic, Uruguay) Emmanuel Benoist (Bern University of Applied Sciences, Switzerland) and Asoke Nath (St. Xavier's College, Kolkata, India)
Information Science Reference • © 2020 • 295pp • H/C (ISBN: 9781799824442) • US $235.00

Advanced Localization Algorithms for Wireless Sensor Networks
M. Vasim Babu (Institute of Technology and Sciences, India)
Information Science Reference • © 2020 • 300pp • H/C (ISBN: 9781799837336) • US $195.00

Social, Legal, and Ethical Implications of IoT, Cloud, and Edge Computing Technologies
Gianluca Cornetta (Universidad CEU San Pablo, Spain) Abdellah Touhafi (Vrije Universiteit Brussel, Belgium) and Gabriel-Miro Muntean (Dublin City University, Ireland)
Information Science Reference • © 2020 • 333pp • H/C (ISBN: 9781799838173) • US $215.00

701 East Chocolate Avenue, Hershey, PA 17033, USA
Tel: 717-533-8845 x100 • Fax: 717-533-8661
E-Mail: cust@igi-global.com • www.igi-global.com

Editorial Advisory Board

Table of Contents

Section 1
Strategies

Section 2
Technologies

Section 3
Study Cases

Detailed Table of Contents

Section 1
Strategies

Chapter 1

Luisa Dall'Acqua, University of Bologna, Italy & LS TCO, Italy

Intelligence analysts are a task force of experts in the field of politics, economics, technology, military, and terrorism analysis. They possess the knowledge, sufficient capacity for imagination, and creativity to relate data predict events. The intelligence approach (basically) tries to reduce the uncertainty of this analysis to forecast the future without being privy to alternatives in the minds of policy decision makers. This chapter intends to describe a new interpretative socio-cognitive paradigm, Orientism, to understand and manage the fluid nature of knowledge, but at the same time to seize and manage the unpredictability and risks of dynamics of risk decision management in relationships complex environment. The new elements are five key factors and criteria to direct and motivate people in the choosing process and following 10 different and key relationships between them.

Chapter 2

Amitabh Anand, SKEMA Business School, Universitie Cote d'Azur,
France & GREDEG, France
Giulia Mantovani, University of Bologna, Italy

To tackle the phenomenon of terrorism, especially the attacks carried out by homegrown terrorists, since 2005 all the EU's member states have adopted the Global Strategy to Combat Terrorism. Focusing on four pillars (prevention, protection, persecution, and response), the strategy provides for security measures to protect against terrorism as a criminal act. What if, instead, we consider terrorism as a social phenomenon, strictly connected to radicalization and resulting from discriminatory experiences and discomfort young second generation immigrants suffer within the European society? Moving in this direction, through the application of the PESTLE analysis to the specific context of Belgium, this study elaborates a counterterrorism policy which takes into account the root and activating factors of radicalization by filling Belgium's gaps in terms of integration policies and which could help reducing the likelihood of occurring radicalization and terrorist attacks episodes.

Cognitive bias among workers can undermine security work and lead to critical misinterpretations of data. Understanding cognitive biases can improve understanding of how employees make decisions. This work analyzes key factors to better understand, predict, and obviate the detrimental bias symptoms, focusing on groupthink and polythink phenomena occurring in security and business decisions. It intends to provide support for the strategic versus tactical hypothesis in a strategic group decision-making, confirming how even in a clear-cut decision, following a groupthink or polythink dynamic, implementation becomes difficult due to a group dynamics at the other end of the decision-making continuum.

This work focused on the method of analysis, to be understood in general terms and following the intelligence cycle as developed by various international realities, with possible variations. This method was exposed, also graphically, before going further into the details of the different phases or the acquisition, processing of data, and news for subsequent dissemination. These procedures have been described in practical terms and from a distinctly private perspective, also providing the necessary connections with the figures responsible for their development up to the description and requirements that the information product must satisfy, also in this case from a customer's perspective.

The notion of the innovation system is connected to the role of leaders and decision makers in the management of the scientific and technological environment. Innovative frameworks of analysis, by approaching science and technology systemically (i.e., in relation to the economy, politics, and society), adapt stress for success. Any research and innovation policy must take account of a complex set of problems. The focus of this work is to analyze the application of tactical strategies in the risk management, looking at the historical ninja training. Their worldview, the "way of the warrior" as an art of war but also as a path of inner knowledge, has also had great importance in artistic production, culture, and the construction of social relations.

Chapter 6

The private information analysis is strictly inherent to the protection of corporate interests. This generally means protecting the company from fraud, theft of industrial secrets, and intellectual capital as well as protecting its cyber architecture. The tasks are delicate and suited to the various corporate interests. This information work would usefully be placed in the national intelligence context by providing a precious link between the national security services and the company itself, to which such an adhesion would be difficult to guarantee in any other way.

Section 2
Technologies

According to various surveys conducted, regardless of how many studies in software development projects have been done, the chance that software development projects may fail remains very high. A relatively new approach to the problem of failure is using the concept of artificial intelligence (AI) to help automate a certain part(s) of the projects in order to minimize the issue. Unfortunately, most of the works proposed to date use AI as a standalone system, which leads to limiting the degree of automation that the overall system can benefit from the technology. This chapter discusses a preliminary work on a novel risk monitoring, which utilizes a number of agent-based systems that cooperate with each other in minimizing risks for the projects. The proposed model not only leads to a high degree of automation in risk management, but this extensible model also allows additional tasks in risk monitoring to be easily added and automated if required.

Over the past years, extended reality (XR) technologies, such as virtual, augmented, and mixed reality, have become more popular in business. Through immersive extended reality experiences, businesses of all shapes and sizes are waking up to the possibilities of using this emerging technology to create new opportunities and support their digital transformation. The aim of this chapter is to present the state of the art of extended reality devices, tools, and applications currently available.

Chapter 9

Artificial intelligence technologies are currently at the core of many sectors and industries—from cyber security to healthcare—and also have the power to influence the governance of domestic industry, the security and privacy citizens. In particular, the rise of new machine learning methods, such as those used in recommendation systems, provides many opportunities in terms of personalization. Big players like YouTube, Amazon, Netflix, Spotify, and many others are currently using recommendation systems to improve their business. Recommender systems are critical in some industries as they can generate income and provide a way to stand out from competitors. In this chapter, a literature review of recommendation systems is presented, as well as the application of recommendation systems in industry.

Chapter 10

At this time of digital, social, technological, and economic transformation driven by increasing diversity and inequality in the world, it is worthwhile to question from new theoretical discussion the individual and collective relationship that we have with the technological world around us, going to the roots of our interactions with technology. This chapter questions our capacity to perform individual and collective agentic learning relationship as in an increasingly technological society. Research questions in this chapter are: How do we deal with augmented and emerging interactions with increasingly complex material and virtual objects? What are the learning implications of a posthumanism deeply embedded with technology?

Chapter 11

Origin of Cyber Warfare and How the Espionage Changed: A Historical
Maria Luisa Nardi, Independent Researcher, Italy

International politics is faced with new and vital issues, linked to aspects such as individual rights, the holding of democracy, the effects of worldwide policies, as well as the geopolitics of technology. The intertwining of technology and international relations is now a fact. Exploring the new and different political challenges posed by new technologies is a factor of transformation of the global society that influence on its actors. Today, an application of technological innovation, digital technology, and artificial intelligence is a steady political field. The focus of this work is to describe over time the notion of information warfare, which has matured and manifested into a form that has a colossal impact on how the contemporary wars are fought, but this has also resulted in the downgrading of strategic side of information warfare or cyber warfare to a decisive tactical force multiplier capable of turning the tides in war.

Section 3
Study Cases

Chapter 12

General George S. Patton and Our Climate Crisis: The Stories People Need –
John Thomas Riley, The Big Moon Dig, USA

The story of General Patton at the Battle of the Bulge is an excellent example of a story with a message that can be applied to our climate crisis. Our climate crisis is the defining problem for human society in the 21st century. Although the current situation is chaotic, as in this story, several positive paths are now clear enough to allow useful plans for a worldwide effort. One alternative to fear is to build a vision of a viable future through stories. Stories have a long history of being a common tool for building unified societal efforts. The stories that society now needs require both a science-based background and believable characters in effective action on our climate crisis. The elements used to build stories, first the background and then the plot, are called beats. The background beats developed here include sea level rise, no-till farming, population peaking, and technology innovation for the period 2020 to 2100. These beats should enable fiction writers to place stories and characters in a world of action on our climate crisis.

Chapter 13

Lobbying a Crucial Mechanism for NGOs to Obtain Funding for Poverty
Idahosa Igbinakhase, University of KwaZulu-Natal, South Africa
Vannie Naidoo, University of KwaZulu-Natal, South Africa
Thea van der Westhuizen, University of KwaZulu-Natal, South Africa

The need to unravel the organizational capabilities of youth-serving NGOs that may influence the replication of successful programmes designed to empower poor youths in order to make these programmes accessible to more youths and more geographical locations has motivated this study. This chapter will highlight the crucial role lobbying plays for NGOs in their efforts to obtain funding for poverty alleviation programs in Nigeria. Lobbying challenges experienced by youth-serving NGOs and factors that influence lobbying capabilities will be also be unpacked and discussed. A quantitative study was conducted on 196 youth-serving NGOs in Nigeria. Simple random sampling was used to collect data. This chapter will highlight the crucial role lobbying plays for NGOs in efforts to obtain funding for poverty alleviation programs. The results of the study indicated that lobbying is an important organizational capability for youth-serving NGOs in their bid to alleviate youth poverty in Nigeria.

Chapter 14

"How dare you!" was the opening line 16-year-old Greta Thunberg used in her address to world leaders at the United Nation Global Summit on Climate Change. This young woman demanded global political and business leaders to listen to her plea, as she firmly believes global systems are in crisis and politicians and business persons alike are not playing their part to resolve our people, planet, and profit crisis. Student protests in response to leadership in higher education institutions have become a generic form of expressing discontent. In a quantitative investigation, this study assessed student perceptions regarding higher education leadership in relation to three core leadership capabilities: a strategic approach, communication and collaboration, and institutional drivers and results. Data collection from students in their final year was done using a combination of simple and stratified sampling. SPSS version 25 was used for data analysis. Findings reiterated a current dichotomy and urge the need for social cohesion between student and university leadership.

Preface

State secrecy, military secrecy, investigative secrecy, office secrecy, banking secrecy, industrial secrecy, are only a part of the institutional obstacles set on the government road of free information, and therefore of the knowledge of public affairs. Knowledge is the true basis of national power.

Intelligence Analysts are experts in the field of analysis (politics, economics, technology, military, terrorism) who possesses knowledge, sufficient capacity for imagination and creativity to relate data, predicts events. They are increasingly requested by the institutional apparatus responsible for national security and public security, by companies, by public and private research centers, and by the armed forces. Specifically:

- Tactical intelligence provides analysis, maps, and data to support an operation or disaster response effort, and fulfilling short term, case-specific needs
- Strategic intelligence takes a "big picture" view of competitor/criminal/ terrorist activity. It focuses on the long-term aims of law enforcement agencies, and, in a criminal context, on crime environment, threats to public safety and order, counter programs, avenues for change to policies, programs, and legislation.
- Operational intelligence typically provides an investigative team with hypotheses and inferences concerning specific elements of illegal operations of any sort. These will include criminal networks, individuals or groups involved in unlawful activities, as well as methods, capabilities, vulnerabilities, limitations and intentions

Intelligence disciplines are rarely completely independent of each other, and their definitions are sometimes driven more by the unique regulatory authorities of intelligence collection agencies than by distinct differences between the collection methods or the material itself.

Today, intelligence research is highly fragmented and distributed across over a dozen disciplines, each leading to theories and empirical findings about specific aspects of intelligence. In addition to economic and institutional problems, it's an issue the accountability and politicization of Intelligence Analyst's activity, and the absence of tuning between Intelligence outcomes and decision-makers actions.

Specifically, Leadership Analysts support policymakers by producing and delivering assessments of foreign leaders and key decision-makers, by examining their worldviews, national ambitions and constraints, and the social context of these leaders. This type of analysts comes from the fields of social psychology and political science and takes a quantitative methodology when conducting analysis. In addition, they can explore quantitative measures such as verbal styles, grammatical choices, and scales for achievement, affiliation, and power provide room for analysis.

On another hand, industrial espionage refers to illegal efforts to collect information about technologies, industries or patents for example. In contrast to corporate espionage, industrial espionage as a term refers to government-sponsored espionage rather than enterprises' own espionage to boost competitiveness. One of the biggest problems concerns incentives for businesses to finance investments in threat prevention and in creating a culture of resilience.

A 21st century approach to decision making requires evaluating new and better methods to measure what matters, diagnosing strengths and weaknesses throughout the process, improving decision maker performance, and involving multiple stakeholders in the process. designing, conducting and conducting it. Numerous issues relating to risk management and assessment have emerged in an increasingly integrated and interconnected global context where each connection is called upon to play a central role in order to improve various aspects of overall safety.

With the rapid spread of information and communication technology worldwide, cyber crime appears to be a potential threat for confidential computer data and systems. Technologically advanced countries like the United States are also victim of this crime.

But new technologies are also an added value to the decision-making and analysis process. They increase awareness in security, including simulation of scenarios involving virtual people and objects. For instance, a simulator can be potentially used to simulate a cyber-attack as well as business training use cases. A possible improvement to this simulator could be the inclusion of artificial intelligence to propose a scenario to the user is also being heavily considered. In the future, the automatic suggestion of a scenario would make the program more efficient in terms of goals achieving. As well as, a comprehensive analysis of countries' vulnerability to 5G related security threats could be a topic for further research.

One of the most important security problems is the warming artic. There is a massive amount of methane frozen in the artic as permafrost and in sub-sea ice. The artic is currently the fastest warming area. If it runs away, then the Earth will simply move to the hothouse mode.

The issue concerns not only safety but also connection between all institutions and governments in a prevention and safeguard actions. And AI (Artificial Intelligence) is likely to be a major factor in addressing our climate crisis. It is a new tool just when we need new tools. A good example of tools is IceSat-1 and IceSat-2. These two satellites measured the thickness of the Greenland Ice sheet from orbit. The National Geospatial-Intelligence Agency (NGA) is already well equipped—in terms of software and expertise—to find intelligence value in this information.

HOW THIS BOOK WORKS

This book proposes a transdisciplinary research, enabling progress towards a complete understanding of intelligence analysis, risk management and applied technology. The proposed Science of Intelligence aims to establish intelligence research as a unified scientific discipline. Furthermore, The book analyzes the concept of threat vs risk, focusing on possible risks identification criteria and the main analytical approaches for the risk management.

A specific sector of application is Security Intelligence, and the book aims to provide a theoretical foundation and empirical support for analyzing the development of a range of techniques (and useful technologies) in this sector.

The analysis consists of key issues, problems, trends, and particularly new emerging ideas and innovation Furthermore, it investigates questions, explanations of terms and concepts in order to probe further thinking.

This comprehensive and timely publication aims to be an essential reference source, building on the available studies on developing 'instruments of analysis' to train managers, analysts, politicians, and researchers. That mains a collective resource with comprehensive knowledge in the development of managerial and intelligence analysis competency, including industries, academics (researchers, lecturers, and advanced students), professional institutions and Governative Departments.

The book consists of three sections and 14 chapters. The first section focuses on some crucial strategies to Intelligence Analysis and decision-making process; the second one focuses on new challenges and technologies to support this process; the last one is a collection of a few study cases to improve the analysis according to several and different points of view.

A brief description of each chapters follows:

SECTION 1: STRATEGIES

Chapter 1: Cognitive Science, Orientism Management (OM), and Intelligence Analysis

This chapter is a review of human factors related to intelligence analysis research and presents multiple cognitive challenges, by an interpretation of a knowledge management framework to improve intelligence analysis quality by reducing the negative impact of cognitive biases. Intelligence approach (basically) try to reduce the uncertainty of this analysis to forecast the future without being privy to alternatives in the minds of policy decision-makers. Specifically, this chapter intends to describe a new interpretative socio-cognitive paradigm, Orientism, to understand and manage the fluid nature of knowledge, but at the same time to seize and manage the unpredictability and risks of dynamics of risk decision management in relationships complex environment. New elements are 5 key factors and criteria to direct and motivate people in the choosing process and following 10 different and key relationships between them.

Chapter 2: Homegrown Terrorism – An Analysis of Its Effects on PESTLE Factors

The chapter, through a simple and smooth language, applies in an innovative way a widely used method in the economic world: the PESTLE analysis. The authors, by acting as if they were managers, thanks to the PESTLE analysis isolated those economic, political and social variables that have proven to be the radicalization engines of young second generation Muslims in Europe, in particular in Belgium, and they propose an alternative counterterrorism strategy which focuses on the reduction of the likelihood of a successful terrorist attack and on the amount of converted individuals. On this basis, "Homegrown Terrorism: an Analysis of its Effects on PESTLE Factors" represents a starting point for the development of a European counter-terrorism strategy which, together with the national strategies, could improve and strengthen the international cooperation in this field, thus bringing to light through the use of the PESTLE analysis those factors that are common to all radicalization and homegrown terrorism's phenomena within European nations.

Chapter 3: Exploring Cognitive Biases, Groupthink, and Polythink Syndrome in Security Decisions and Business Outcomes

A group decision-making dynamic is based on different members in a decision-making unit espouse a plurality of opinions and offer divergent policy prescriptions, which can result in intragroup conflict, a disjointed decision-making process, and decision paralysis as each group member pushes for his or her preferred policy action. Cognitive bias among workers can undermine security work and lead to critical misinterpretations of data, warns. Understanding cognitive biases can improve understanding of how employees make decisions. This work analyzes key factors to better understand, predict, and obviate the detrimental bias symptoms, focusing on groupthink and polythink phenomena occurring in security and business decisions. It intends to provide support for the strategic versus tactical hypothesis in a strategic group decision-making, confirming how even in a clear-cut decision, following a groupthink or polythink dynamic, implementation becomes difficult due to a group dynamic at the other end of the decision-making continuum.

Chapter 4: Intel Cycle for Private Professionals – Acquisition, Management, and Dissemination of Information

Intel cycle is a powerful tool for implementing and obtaining information results from an organized system that could be built inside a private organization or bought as a product from intelligence professionals. Being adapted to a private environment such as a business in quite every type of commercial aims, intel cycle needs to be performed differently from what could be usual in a public organization or in a military operation. The chapter describes the key-points where doctrinal assumptions could be wrong and how the entire cycle should be applied to obtain information from data that are commonly around business areas and for this reason some principles are the same of business intelligence. Acquisition and management are also described with a particular focus on how an out-sourced professional could work in a compatible way with every type of company needing information for its decision-making process

Chapter 5: Tactical Art of Risk Management in the History of Ninja

The notion of innovation system is connected to the role of leaders and decision-makers in the management of the scientific and technological environment. Innovative frameworks of analysis, by approaching science and technology systemically (i.e. in relation to the economy, politics, and society), adapt stress for success. Any research and innovation policy must take account of a complex set of problems. The focus of this work is to analyze the application of tactical strategies in the risk management, looking at the historical ninja training. The jobs of a ninja are divided into the two main categories of performing espionage and strategy. Espionage is similar to the job of modern spies, wherein one carefully gathers intelligence about the enemy and analyzes its military strength.

Chapter 6: Private Intel for Corporate Protection

As a matter of fact, private companies that work in a global economy need to protect their interests in a very dynamic business environment and many risks that few decades ago were limited to big multinational holding are now to be taken in consideration even for small groups selling their products online or needing to travel in other countries. The chapter is about how private intel could perform better than the government in adherence with the risks that a company should work with selling its products. Moreover, every paragraph is about the most frequent crimes that could be performed against corporate interests. Fraud, theft of industrial secrets, cyber-attacks and assault to foreign representations require delicate tasks that should be analyzed in consideration of safeguarding the economic affairs and linking the protection of the business with national interests. The output would be a useful cooperation in a challenging world.

SECTION 2: TECHNOLOGIES

Chapter 7: Agent-Based Approach for Monitoring Risks in Software Development Projects

According to various surveys conducted, regardless of how much researches in software development projects have been done, the chance that software development projects may fail is remain very high. A relatively new approach to the problem of failure is by using concept of Artificial Intelligence (AI) to help automate a certain part(s) of the projects in order to minimize the issue. Unfortunately, most of the works proposed to date use AI as stand-alone system, which lead to limiting degree of automation that the overall system can benefit from the technology. This chapter discusses a novel risk management model, which utilize a number of agent-based AI systems that cooperating with each other in minimizing risks for the projects. The proposed model not only leads to high degree of automation in risk management, but this extensible model also allows additional tasks in risk management to be easily added and automated, if required.

Chapter 8: State of the Art of Extended Reality Tools and Applications in Business

This chapter describes the main Extended Reality technologies nowadays available (Virtual Reality, Augmented Reality, Mixed Reality) and how these technologies can be applied to business. Furthermore, a list of state of the art Extended Reality devices currently available as well as a comparison of these devices using validated metrics. Finally, some use cases of Extended Reality application developed and used in several industries is presented. This chapter aims to be a useful guide to the readers towards the potential of such technologies.

Chapter 9: Literature Review of Recommendation Systems

This chapter provides and overview on Recommendation Systems, a specific field of Artificial Intelligence commonly used to provide recommendation of items to the user using a variety of recommendation approaches: collaborative filtering-based recommendation (collection of data from similar users to the target user), content-based recommendation (collection of data from keywords related to items). The chapter then illustrates examples of existing recommendation systems in literature, and finally presents state of the art recommendation systems in Business.

Chapter 10: Augmented and Emerging Transformative Interactions With Technology – Learning in Post Humanism

The everyday meaning of the term 'technology' itself has morphed so quickly in recent years that it has become virtually synonymous with the digital technologies transforming patterns of human life globally. Currently a part of the community of researchers in psychology engages in evaluating and analyzing these technologies in people's lives: the intertwining of psychology and technology is gaining considerable space. Terminology like Humanism, Transhumanism and Hyper humanism (Post-humanism) and link with Intelligence Augmentation emerge in the actuality. This chapter explores Intelligence Augmentation as part of a complete understanding of intelligence analysis.

Chapter 11: Origin of Cyber Warfare and How the Espionage Changed – A Historical Overview

Today, an application of technological innovation, digital technology and artificial intelligence are a steady political field. Nascent threats like transnational cyber terrorism and information warfare exist alongside the positive aspects of globalization. The focus of this work is to describe over time the notion of information warfare, which has matured and manifested into a form which has a colossal impact on how the contemporary wars are fought, but this has also resulted in the downgrading of strategic side of information warfare or cyber warfare to a decisive tactical force multiplier capable of turning the tides in war. Exploring the new and different political challenges posed by new technologies is a factor of transformation of the global society, that influence on its actors.

SECTION 3: STUDY CASES

Chapter 12: General George S. Patton and Our Climate Crisis – The Stories People Need: Building New Myths for a Sustainable Earth

In a report, released by the "National Security, Military and Intelligence Panel (NSMIP)" of the Center for Climate and Security, experts warned of *High-to-Catastrophic* threats to security from climate change. The panel analyzed the globe by the Center for Climate and Security (CCS), an institute of the Council on Strategic Risks (CSR), in partnership with the Henry M. Jackson Foundation (HMJ) and the Environmental and Energy Study Institute (EESI). NASA, and particularly at the Goddard Space Flight Center in Maryland, builds and flies scientific instruments for space that monitor parameters critical to our climate crisis. An important lesson about today's climate crisis can be taken from General Patten's response to the Battle of the Bulge. Detailed planning started the moment a crisis is identified may save the day when the need for action becomes widely understood. Society is at a similar point with our climate crisis. The problem is well understood by specialist but the public is not yet ready for the massive action required. Current efforts to build resolve have been based on technical presentations and rising fear. These have not been successful. An alternative is to generate stories, especially for young people, about a future of adventure where believable characters take on real problems and persevere. Writing such stories will require both technical expertise to envision the near future under challenging conditions and the ability to write. These skills are rarely found together. The bulk of the chapter is then technical descriptions of what is likely to happen matched with resulting story elements, hopefully to help this process along

Chapter 13: Lobbying a Crucial Mechanism for NGOs to Obtain Funding for Poverty Alleviation Programs in Africa

Nigeria is one of Africa's biggest developing nations in the African continent, which has a growing youth population. Nigeria is facing a serious crisis due to the prevailing increase in youth poverty. The state of increasing poor youths in Nigeria is causing concern despite efforts by youth-serving NGOs to bring respite to the youth through various youth poverty alleviation programs. This chapter highlights the crucial role lobbying plays for NGO's in their efforts to obtain funding for poverty alleviation programs in Nigeria. Lobbying challenges experienced by youth-serving NGOs and factors that influence lobbying capabilities are also unpacked and discussed.

Chapter 14: Dichotomy and Violent Student Protests – Perceptions From Students

Student protests in response to leadership in higher education institutions have become a generic form of expressing discontent. In a quantitative investigation, this chapter assesses student perceptions regarding higher education leadership in relation to three core leadership capabilities: a strategic approach, communication and collaboration, and institutional drivers and results.

Luisa Dall'Acqua
University of Bologna, Italy & LS TCO, Italy

Irene Maria Gironacci
Swinburne University of Technology, Australia

Acknowledgment

We would like to acknowledge the help of all the people involved in this project. Without their support, this book would not have become a reality.

A special thank is for Eng. John Tom Riley (The Big Moon Dig, USA), Dr. Varsha PS (Visvesvaraya Technological University Belagavi, Karnataka) and Dr. John Paez (Universidad Distrital "Francisco Jose de Caldas", Colomba) regarding their in-depth and fine-tuning analysis of reviewed chapters.

We wish to acknowledge the very valuable help and encouragement I received from my Colleagues and friends. Most of the authors also served as referees; I highly appreciate their double task.

A special thank is for the students of Luisa dall'Acqua at the University of Bologna (Italy), regarding their hard work to test laboratories and to review the proposed literature.

We wish to place on record our deep appreciation and thanks to IGI Global Assistant Development Editors for their support, cooperation and attention to detail to bring out the publication of this book in time.

Lastly, we wish to thank our families for the understanding and support in providing us with all the necessary facilities to enable us to complete our work and above all, we are immensely thankful to the Almighty.

University of Bologna, Italy & LS TCO, Italy

Irene Maria Gironacci
Swinburne University of Technology, Australia

Section 1
Strategies

Chapter 1
Cognitive Science, Orientism Management (OM), and Intelligence Analysis

Luisa Dall'Acqua
University of Bologna, Italy & LS TCO, Italy

ABSTRACT

Intelligence analysts are a task force of experts in the field of politics, economics, technology, military, and terrorism analysis. They possess the knowledge, sufficient capacity for imagination, and creativity to relate data predict events. The intelligence approach (basically) tries to reduce the uncertainty of this analysis to forecast the future without being privy to alternatives in the minds of policy decision makers. This chapter intends to describe a new interpretative socio-cognitive paradigm, Orientism, to understand and manage the fluid nature of knowledge, but at the same time to seize and manage the unpredictability and risks of dynamics of risk decision management in relationships complex environment. The new elements are five key factors and criteria to direct and motivate people in the choosing process and following 10 different and key relationships between them.

INTRODUCTION

A long tradition of studies analyzed the risk components (i.e. logical-probabilistic, cognitive, regulatory, socio-systemic, and socio-cultural), inherent in a decision-making process. The multiple variables, able to cause an unstable condition of unpredictability in a decision-making process, found a catalytic function of

DOI: 10.4018/978-1-7998-4339-9.ch001

management in the information factor, or factor 'k', in the regulatory role of external agents (social environment) and the cooperation between action makers.

Worldwide Analysts have common problems and similar challenges, such as:

- Understanding and interpretation of information by management of intelligence
- Competition with media and other information brokers who communicate and disseminate information on world events instantaneously
- Overabundance of information
- Level of knowledge and application of technical analysis, scientific methodologies, tools, techniques, for different contexts, "clients" and intelligence products
- The effective use of the analysis in the decision-making process
- Intelligence estimable to design future developments, allowing the development of strategic plans

Richard Betts (2007) has made the greatest contributions to shifting the evaluative metric from the unattainable ideal of accuracy to something more realistic with his argument that intelligence failures, consisting of either inaccuracy or surprise, are inevitable. Betts' argument is a sophisticated one which acknowledges that

The Analyst is a real *risk manager* that establishes proceedings towards analysis, design, development, and evaluation of decision-making effects. The paradigm requires a *complex decision screenplay* (scenario): a macro project (about operation modes), a micro project (about contents and activities types), and scripts of activity sequences.

He designs in phases and dynamic structures, deciding on

- *Declarative knowledge*, which describes "how things are", in a format that may be manipulated, decomposed and analyzed by its reasoners. Declarative knowledge tends to be flexible and broadly applicable
- *Procedural knowledge*, is related to the procedure how to perform actions. Procedural knowledge tends to be more fluent and automatic
- *Propositional thoughts*, which translates experience into knowledge semantics
- *Mental images*, which can recognize and identify the information retained. It allows "factual knowledge", an important skill area for a self-managing set of attitudes and behaviors
- *Narrative thought,* able to interpret own experience, comparing it with the experience of others.

State-of-the-art ICT-enabled knowledge management environments provide an advanced experience where team-works are lead figures, and their human knowledge behaviors, cognitive preferences, and human characteristics are recognized, considered, monitored, recorded, and modeled. This facilitates the capability to personalize, adapt, and improve the knowledge management processes in tune with individual preferences, characteristics, and preferred learning styles/habits.

Personal Knowledge Management (PKM) is an open question about what is the PKM roles and values in different individual, organization, and social context. The main related literature by different scholars provides insight into the definition and nature of PKM. A valuable synthesis of the more significant designs is the conceptual model of PKM 2.0,

developed by Cheong & Tsui (2010). Authors reviewed the results of a global survey about the roles and values of the main PKM frameworks (Cheong&Tsui, 2010): from mere individual activities to outcome/impact-oriented; from information handling skills to personal competencies, sensemaking, and self-reflection; from individually focused to a community and social collaborative focused.

This evolution led. towards the design of a comprehensive PKM model that encapsulates the need for personal information management, knowledge internalization, transferring of knowledge and knowledge creation, and learning, Key identified issue remains an alignment of the appropriate technologies. The outcome was the definition of four core components of PKM: Personal Information Management (PIM), Personal Knowledge Internalisation (PKI), Personal Wisdom Creation (PCW), and Inter-Personal Knowledge Transferring (IKT). The PKM 2.0 framework focuses on both individual and interpersonal interactions (Cheong&Tsui, 2011)

Methods, strategies, and tools to support, enhance, adapt and personalize the knowledge processes to make the action makers aware and having control, step by step, of their own decisional path, are a challenge for designers and trainers. Quoting Goldsmith: *We're trying to manage something-knowledge-that is inherently invisible, incapable of being quantified, and borne in relationships, not statistics […] Our most important work is to pay serious attention to what we always want to ignore: the human dimension* (Goldsmith, et al., 2004, 57).

Between others, we focus on those who propose active roles of the agents – e,g. ASSURE, a model designed for knowledge managers. It incorporates Gagné's (Gagnè, 1985) events of instruction to assure effective use of media in instruction (Marschark et al. 2002) – and in a network of connections – e.g. the PENTHA ID model (acronym of Personalization, Environment, Network, Tutoring/Training, Hypermedia, Activity), which focuses on dynamic relationships and patterns among "complex agents" in the knowledge management process, rather than the static properties of isolated objects (dall'Acqua, 2011).

This analysis refers to the Orientism Management (OM) concept (dall'Acqua, Md Santo, 2014) to describe the decision-making under risk. The focus of the OM is specifically to orient people to manage decisions in unpredictability conditions in a multi-user environment context. It intends to propose a new solution to the demand for "innovative and creative decision-making" to make choices, to open to the change of perspective, to manage relationships and complex environments, basing on the conception of a new model of behavior and management of the simultaneity of how people process information.

The Orientism framework proposes a new scenario of activities, to improve the people's ability to contextual changes in natural-, social-, artificial multi-user environments, with multiple reference points and multi-interpreting paradigms. Furthermore, it proposes a new solution to the demand for "innovative, creative, and leadership" education to make choices, to manage their own life, relationships, and complex environments.

The model is based on intertwined 10 Knowledge Managements typologies, each based on areas of development and improvement of own personal leadership. In a corporate politics perspective, Orientism Management becomes OMS (Orientism Management Strategy), OMP (Orientism Processes Organization), and OMT (Orientism Management Tools).

INTELIGENCE ANALYSIS CYCLE

Intelligence Analysts are a task force of experts in the field of politics, economics, technology, military, terrorism analysis. They possess the knowledge, sufficient capacity for imagination, and creativity to relate data, predict events. They are increasingly requested by the institutional apparatus responsible for national security and public security by companies, by public and private research centers, by the armed forces. Specifically:

- **Strategic intelligence** takes a "big picture" view of competitor/criminal/terrorist activity. It focuses on the long-term aims of law enforcement agencies, and, in a criminal context, on
- Crime environment
- Threats to public safety and order
- Counter programmes
- Avenues for change to policies, programmes, and legislation.
- **Tactical intelligence** provides analysis, maps, and data to support an operation or disaster response effort, and fulfilling short term, case-specific needs

- **Operational intelligence** typically provides an investigative team with hypotheses and inferences concerning specific elements of illegal operations of any sort. These will include criminal networks, individuals or groups involved in unlawful activities

The complex phases, in which the information security activity is articulated, are called **"Intelligence Cycle"**: it consists of 6 standard steps, that raw data and information valued-added intelligence, methods, capabilities, vulnerabilities, limitations and intentions

Figure 1. Analyst's role

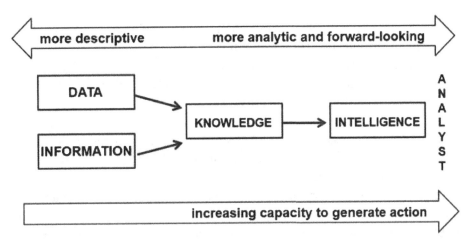

The Intelligence Analyst participates in the cycle at various points:

- In the obvious phase of **analysis** and **reporting**
- In the **data collection phase** determining the type of information necessary for that specific problem
- In the **planning phase**, determining the type of analysis required

The intelligence cycle drives the day-to-day activities of the intelligence community (IC). It is a cycle because there is no solution of continuity between the response to needs the new request for information deriving from the previous elaboration.

Planning and direction. The intelligence cycle is caused by a management decision. the products of intelligence analysis can assist in developing strategic plans

Figure 2. Classical intelligence cycle
(*Source: dall'Acqua, 2019*)

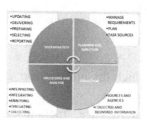

to tackle current problems and to prepare for anticipating ones. The contribution to the problem situations should be:

- Problem (or opportunity) identification (Problem finding)
- Problem classification (Problem setting)
- Problem decomposition (Problem analysis)
- From not programmed to programmed problems (refined problem analysis)
- Problem ownership (accountability)

Collection management is the process that aligns intelligence needs with information collection and processing capabilities, and assets within the various intelligence collection disciplines.

Analysts receive the information, control the data gathering activities pursued by the information collection services, process the data obtained by collectors, analyze the information, inform the users about the required questions. Main actions are:

- Correcting information or material that was supplied
- Adding missing information that should have been supplied
- Clarifying information provided that should have been clear

Analysis and Processing. Intelligence is produced from data information though recording of information for comparison with other items by hand, an assessment of information in order to determine the value of intelligence, and an interpretation of information concerning other information and intelligence hand in order to reach a conclusion as to its meaning.

The analysis is a central element of the intelligence cycle to provide the users with analysed and assessed information (intelligence knowledge management), to help in decision-making, and to uncover and define possible threats, risks and challenges (for a decision maker, a company, a State).

Figure 3. Analytic processes

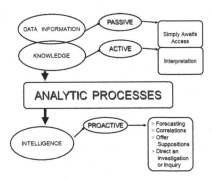

Intelligence Analysis Biases

Intelligence analysts can fall in cognitive biases. Cognitive biases are a mistake in reasoning, evaluating, remembering, or other cognitive processes (see chapter 2). They are mental errors caused by our simplified information processing strategies, and can be cultural, emotional or intellectual predisposition toward a certain judgment, organizational bias, and bias that results from one's own self-interest.

Cognitive biases are similar to optical illusions in that the error remains compelling even when one is fully aware of its nature. But an awareness of biases, by itself, does not produce a more accurate perception.

In the case of Intelligence Analysis, the main types of cognitive biases in synthesis are:

Vividness Vivid, concrete, and personal information has a greater impact than pallid, abstract information that may actually have substantially greater value as evidence

Absence of Evidence estimate potential impact of missing data and adjust confidence in judgment. Using of fault trees

Oversensitivity to Consistency "out of sight, out of mind" highly correlated or redundant information, or drawn from a very small or biased sample

Law of Small Numbers tendency to place too much reliance on small samples

Coping with Evidence of Uncertain Accuracy that is Misunderstanding, misperception, incomplete story, source bias, distortion in the communication chain, misunderstanding and misperception by the analyst

Persistence of Impressions Based on Discredited Evidence Impressions tend to persist even after the evidence that created those impressions has been fully discredited

Biases in Perception of Cause and Effect When inferring the causes of behavior too much weight is accorded to personal qualities and dispositions of the actor and not enough to situational determinants

Bias in Favor of Causal Explanations People expect patterned events to look patterned and random events to look random, but this is not the case. Random events often look patterned

Bias Favoring Perception of Centralized Direction. It is the tendency to see the actions of organizations as the intentional result of centralized direction and planning. Accidents, unintended consequences, coincidences, and small causes leading to large effects are perceived as coordinated actions, plans and conspiracies

Similarity of Cause and Effect Rule of thumb people use is to consider the similarity between attributes of the cause and attributes of the effect. Assumption that big events have important consequences, does not apply

Internal vs. External Causes of Behavior. A fundamental error made in judging the causes of behavior is to overestimate the role of internal factors and underestimate the role of external factors

Overestimating Our Own Importance Individuals and organizations tend to overestimate the extent to which they successfully influence the behavior of others: familiar with own efforts, much less with factors that influenced the other's decision

Illusory Correlation. It does not necessarily imply causation. For example, two events might co-occur because they have a common cause, rather than because one causes the other. But when two events or changes do co-occur, and the time sequence is such that one always follows the other, people often infer that the first caused the second.

ORIENTISM MANAGEMENT STRATEGY (OMS)

Orientism is an innovative multidimensional knowledge management approach, Orientism view is a new conception of the Knowledge Management: it moves towards a knowledge awareness, extension of own horizon points of perspective and meanings management, in a network of relationships, starting from own strength points and profile, and consciousness transfer in a knowledge interface phenomenon.

New variables, factors and criteria are designed to direct and motivate the mind in the decisional process, in self-reference, to be considered in a lifelong guidance to have success in choices, assumptions of responsibilities and achievement of objectives, over the uncertainty.

The approach is contextualized in the experience of people and their own environment, to enable a person to face the problem positively and to develop strategies to manage situations, to mediate complex relationships through task facing orientation, and it is based on:

- The vision of the decision-making itself like an understanding process, choosing what to learn And the meaning of incoming information, seen through the lens of a shifting reality;
- the management of larger pieces of human experiences to be put together to achieve success;
- The management of a complex network with numerous typologies of nodes/connections, such as information, competences, intelligences, people and interpretations;
- The adaptation of the knowledge management/learning attitude to activate orienting reflex phenomena and to develop a critical mind;
- The definition of the needed supporting learning process; the develop of analytical and aware skills;
- The definition of profile and action modality of supporting human and cognitive tutoring;
- The understanding whether and how an environment, a digital tool, specifically designed, can promote the processes of subjective orientation

The approach consider three levels of analysis.

Knowledge level. This level is focused on
  - Generating a significant flux of communications and coordination of actions in order to facilitate the act of processing meaning (by interactions)
  - Implementing cooperation through KM strategies, such as: sharing, different level of specialization of the agents, collection or creation of content and sub-division of the work (distributed allocation)
  - Managing factual information and access content, as well as procedural knowledge of best practices, working towards a "reduction of complexity"
  - Finding related Information and then integrating distributed knowledge
  - Realizing and managing re-generation and re-purposing of different knowledge patterns (spirals) emerging in different forms
  - Realizing and managing awareness of knowledge and data meaning management in a network of relationships
  - realizing and managing consciousness transfer in an optimized e-learning environment

User(s) level. This level is focused on:
  - Realizing a degree of connectedness, through a high density of connected users, speed and flow of shared information, plasticity and frequency of created connections

- ○ realizing periodically interaction between all the Agents, to understand problems, mitigate risks and Remove the roadblocks
- ○ Managing a complex network with numerous typologies of nodes and connections of knowledge, competences, communication, representations, relationships, technologies and many different paradigms to work

Technology (e-environment) level. This level is focused on:

- ○ Facilitating information management by archiving all communications and interactions within an e-environment to access and share for future activities. The environment is a mix of PLE (Personal Learning Environment), PKE (Personal Knowledge Environment), and PWE (Personal Work Environment), able to support social networking activities as well as collaborative learning, supported by an intelligent system
- ○ Enabling an effective capture of the tacit knowledge of Agents (e.g., experience, intuition, creativity) that is missed with traditional knowledge management systems, that focus on document archiving (i.e., explicit knowledge)
- ○ Promoting communication and logistical coordination among (geographically distributed) workforce members through the use of communities of practice (CoPs) and collaboration tools
- ○ Scanning and reporting pathways of individual/social actions
- ○ Facilitating an intelligent and creative learning/business atmosphere that will allow Agents (employees) freedom to capture the knowledge that is up to date and accurate

This approach is scientifically based on the following theories.

Design Human Engineering, DHE. It is considered for the definition of criteria to improve the people's ability of contextual changes, to design knowledge/learning strategies to apply. This theory is the evolution of the well-known Neuro Linguistic Programming (NLP) theory (Bandler et al, 2013):

- While NLP is based on the replication of human behavior (modeling), the DHE is based on the creation of new models.
- While NLP analyzes the sequence of access to certain information, the DHE takes into consideration the simultaneity of how we process information.
- While NLP deals with divide human behavior into smaller and smaller pieces, the DHE is the model by which larger and larger chunks of human experience are put together to achieve success.

Strength point of the theory is that it not only intends to allow creating of new communication flux, strategies and skills, but also intends to let user create better motivation strategies to accomplish their own tasks.

Nature Knowledge Theory, NKT

It is considered for the definition of Nature and Human Knowledge, to design a semantic interpretation of the knowledge process. It is a transdisciplinary approach (Md Santo et al., 2014), proposing a holistic vision of the KM process dynamic, and reverses the prospective, proposing a so defined "not management technique": its role is to give "final touch by blowing spiritual enrichment" to the agents, through contextual interaction of KM components. The organization is interpreted like a living mechanism, having interior own consciousness, wherein each agent works with own specific profile, as well as each tool, works with its specific functions, having to be orchestrated in a "Nature Knowledge continuum", through comprehending the Knowledge Base of a Global Complex System. This approach evolves in Nature Knowledge Theory or NKT.

It is the evolution of the Human System Biology-based Knowledge Management (HSB-KM) model framework. The main goals are an Establish Taxonomy of Enterprise Process Business (indicating Complexity aspect of Risk Management) based on Process Classification Framework (PCF) method and proceed to strongly recommended Community of Practice (CoP) and Learning Organization (LO), as modern trending issues before developing it to further usual themes of management tools.

The framework dedicates attention to different "plans" in the decision-making process:

- **Prescriptive Plan:** How Policymaker should reason
- **Descriptive Plan:** How they reason
- **Social Plan:** What type of reasoning motivates the decisional action in terms of efficacy and efficiency
- **Communicative Plan:** What type of reasoning is recognizable
- **Management Plan:** What conditions guarantee "order" in a process, against networking, understanding and learning "chaos"
- **Tutoring Plan:** How Policymaker can be supported in their choosing process
- **Historical Plan:** How a diachronic vision (history) of the issues and own previous experiences can lead decisions
- **Comparative Plan:** How a synchronic vision (comparing transversal situations and conditions) can lead decisions
- **Creative Plan:** How to innovate

- **Simulation Plan:** How to simulate cases study

The result is an innovative framework, Orientism Management (OM), based on 5 factors (vertices in the figure 4).

Figure 4. Orientism management (OM) diagram

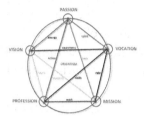

The vertices represent the profile variables to be considered in a training guidance.

- **Profession Vertex:** It is an openly declaring, according own thought and identity; specific knowledge, training and skills towards own employment. It is the representation of people as policy decision-makers.
- **Vision Vertex:** It is an aware semantic interpretation of reality and/or own will. It leads the thought towards of a meaning schema of actions
- **Passion Vertex:** It is a powerful emotion. It pushes a person towards a target with force and determination.
- **Vocation Vertex**: It is a strong feeling of suitability to act in some context. For it people regard themselves as particularly worthy. It requires great dedication.
- **Mission Vertex:** It is a statement of a reason for existing. It motivates people to perform a service.

Table 1. Variables (vertices) and domains

Vertices' name	Domains
Profession vertex	the Work, the Skills, the Action, the Future of people
Vision vertex	the Future, the Purpose, the Awareness, the Energy of people.
Passion vertex	the Energy, the Spirit, the Love, the Action of people.
Vocation vertex	the Spirit, the Love, the Awareness, the Role of people
Mission vertex	the Role, the Work, the Love, the Purpose of people

The vertices represent the added subjective components to orient, train and activate choice processes.

- **Spirit** factor is the synthesis of the relationship between own personal investment and powerful being pushed towards a target (Passion) and own deep feeling and dedication (Vocation).
- **Energy** factor is the synthesis of the relationship between own personal investment and powerful being pushed towards a target (Passion) and semantic interpretation of reality (Vision).
- **Awareness** factor is the synthesis of the relationship between own semantic interpretation of reality (Vision) and own deep feeling and dedication (Vocation).
- **Love** factor is the synthesis of the relationship between own personal investment and powerful being pushed towards a target (Passion) and own reason to perform (Mission).
- **Action** factor is the synthesis of the relationship between own personal investment and powerful being pushed towards a target (Passion) and identity as a policy decision-maker towards an employment (Profession)
- **Purpose** factor is the synthesis of the relationship between own semantic interpretation of reality (Vision) and reason to perform (Mission).
- **Skills** factor is the synthesis of the relationship between own deep feeling and dedication (Vocation) and own identity as policy decision-maker towards an employment (Profession)
- **Future** factor is the synthesis of the relationship between own identity as policy decision-maker towards an employment (Profession) and semantic interpretation of reality (Vision).
- **Role** factor is the synthesis of the relationship between own deep feeling and dedication (Vocation) and own reason to perform (Mission).
- **Work** factor is the synthesis of the relationship between own identity as policy decision-maker (Profession) and own reason to perform (Mission).

The focus of the Orientism Management is specifically to orient people to manage decisions in unpredictability conditions in multi-user environment context. It intends to propose a new solution to the demand for "innovative and creative leadership" to make choices, to open to the change of perspective, to manage relationships and complex environments, basing on the conception of a new model of behavior and management of the simultaneity of how people process information.

OM Knowledge Management typologies

The result of this analysis is an Orientism Management (OM) concept, based on intertwined 10 Knowledge Managements typologies, each based on areas of development and improvement of own personal leadership:

Knowledge Management with Consciousness (Low) (KMC/l). It focuses on the learning "to know what" that the Agent needs to manage. It is based on the empowering of Energy-, Action-, Future factors (green-yellow-red triangle in the schema), according to Passion, Vision and Profession of the Trainee.

Knowledge Management with Consciousness (Medium) (KMC/m). It focuses on the learning "to know how" that the Agent needs to manage. It is based on the empowering of Role-, Skills-, Work factors (violet-blue-black triangle in the schema), according to Vocation, Profession and Mission of the Trainee. To support this knowledge/orientation management,

Knowledge Management with Consciousness (High) (KMC/h). It focuses on the learning "to know where" that the Agent needs to manage. It is based on the empowering of Action-, Love-, Work factors (red-orange-violet triangle in the schema), according to Profession, Passion and Mission of the Trainee.

Knowledge Management with Meaning (KMM). It focuses on the learning "to know why" that the Agent needs to manage. It I based on the empowering of Purpose-, Future-, Work factors (azure-yellow-violet triangle in the schema), according to Profession, Vision and Mission of the Trainee.

Knowledge Management with Feeling (KMF). It focuses on the learning "to know moving (towards)" that the Agent needs to manage to activate a change of perspective or action. It is based on the empowering of Role-, Love-, Spirit factors (pink, black, orange triangle in the schema), according to Profession, Vision and Mission of the Trainee.

Knowledge Management with Will (KMW). It focuses on the learning "to know experiencing", process that the Agent needs to activate and control. It is based on the empowering of Action, Skills-, Spirit factors (red, blue, pink triangle in the schema), according to Profession, Vision and Mission of the Trainee

Knowledge Management with Understanding (KMU). It focuses on the learning "to know enabling" that the Agent needs to become. It is based on the empowering of Awareness, Skills, Future factors (brown, blue, yellow triangle in the schema), according to Profession, Vision and Mission of the Trainee

Knowledge Management with Personalization (KMP). It focuses on the learning "to know changing" for Agent part. It is based on the empowering of Role, Awareness, Purpose factors (brown, black, azure triangle in the schema), according to Vocation, Vision and Mission of the Trainee.

Knowledge Management with Availability (KMA). It focuses on the learning "to know opening" towards people, environment, prospective and perspectives, interpretations for Agent part. It is based on the empowering of Awareness, Energy and Spirit factors (brown, pink, green triangle in the schema), according to Vocation, Vision and Mission of the Trainee, with high attention to the comparison devoting" towards work, goals, relationships for Agent part.

Knowledge Management with Synergy (KMS). It focuses on the learning "to know devoting" towards work, goals, relationships by the Policymaker. It's on the base of all plans, specifically it's part of social plan. It is based on the empowering of Purpose, Energy and Love factors (green, orange, azure triangle in the schema), according to Vocation, Vision and Mission of the Trainee, with high attention to the comparison.

OM Rules and Logical Relations and Training

Consequently, according to OMS, and considering the decision-making itself as a learning process. Choosing what to learn and the meaning of incoming information seen through the lens of a shifting reality, the decision-maker should follow rules and logical relations to manage the uncertainty of the decision-making under risk of failure, which consists of:

- A **stable structure,** representing:
  - The decision domain, *epistemological* rules and *logical* connections
  - The adopted *decision-making l* model to be applied (theory driven, method driven, problem driven)
  - The *assessment* rules, including a selection of right/wrong actions
  - The *training* and *tutoring modes* rules
- A **flexible structure**, representing:
  - *Semiotic* rules
  - *Selection* rules, responsible for selecting the appropriate decision-making nodes
  - *Sequence* rules, to apply a proper presentation order of the content in question
  - *Collaborative path* rules, in relation to the learning objectives of the course
- An **adaptive structure**, representing:
  - *Evolution* rules of the decisional condition, cognitive state and his/her political decision preferences
  - *Individualized path* rules, finalizing the ability to let achieve the defined objectives

○   *Personalized path* rules, depending on achievement of decision-makers cognitive excellence

Specifically, OM framework founds a valid training support in PENTHA ID approach (Dall'Acqua, 2014). This approach lets a management as follows (see Table 3):

Knowledge Management with Consciousness (Low) (KMC/l). To support this knowledge/orientation management PENTHA suggests, between others, Fading tutoring/training mode, a method for adjusting and adapting the knowledge/ orientation path according to the achievements of the decision-maker until the proof of his positive capability in full autonomy.

Knowledge Management with Consciousness (Medium) (KMC/m). To support this knowledge/ orientation management, PENTHA suggests several tutoring/ training modes, such as:

- Scaffolding, a method which favours the adaptation of the knowledge/ orientation path, a reflection on the actions developed by the decision-maker, stimulated by the Trainer/Tutor
- Modeling, a method according to which the Tutor/Trainer demonstrates how to perform a task
- Performing, a method according to which the Tutor/Trainer motivate the decision-maker, stimulating his/her own attitude and disposition to the work

Knowledge Management with Consciousness (High) (KMC/h). To support this knowledge/orientation management, PENTHA suggests, between others, Narrating tutoring/training mode, a method based on a) the basic idea of the tutoring/training role is to introduce a topic to attract the attention of the Trainees, the appreciation of different learning styles and different forms of intelligence; b) the basic idea of the learning aspect is to encourage the Trainees to verbalize their own experiences, to activate a process of working self-reflection/evaluation.

Knowledge Management with Meaning (KMM). To support this knowledge/ orientation management, PENTHA suggests several tutoring/training modes, such as:

- Coaching, a method according to which the Tutor/Trainer actively supports the Trainee, primarily motivating and analysing the Trainees performance, providing feedback, reflecting together on assignments to stimulate discussion about the method adopted
- Norming, a method aimed at high performing guideline, towards effective work and collaborative behavior

Knowledge Management with Feeling (KMF). To support this knowledge/ orientation management, PENTHA suggests, in addition to the above Coaching, Narrating and Fading tutoring/training modes, also to the more specific Reflecting mode, a method based on the pushing the Trainees to compare their own difficulties with an Expert, encouraging them to perform pull actions. Reflection is the vehicle for critical analysis, problem-solving, synthesizing of opposing ideas, evaluation, identifying patterns and creating meanings.

Knowledge Management with Will (KMW). To support this knowledge/ orientation management, PENTHA suggests, the above Fading and Performing.

Knowledge Management with Understanding (KMU). To support this knowledge/orientation management, PENTHA suggests, in addition to the above Coaching, Narrating, Scaffolding, Reflective and Fading tutoring/training modes, also to the more specific Exploring mode, which aims to lead the Trainees to solve problems with new or alternative solutions. The construction of knowledge occurs through the observation and the transformation of own or other experiences.

Knowledge Management with Personalization (KMP). To support this knowledge/orientation management, PENTHA suggests, in addition to the above Scaffolding, also to the more specific Storming mode, regards effective communication, and conflict resolution support and training.

Knowledge Management with Availability (KMA). To support this knowledge/ orientation management, PENTHA suggests the above Scaffolding and Fading tutoring/training modes.

Knowledge Management with Synergy (KMS). To support this knowledge/ orientation management, PENTHA suggests the above Scaffolding and Fading tutoring/training modes.

CONCLUSION

The proposed approach interprets the fluid nature of the decision-making process, looking at knowledge and knowledge activities as dynamic, adaptive and self-regulative, based not only on well-known explicit curricular goals, but also on unpredictable interactions and relationships between players. The knowledge process is emerging in human and biological, social and cultural environments. This process is oriented toward the generation of an "order in the chaos" of complex and dynamics management, to orient on the internal "diversity", the variety of backgrounds, interests, knowledge, skills and the whole personality of the trainees, individually or within in a work team.

The chapter intended to describe a new interpretative socio-cognitive paradigm, Orientism, to understand and manage the fluid nature of knowledge, but at the same

Table 3. 10 KM typologies (OM model) with related focused tutoring modes

Knowledge Management	Learning	To empower	According to	Focused Tutoring Modes
with (Low) Consciousness KMC/l	*to know what*	Energy, Action Future	Passion, Vision, Profession	Forming
with (Medium) Consciousness KMC/m	*to know how*	Role, Skills, Work	Vocation, Profession, Mission	Scaffolding, Modeling, Performing
with (High) Consciousness KMC/h	*to know where*	Work, Action, Love	Profession, Mission, Passion	Narrating
with Meaning KMM	*to know why*	Work, Purpose, Future	Profession, Vision, Mission	Coaching, Norming
with Feeling KMF	*to know moving*	Role, Love, Spirit	Vocation, Mission, Passion	Coaching, Reflecting, Fading, Narrating
with Will KMW	*to know experiencing*	Action, Skills, Spirit	Passion, Profession, Vocation	Fading, Performing
with Understanding KMU	*to know enabling*	Awareness, Skills, Future	Vision, Vocation, Profession	Coaching, Narrating, Exploring, Reflecting, Scaffolding, Fading
with Personalization KMP	*to know changing*	Role, Awareness, Purpose	Vocation, Mission, Vision	Storming, Scaffolding
with Availability KMA	*to know opening*	Awareness, Energy, Spirit	Vision, Vocation, Passion	Storming, Fading
with Synergy KMS	*to know devoting*	Purpose, Energy, Love	Passion, Vision, Mission	Fading

time to seize and manage the unpredictability and risks of dynamics of risk decision management in relationships complex environment. New elements are 5 key factors and criteria to direct and motivate people in the choosing process and following 10 different and key relationships between them.

The goal is to support analysts, decision-makers and trainers to manage decisions in stable, flexible and dynamic conditions and unpredictability.

ACKNOWLEDGMENT

The author wishes to express sincere esteem and gratitude to Dr. Md Santo, awarded international Knowledge Management expert, founder of Nature Knowledge Theory

(NKT), to have inspired the scientific base of the complex concept and to be a valuable research partner in innovative projects.

REFERENCES

Bandler, R., Robert, A., & Fitzpatrick, O. (2013). *An Introduction To Nlp*. Harper Collins Publishers.

Betts, R. (2007). *Enemies of Intelligence: Knowledge and Power in American National Security*. Columbia University Press.

Cheong, R. K. F., & Tsui, E. (2010). The Roles and Values of Personal Knowledge Management: An exploratory study. *VINE Journal of Information and Knowledge Management Systems*, *40*(2), 204–227.

Cheong, R.K.F., & Tsui, E. (2011). From Skills and Competencies to Outcome-based Collaborative Work: Tracking a Decade's Development of Personal Knowledge Management (PKM) Models, Knowledge and Process Management. *The Journal of Corporate Transformation, 18*(3), 175-193.

dall'Acqua, L., & Santo, M. (2014). Orientism, the basic pedagogical approach of PENTHA ID Model vs. 2, to manage decisions in unpredictability conditions. *Proceedings of World Congress on Engineering and Computer Science WCECS2014*, *1*, 316-21.

dall'Acqua, L. (2011). Didactical suggestion for a Dynamic Hybrid Intelligent e-Learning Environment (DHILE) applying the PENTHA ID Model. In *AIP, Conference Proceedings, Special Edition of the WCECS2010* (Vol. 1373, pp. 159-173). Academic Press.

dall'Acqua, L. (2014). Needs and strategies of KM in a multi-user environment: PENTHA Model view and analysis. *Jekpot KM19*.

dall'Acqua, L. (2019). Scientific Intelligence, Decision-Making and Cyber-Security. In *Forecasting and Managing Risk in the Health and Safety Sectors*. IGI Global.

Gagné, R. M. (1985). *The Condition of Learning and Theory of Instruction*. CBS College Publishing.

Goldsmith, M., Morgan, H., & Ogg, A. (2004). *Effectively Influencing Up:Ensuring That Your Knowledge, Makes a Difference. In Leading Organizational Learning*. Jossey-Bass.

Hasted, G. P. (1987). The New Context of Intelligence Estimating: Politicization or Publicizing? Intelligence and Intelligence Policy in a Democratic Society. Transnational Publishers, Inc.

Marschark, M., Lang, H. G., & Albertini, J. A. (2002). *Educating Deaf Students: From Research to Practice*. University Press.

KEY TERMS AND DEFINITIONS

Intelligence Analyst: The professional is an intermediary between abstract knowledge and political action. He or she translates that information into a form which is both understandable and usable by the non-expert. Deference to the professional typically rests upon the presumption that compromise and negotiation, the hallmarks of political deliberation, have no significant impact on the manner by which professionals arrive at their conclusions. Rationality and objectivity are held to guide their analysis of information (Hastdet, 1987). Sometimes intelligence and intelligence analysis is ignored by decisionmakers, and sometimes intelligence—or intelligence analysis—is changed or distorted to be more consistent with (or in opposition to) the interpretation that the decisionmakers would prefer.

Orientism Management Framework: Is a new multi-dimensional KM approach to improve the people's ability to manage decisions and own change of perspective, according to natural, social, artificial environments, in personalized multi-user dynamic, assigned value to multiple reference points and multi-interpreting paradigms.

PENTHA Model: Is an ID Knowledge Design Model focused on designing the KM environment, defining the (didactical) rules for an Intelligent Tutoring System, facilitating person's change and enhancement,

Chapter 2
Homegrown Terrorism:
An Analysis of Its Effects on PESTLE Factors

Amitabh Anand

iD https://orcid.org/0000-0001-6649-6422

SKEMA Business School, Universitie Cote d'Azur, France & GREDEG, France

Giulia Mantovani

University of Bologna, Italy

ABSTRACT

To tackle the phenomenon of terrorism, especially the attacks carried out by homegrown terrorists, since 2005 all the EU's member states have adopted the Global Strategy to Combat Terrorism. Focusing on four pillars (prevention, protection, persecution, and response), the strategy provides for security measures to protect against terrorism as a criminal act. What if, instead, we consider terrorism as a social phenomenon, strictly connected to radicalization and resulting from discriminatory experiences and discomfort young second generation immigrants suffer within the European society? Moving in this direction, through the application of the PESTLE analysis to the specific context of Belgium, this study elaborates a counterterrorism policy which takes into account the root and activating factors of radicalization by filling Belgium's gaps in terms of integration policies and which could help reducing the likelihood of occurring radicalization and terrorist attacks episodes.

DOI: 10.4018/978-1-7998-4339-9.ch002

INTRODUCTION

The Global Strategy to Combat Terrorism was issued by the European Union in 2005 and it is focused on 4 pillars: prevention, protection, persecution and response. To tackle the phenomenon of terrorism and in order to try to reduce its frequency, especially the attacks carried out by homegrown terrorists, the first pillar of the strategy deals with the increased border and weapons market control, the constant monitoring of the online propaganda and the criminalization of every action and monetary support to foreign fighters. Terrorism is considered by the European Union as a criminal act, uncoupled from radicalization. What if we consider it as a social phenomenon, resulting from radicalization and originating from discriminatory experiences and discomfort young second generation immigrants suffer within the European society? If we move in this direction, we can elaborate counterterrorism policies which take into account the root causes of terrorism and which could help reducing the likelihood of occurring radicalization and terrorist attacks episodes. Through the application of the PESTLE analysis to the specific context of Belgium, we have analysed the living condition of the young Muslims of second generation within the European society and its emergence in the political, economic, social, technological and legal discriminations which they experience on a daily basis and which, functioning as predisposing factors, enable them to tackle the path of extremism as the only way out of the isolation and poverty they experience. From this study we aim to provide the possibility to develop a counterterrorism strategy which addresses the root and activating factors of radicalization considering Belgium as a case. We identify the gaps in terms of integration policies, thus helping diminishing radicalization and terrorism phenomenon.

EU Counter-Terrorism Strategy

The latest data collected by Europol in TE-SAT Report show how, since 2006, the frequency of jihadist-style terrorist attacks in Europe has increased, while their sophistication and their planning has decreased (Europol, 2018, p.4). This phenomenon's trend seems to be linked to the new threat Europe has been facing since the 2005 London bombings: the homegrown terrorism. To tackle the new evolution of terrorism characterized by second or third generation young immigrants, born and/or raised in the West, that independently (without direct support from international terrorist organizations) and ideologically driven by the political Islam, decide to attack their own country (Nelson, 2011, pp. VII, 11), the European Union has implemented the "EU Counter-Terrorism Strategy" to combat the global terrorism (European Council & Council of the European Union, n.d.). All EU Member States have transposed the four-pillar counterterrorism strategy into their national legislation.

In particular, the four pillars deal with prevention, protection, persecution and response to terrorism (European Council & Council of the European Union, n.d.). Leaving aside for a moment how the European Union intends to address the issue of radicalization with the prevention pillar, Member States are called upon to protect their own citizens and national infrastructures against possible terrorist incidents with measures such as "securing external borders, improving transport security, protecting strategic targets, reducing the vulnerability of critical infrastructure" and the adoption of the regulatory directive on the passenger name record (PNR).[1] EU's objective is to hinder the physical and economic capacity of terrorists to plan and carry out attacks. To this end, not only Member States must strengthen their resilience towards threats, but also the exchange of information at supranational level both within the Union and with third countries must be enforced.[2] Anyway, if a bombing occurs on the national soil, it is essential to the European Union that the State is capable to deal with the attack's consequences, to respond to the citizens' needs, by improving risk analysis, the coordination of civil protection and security bodies, implementing a crisis management plan at European level.[3]

Let us concentrate on the prevention pillar, it appears clear that the European Union regards terrorism as a criminal act which must be addressed by identifying and limiting recruitment attempts and those which it (mistakenly) regards as the radicalization's root causes (European Council & Council of the European Union, n.d.). The EU sets up measures to prosecute recruiters and who provides economic and physical support to foreign fighters and to improve the traceability of weapons, border controls and the fight against online propaganda (European Council & Council of the European Union, n.d.). These objectives, however, show that Member States don't consider radicalization as a phenomenon from which terrorism originates, but rather as an event that allows the phenomenon to grow and expand through propaganda and networking. By considering radicalization as a set of factors that are functional to the subsistence and expansion of terrorist cells, it means to observe from a single perspective a multi-faceted and complex problem which originates from the relationship that the individual has with his origin society and from the personal experiences that he lives in it.[4] For this reason, we see radicalization as a "process in which individuals adopt extreme political, social and/or religious ideals and aspirations, and where the attainment of particular goals justifies the use of indiscriminate violence", engendered by the existence of political, economic or social root causes, which lead the individual to approach extremism, and of trigger factors (the ones considered by the EU as root causes), that is all those elements within the social fabric (i.e. recruitment networks and terrorist organizations) that enable the individual to physically plead his cause (Wilner & Dubouloz, 2010, p.38).

In this context, therefore, since we identify in the prevention pillar the loophole of the "EU Counter-Terrorism Strategy", it is proposed an innovative approach to address the problem of radicalization, in order to make it possible to identify in a simple and detailed way the real root causes of this phenomenon and thus reinforcing the effectiveness of the strategy: PESTLE analysis.

Understanding PESTLE Analysis

PESTLE analysis is a tool for the economic and strategic evaluation used by organizations, companies and managers to understand which might be the best short- and long-term strategies to adopt in a foreign context where they aim to expand their goals and where there are several (positive or negative) impacting factors that cannot be controlled by the company itself (Team FME, 2013, pp.6-7).

This method of analysis was invented in 1967 by Professor Francis Aguilar who in his book "Scanning the Business Environment" applied, for the first time ever, the ETPS analysis, later called PESTLE analysis (Ealing, 2018, pp.1-2).

We can use different names to refer to PESTLE analysis depending on the variables that are taken into account. In fact, as we can notice, PESTLE is the acronym of the five variables of interest for a good business strategy: Politics, Economy, Society, Technology, Legality and Environment (Team FME, 2013, pp.8-9).[5] From a political point of view, the manager assesses the foreign government's stability and its policies on employment, taxation and regulation of corruption (Team FME, 2013, pp.12-13).

The economic factors considered are the macroeconomic aspects such as inflation levels, taxation and exchange rates and the cost of living or the credit and insurance system (Team FME, 2013, pp.13-14).

Societal variables measure the level of education and life satisfaction of potential consumers, analyze demographic trends and social mobility opportunities (Team FME, 2013, p.15). Technological aspects are related to the use of innovations for productive goals and the policies that support this sector (Team FME, 2013, pp.16-17).

The legal and environmental aspects, in the end, concern laws and regulations that could pose an obstacle to the business operation in several matters (Team FME, 2013, pp.18-19).

Since this study consider terrorism as the outcome of a social process such as that of radicalization where come into play political, economic, social, technological and legal variables that impact on the life of the individual by bringing him more or less closer to the Islamic extremism, the authors can play the role of business manager and apply PESTLE analysis to the issue of terrorism to try to identify the causes that, to varying degrees, contribute to its development, thus enabling them

to elaborate an effective counterterrorism policy to tackle the real root causes from which this phenomenon originates.

The issue of terrorism, in particular homegrown terrorism, can be addressed by applying PESTLE analysis with a dual perspective: the assessment of the impact of terrorism on the PESTLE variables and the identification of the PESTLE variables which contribute to the growth of the phenomenon and foster the development of the vicious circle radicalization-terrorism.

PESTLE Analysis Applied to Terrorism

Whenever a terrorist attack occurs, immediate and long-term consequences are generated. Naturally, in the immediate post-attack we are faced with destruction, fear and death. However, if at first sight violence and the sense of powerlessness impress us, while these feelings fade away the long-term consequences pour into various sectors of the affected nation. In fact, by using PESTLE analysis, it is possible to confirm that political, economic, technological, social and legal variables of the target are negatively affected as a result of a terrorist attack.

From a political point of view, terrorism can "exacerbate the likelihood of some governments failure" (Williams, Koch & Smith, 2013, p.343). The study of Laron Williams, Michael Koch and Jason Smith (2013, pp.347-348) found out that right-wing governments are less likely to fall after a terrorist attack because left-wing one are interventionist and react in a stronger way, thus reinforcing the electoral consensus around them, trying to answer to the society's needs of security and reassurance. Moreover, as external and critical event, terrorism generates three important reactions within the targeted political context: all the political parties tend to coalize to react and condemn the attack, the political agenda is revised and the anti-terrorism and security measures are prioritized, the public opinion will punish the party in charge at the moment of the attack by voting the opposition in the next elections (Williams, Koch & Smith, 2013, pp.346-347).

The political instability generated by a terrorist attack then creates a warmer climate for renewed attacks and national economic problems.[6] Terrorism has five short- and long-term economic consequences. To better understand them, we use the example of the economy of the United States in the immediate aftermath of 9/11. Surely, the physical destructions of production facilities, transport systems and infrastructure are the first direct consequences of a terrorist attack (Ross, 2019). The World Trade Centre attacks are a good and clear example. In fact, the collapse of the Twin Towers caused thousands of deaths and injuries and the blockade of several American airports and port systems (OECD, 2002, p.128).

The economic instability could also spill over to the financial sector, prompting investors to redirect their investments elsewhere and Central Banks to take emergency measures such as infuse a large amount of liquidity into the system and introduce additional financial and fiscal regulations (Ross, 2019; OECD, 2002, pp.122-124). Also the general country's wealth can diminish when the affected areas experience a declining trend in tourism and the reluctance of insurance companies to offer policies against terrorist acts (Ross, 2019). The US case shows insurance companies suffering losses of between $30 billion and $58 billion in compensation and reducing the number of covered accidents and matters while raising insurance rates (OECD, 2002, pp.124-128).

The increased security measures have a major economic impact on the state expenditure too. In fact, strengthening borders and means of transport controls and disposing reconstruction plans means requiring a greater amount of money for the technological improvement and control and to pay the additional staff to carry out these tasks. Moreover, these measures have also an indirect impact on government coffers by slowing down the trade's speed and its profit-making abilities (Ross, 2019; OECD, 2002, pp.128-132). Lastly, state's foreign skepticism and nationalism resulting from an attack can cause economic losses. In fact, by closing borders and tightening migration policies, countries may see their production fall as a result of a smaller labor force available (Ross, 2019).

We can assess the impact of the short- and long-term consequences of terrorism within society too. In the immediate aftermath of the attacks the society tends to strengthen its bond and showing internal solidarity against every government attempt to negotiate with terrorists. At the same time the collectivity deals with decreasing living standards resulting from the increasing private expenditure demanded by the government to implement new counterterrorism policies and measures. In fact, by raising taxes to collect funds to implement the new security measures, the government will force its citizens to invest less in their interests.

People's life standards and life quality decreases not only in economic terms, but also in terms of freedom and usability (Greisman, 1979, pp.139-140). Indeed, there'll be more controls and limited freedom of movement both for people and goods, making travels longer and complicated due to congestion and huge waiting times.

Socially speaking, on the other hand, terrorism generates a spiral of growing insecurity and social closure (Greisman, 1979, pp.141-146). This is another form of reduction in people's life quality which forces the collective to change its habits by don't trusting the neighbor, avoiding public and crowded places and seeking private security in the form of neighborhood patrols and weapons detention.

However, the most worrying social impact is the psychological or physical reaction to an attack. Many have developed mental illnesses and behavioral disorders, insomnia, panic attacks, self-harm and heart problems, alcoholism, addiction to smoke or illicit substances (Greisman, 1979, pp.143-144; Grieger, 2006, 1-2).

Moving on, the introduction of technology into our daily lives has had positive effects on the ability to communicate remotely, be connected with people around the world, obtain information and produce faster and in exponential quantities. These benefits are available to everyone, including terrorists who are increasingly introducing technological elements to plan and conduct their attacks. Then, it is not by coincidence that today we talk about cyberterrorism as a growing threat coming from states and non-state entities such as terrorist organizations.[7] If the latter can use the power of the recent technologies, they could cause damage to a greater extent than the current physical and direct attack as they would disrupt the entire functioning of the nation.[8]

Terrorists are also adept at exploiting new social media such as Facebook, YouTube and Twitter for propaganda, fundraising and recruitment (Europol, 2018, pp.30-33; INFOSEC, 2018). The evolution of communication towards anonymity and end-to-end encryption has made communications safer and less subject to interference and interception, but it is precisely for this very reason that today it is much more difficult to identify terrorists and foil planned attacks (INFOSEC, 2018; The National Interest, 2019).

Lastly, terrorism also impacts on antiterrorism laws and legislative measures. In the Western world both the European Union and the United States developed counterterrorism strategies focusing on four pillars: prevention, protection, prosecution and response. As said in the previous paragraphs, the European Union's Counterterrorism Strategy provides for a four pillars plan which consists of increasing regulation and monitoring on the possessions of arms, borders and online activities, the criminalization of recruitment and support to foreign fighters and protective measures to secure citizens and at-risk infrastructures and to improve the exchange of information among European and third countries (European Council & Council of the European Union, n.d.). In turn, the President of the United States Donald Trump, in October 2018, issued the new US Counterterrorism Strategy. Despite adopting an America first approach (which requires the accordance of each point of the strategy with the national interests and US capabilities), the President aims to prevent radicalization by improving the mechanisms of mutual assistance, information exchange and coordination of local and federal authorities and by strengthening border controls and legal provisions for anyone linked or suspected to have connections with terrorism (Trump, 2018, pp.11-24).

Once again, through these additional regulations and security measures, terrorism impacts on civil liberties which, as the Office of the United Nations High Commissioner for Human Rights points out, must be respected and safeguarded even when it comes to counterterrorism policies projects (OHCHR, 2008, pp.19-25).[9]

The Case of Belgium

On the wave of the 22 March 2016 Brussels attacks, the city of Brussels and, more generally, Belgium turned from being safe haven for bombers to being targets of their attacks (BBC News, 2016; Cruickshank, 2017). Suddenly Belgium was identified as a place par excellence where angry, frustrated and isolated second-generation young people join recruiters, hoping to get a payback by adhering to radical Islam. What are the causes that drive them to commit these acts? Can we ever remedy the growing threat of homegrown terrorists? Can we develop effective counterterrorism strategies to deal with the root causes of radicalization? This study provides an answer to these questions by applying a PESTLE analysis to the social, political and economic fabric of Belgium to identify and try to solve the root and activating causes of radicalization.

Why Belgium?

Authors' choice to select Belgium as case study is not random. In fact, it has features that on the one hand make this country the perfect place where a homegrown terrorist can move freely and easily get hold of weapons and funds and on the other it is characterized by contradictions and difficulties which favorite the discrimination and the isolation of anyone who is not properly Belgian, fostering a growing spiral of hatred and resentment towards the nation itself.

This paragraph is focused on what authors believe to be the five factors that make Belgium the heart of European terrorism and which prompted them to conduct a detailed analysis which could explain why Belgium has high radicalization rates and why it is the European nation with the greatest per capita number of foreign fighters leaving for Syria (Kroet, 2016).

Geographically, Belgium is at the heart of the Schengen area. This means that young second-generation homegrown terrorists who are born and raised in Belgium, as European citizens, can move freely and unhindered from one EU's country to another (Baudet, 2019). In this connection, then it would be explained why the 2015 Paris bombing's terrorist network managed to create undisturbed ties linkes with the Brussels' one and it had its headquarter in Molenbeek, a Muslim majority Brussels's neighborhood.

We can also find signs of Saudi influence in Belgium. As is well known, Saudi Arabia is a country sponsor and supporter of terrorism and in Belgium there are several mosques whose construction was financed by the Saudi (Baudet, 2019). Among the others, Saudi Arabia financed the creation of the oldest and largest mosque of Brussels, the one located in the Cinquantenaire Park. This Saudi influence represents the second factor that helped fostering the birth of fertile and prolific soil for the radicalization of Belgian Muslims (Baudet, 2019).

Again, for a long time federal, regional and local authorities have underestimated the importance of developing effective and accurate integration policies, thus contributing to the creation of unbridled ghettos in Belgian cities (Baudet, 2019). Here, it is not surprising that this mixture of complexity and negligence of the administrative and security apparatus has contributed to the proliferation of radicalized individuals and to the growth of the first terrorist network that has been able to expand and to gather followers undisturbed: the network of the Francosyrian Sheikh, Bassam Ayachi.

The lack of good integration policies has also made it difficult, if not impossible, for 4% of the Belgian population of non-European origin to enjoy the same rights and opportunities as the Belgian and European citizens, thus aggravating the condition of socio-economic inequality that young people of the second generation experience every day.

Lastly, Belgium is also the place where terrorists can easily obtain arms of any kind because of the large illegal weapons market the country developed during late 1990s, after the end of the Caucasus and Balkans wars, when the Albanian and Chechen mafia moved to its territory (Baudet, 2019).

PESTLE Analysis Applied to Belgium

In order to fully understand the phenomenon of radicalization in Belgium, it is essential to conduct a thorough study of the social, economic and political context of the nation aim at understanding how second generation young people fit into it and why one can speak of radicalization as a generalized phenomenon in Belgium rather than a problem that affects only Brussels and the ghetto district of Molenbeek.[10] To conduct the research and identify the real root causes of radicalization to address and restrict, this study applied the PESTLE analysis grid.[11]

In relation to political variables, Belgium has five major problems related to radicalization.

Certainly, the lack of executive power for 541 days and, subsequently, the political instability Belgium experienced between 2010 and 2013 may have contributed to create breeding ground for the settlement of the future terrorist recruitment networks (Waterfield, 2011). It is not by coincidence then that the absence of a strong and efficient government and police forces favored, in those years, the emergence and growth of the Zerkani's network in the district of Molenbeek (Van Ostaeyen, 2016.).

Here there are the conditions supported by the theorists of the networks who affirm that the networks of affiliated people surrounding a single individual and their ability to promote an extremist ideology in a fascinating and effective way plays a key role in fostering the radicalization process (Wiktorowicz, 2004; Sageman, 2008, pp.225-228).

A second problem for Belgium is its geopolitical configuration. In fact, it is a Federal State governed by a parliamentary monarchy where we can identify three levels of authority (federal, community, regional) and 12 legislative institutions. The legislative tasks are divided by issue among the three levels, but in some matters (i.e. integration issues) at regional level there is an overlapping of tasks and a high risk to enact different policies on the same subject, thus creating a legislative chaos which slows down the elaboration and implementation of laws and favorites the adoption of inefficient policies that, sometimes, can be urgent (Wonderful Wanderings, 2015).

The third problem, complementary to the second, is that of late migration policies.

Since the 1960s, Belgium has signed bilateral agreements with two North African countries: Morocco and Turkey.[12] From here migratory flows increasingly involved populations of North African origin who settled in the ghetto districts of the major cities (Timmerman, Vanderwaeren & Crul, 2003, pp.1065-1067; Martiniello, 2003, p.230).

The Belgian Government did not regulate the question of migration until 1974, when the Council of Ministers opted for the "doctrine of zero immigration" (Martiniello, 2003, p.225).[13]

This lack of migration policies has left immigrants, since the 1960's, without rights and obligations (Timmerman, Vanderwaeren & Crul, 2003, pp.1065-1067; Martiniello, 2003, p.225).

Not only, alongside the problem of migration policies, there is also the integration policies one.

Integration policies are a regional responsibility and each legislative body has different views on the issue of immigration.[14] However, despite the differences, the Belgian integration policies tend to the assimilation and *"imburgering"*.[15] These practices strengthen the sense of isolation and ghettoization experienced by the young second generation immigrants and increase the hatred and mutual suspicion existing between them and the rest of the society (Mandin, 2014, pp.8-12; Martiniello, 2003, pp.230-231). These effects of isolation and discrimination seem, therefore, confirm the vision of existing literature about the social causes of radicalization: French Sociologist (Dalgaard-Nielsen, 2010, p.799) and Susan Samata (2016, pp.1-10) theories (refer to identity and language friction experiences), the Pathway of Borum (2003, pp.7-9) (refers to the perceived social disadvantage) and NYPD (2007, pp.19-43) and Transformative Learning Approach (Wilner & Dubouloz, 2010, pp.45-50) theories (refer to personal crisis experienced as result of discrimination or traumatic events).

Finally, also the lack of political representation and the absence of political rights for the non-radicalized Muslim community are a problem (Muslims in Belgium, 2008, pp.127-133).[16]

This political exclusion and isolation are mainly due to the strengthening of nationalist parties in each Belgian region which not only want to preserve the integrity of their belonging territory, but they also describe the entire Muslim community as a hotbed for terrorists and promote its eradication from the Belgian society (Muslims in Belgium, 2008, pp.127-133).[17]

It is not surprising, then, that those who feel socially and politically disadvantaged could approach an extremist path aimed at attacking the "Western oppressors" who deny them their freedom of expression and consider them as terrorists.

The bad consequences of failed and belated integration policies can be perceived also from an economic point of view.

The Belgian educational system provides that children go to neighborhood schools and, as result, in most cases immigrant families that experience financial problems and live in ghetto district have no choice but to send children in qualitatively less good schools, with demotivated teachers and with high concentration of problematic and same nationality students.

In addition, the Belgian educational system after two years of common secondary school, sorts out pupils in three different types of high schools, based on their grades. Here, because of their language problems, the biggest part of the second young generation immigrants is obliged to attend vocational schools which, if they graduate, grants them a less-renowned and a lower-paid diploma with respect to higher education or technical school qualification (Timmerman, Vanderwaeren & Crul, 2003, pp. 1085, 1078-1080). So, to low educational levels correspond low salaries and the impossibility to improve one's economic condition. Low educational levels can also be the reason why among young second generation immigrants are registered high unemployment rates. However, some studies seem to confirm that they are due to discriminatory episodes they keep suffering while applying for a job in the Belgian labor market. If that is the case, the biased Belgian educational and work systems, which don't provide economic and social mobility for young second generation immigrants, can be identified as PESTLE economic variables that confirm Moghaddam's "Staircase to Terrorism" (2005, pp.161-169), which identifies in the impossibility of a way out from the perceived condition of deprivation the radicalization process' trigger, and that, for this reason, must be addressed (Timmerman, Vanderwaeren & Crul, 2003, pp.1070-1078).

Socially, the Muslim community can't exercise its religious and civil rights because it has problems obtaining licenses and permits to open mosques, to celebrate their traditions and religious beliefs. Indeed, although Islam is recognized as religion by the State since 1974 and Belgium's principle of state neutrality in religious matters is applied until "this freedom is used to commit offenses", the Government has imposed a series of bans on certain religious rituals and traditions, including the Muslim ritual of animal slaughterers (Schreuer, 2019).[18]

This, of course, encourages individuals to act in secret and forbidden ways. For example, we can find several mosques masked as cultural centers where, instead, are active uncontrolled and unmonitored groups of radicalized people.

Another big problem of Belgian cities is the presence within their neighborhoods of big ghettos of nationalities where local and federal authorities have no power (and do not even seek to achieve it) and where the law in force is that of the nation from which the majority of those who live there come (BBC News, 2015; Traynor, 2015). This tendency to ghettoization is due not only to racial hatred and suspicion that Belgian citizens have towards non-Belgian, but also to the ease with which can be created and can grow terrorist networks, by exploiting the poverty, the sense of humiliation and the will of redemption that in great quantity are present there.[19]

As regards PESTLE analysis' technological aspects, we can say with certainty that also the terrorists coming from Brussels have access to the internet and use the new tools to communicate in an encrypted and untraceable way. A great example of the technological power that terrorist possess nowadays is the one of the Brussels 2016 bombers. They used the internet to get hold the triacetone triperoxide, essential to assemble the nail bombs they used in the attacks, and, although their communications and knowledge were mostly offline thanks to Zerkani's network and their residence in Molenbeek, most likely, they used encrypted message apps to communicate and they radicalized both in Syria and online through jihadist propaganda (BBC News, 2016).

Once again, it should be stressed that the use of technology by terrorism is a growing counterterrorism problem as the likely terrorists are increasingly difficult to trace due to new methods of encrypted communication and the easy availability of ingredients to build explosive devices.

Legislatively speaking, finally, Belgium has transposed the EU's "Global Strategy to Combat terrorism" of 2005. As provided for in the strategy, Belgium's counterterrorism efforts have focused on the development of prevention, protection, persecution and response to terrorism.

During the period 2015-2016, the Belgian Government revised the Belgian Criminal Code and the Criminal Procedures to criminalize as terrorist acts foreign fighter trips abroad and to increase the investigative methods available to the counterterrorism intelligence (Elnakhala, n.d.). In addition to the already existing measures to prevent radicalization and improve security in relation to extremism and cyberterrorism such as the Community-oriented policy of 1990, the Plan R against Radicalism, the National Security Plan and the Integral Safety Note, in 2015, after the January and November Paris attacks, were issued thirty counterterrorism measures and the FTF circular, regulating the cooperation between federal and local authorities in foreign fighters issues (Elnakhala, n.d.). Belgium also takes part into the Strategy to Combat Terrorism Financing and into the European Union's RAN initiative which provides for the creation of grassroots networks of volunteers and experts sharing their work experience with radicalized or at risk of radicalization individuals (Elnakhala, n.d.). Again, Belgian Government uses a judiciary approach in the prosecution of terrorist perpetrators, thus ensuring fair trial and avoiding preventive detention (if not in special cases and defined by law) to suspects (Elnakhala, n.d.).

However, despite the innumerable counterterrorism measures adopted, Belgian security and intelligence systems have major operational, communication and cooperation difficulties with their foreigners' counterparts and among themselves. This is indeed mostly due to the parochialism culture, the police's local fragmentation and the lack of funds and personnel to carry out the increasingly high number of counterterrorism activities (Lasoen, 2017, pp.473-476; Lasoen, 2018, pp.2-6).

In fact, Belgium's has three fundamental security and intelligence problems which can be considered as a result of a political failure.

First of all, the successive governments over the years had too much confidence that Belgium, despite the enormous problems within the security apparatus, was safe and far from terrorist attacks. This means the Ministerial Committee and the auxiliary bodies put little attention while drafting safety standards and failed providing clear guidelines on the modalities and powers of action (Lasoen, 2017, 480-481).

Another fundamental problem is the discrepancy between the objectives and tasks assigned to intelligence and its resources in terms of instrumentation, funding and human capital allocated by political power. Belgian intelligence's wages are low, there are no staff and no budget to carry out data collection and train new agents.[20] Finally, the biggest problem undermining the proper functioning of intelligence agencies: the lack of cooperation. In Belgium, within the public administration there's the tendency to adopt parochial attitudes. This culture of rivalry and organizational isolation can be found both between governmental and intelligence and from intelligence vis-à-vis third countries (Lasoen, 2017, pp.475-476).

One again, the lack of communication and the mismanagement of funds would explain why local authorities failed to understand, before the Brussels attacks, the existence of terrorist recruitment networks and the connection between the cell of Paris and the one of Molenbeek.

PESTLE Analysis Applied to e-Government and the Cyber-Terrorism Threat

Again, we can provide a further and more general example of the application of PESTLE analysis to terrorism in a world where the above-mentioned problem of cyberterrorism is growing and increasingly threatening e-Government world.

In the previous paragraphs we introduced the topic of cyber-terrorism as a phenomenon which, according to Dorothy Denning, consist of terrorist attacking or menacing to attack "computers, networks and the information stored therein to intimidate or coerce a government or its people in furtherance of political or social objectives" (Weimann, 2004, p.4). Today, in the era of e-Government, it is a growing threat that no government has to underestimate. When we talk about e-Government, we refer to "the use of information and communications technologies (ICTs), and particularly the Internet, to achieve better government, transparency, accountability, effectiveness, participation, and consultation" (OECD, 2003, pp. 24, 41). This tool surely has a big positive impact on the development of the society, but it also appears as an attractive target for a large-scale terrorist attack, aimed at destroying and undermining technological, emergency and security infrastructures of a country.

Governments can use PESTLE analysis approach to evaluate the effects of e-Government on their societies and to assess the possible impact on their territories of a cyber terrorist attack. Democratic and politically stable countries through the use of e-Government manage to strengthen public policy in terms of efficiency and the provision of services. Furthermore, from a legal point of view, it creates strong institutions based on strict rules and guidelines for the protection of copyright, rights and personal data (Ha and Coghill, 2008, p.115). From an economic point of view, governments that invite and support private sectors to adopt e-commerce measures are more easily able to obtain profits and access to foreign markets. In addition, e-Government makes more efficient and time-saving purchase operations, request and presentation of documentation and monetary movements (Ha and Coghill, 2008, p.116-117).

On a social level the use of e-Government is essential to increase citizens' knowledge of society and to improve their participation in the life of the nation (Ha and Coghill, 2008, p. 117 - 118). Governments with more advanced and resilient technological infrastructures manage to develop a more efficient and resistant e-Government service to cyber and terrorist attacks (Ha and Coghill, 2008, p.117).

The positive effects seen so far, however, are questioned when on the government impacts an external environmental variable: a terrorist cyber-attack. Cyber-attacks are as destructive as the common ones and may involve, as has already happened in the past, attacks on airport computer systems, emergency telephone lines, waste disposal systems and gas transport (Terzi, 2019, p.229). When this happens governments inevitably lose population's confidence towards the use, usefulness and effectiveness of the e-Government, there could be huge economic losses resulting from the loss of sensitive data or disruption of business relationships and social losses resulting from the devastating impact of the attack and the today world's technological dependence (Lee and Rao, 2005, p.2).

Therefore, PESTLE analysis shows how cyber-terrorism represents a threat to the implementation and resilience of e-Government. Since this tool is essential for every government to make its business more efficient, effective and transparent, it is essential to use an IT risk insurance approach based on the creation of international counter-terrorism policies which insist on the strengthening of the network and investment in competent and highly specialized personnel in computer security (Terzi, 2019, pp. 238 - 239).

CONCLUSION

As shown by PESTLE analysis, the increasing security problems and the political instability of Belgium have a major impact on its economy and society. Against this background, the persistent feeling of insecurity and the additional danger of radicalization within Belgium can generate, in the first place, major economic losses in tourism, an increase in the emigration rates and the reduction of foreign direct investment (Ross, 2019). Secondly, since the fear drives individuals to look at each other suspiciously and to seek justice from themselves, there can be also social problems which end up isolating even more the marginalized people who will find refuge in radicalization (Greisman, 1979, pp.141-146).

To remedy these closely related to radicalization problems, Belgium needs a brand-new counterterrorism policy. It must focus on the treatment of the social and economic roots of radicalization and, to do that, in first analysis it should worry about Belgium's integration and migration policies. They should be revised and corrected. In fact, it would be desirable to develop, at federal level, integration programs based on facilitating the simple acquisition of the Belgian language and culture and the entry into the labor market, thus eliminating the *inburgering* efforts and promoting religious freedoms and the exercise of economic activities. This fresh approach to integration would enable immigrants and second-generation children to feel free and at home in the arrival territory where they could live their dual identity of European citizens with democratic and Western values, on one hand, and, on the other, as third countries citizens whose culture remains intact and can be exercised within its own private sphere. It is also necessary to respect the political rights of the Muslim community, allowing it to create political groups which can participate in the elections. Of course, the granting of these rights must be monitored since it is known that within the Belgian community there are many radicalized and politically active Muslims who want to impose Sharia.[21]

A good counterterrorism policy must also take into account that radicalization and terrorism can generate economic losses due to the decline in tourism, the cost of additional security measures and the loss of foreign investment.

That is why is essential to focus on the prevention of terrorism by addressing the economic motivations that can drive an individual towards radicalization. If it is true that radicalization can derive from economic inequality and poverty experienced by an individual, then it is good to act at the root of this social inequality: the educational system. We have already seen that low incomes and the economic paralyses are strictly connected to the second-generation immigrants' low educational levels. At this point, it is therefore clear that a reform of the educational system is needed. This study proposes the inclusion of the second or third generation young people into classes with a low percentage of foreigners, so to enable them to learn quickly and better the Belgian language and to obtain better grades, without jeopardizing their future educational career. Also, vocational schools (which usually have a higher concentration of second-generation immigrants) should be reformed. There should be employed more motivated teachers, able to cope with problematic students and who possess basic notions of the Arabic language.

One should also lay hands on the Belgian society. Indeed, the Belgian citizens must be educated to inclusion and equal opportunities and must be aware of the economic and social losses that isolation and radicalization can provoke. In addition, this re-education process could also contribute to reduce unemployment rates among second-generation young people and to give them greater recognition in terms of civil rights and freedoms of expression. Another, and maybe too ambitious, proposal could be the elimination of ghettos.

Last but not least, we have to consider legal aspects. The fragmented structures of the police and intelligence services need to be reconstructed since they make it difficult for these two bodies to carry out an essential task: the exchange of information.

It is not feasible for a state where there are many radical Muslims and which is so prone to terrorist episodes that the security structures cannot communicate because they collect data and information in a different way, have at their disposal different instruments and still have deep-rooted in themselves the culture of parochialism which prevents them, voluntarily and otherwise, from cooperating.

Considering all these loopholes it is then strongly recommended to develop a legislative reform, establishing a single federal intelligence corps and a single federal police corps that will command and coordinate the regional and federal corps under their control. Also federal funding are needed to recruit and train new staff, hiring experts in cybersecurity and with knowledge of the Arabic culture and language and for the creation of new digital tools aimed at improving the exchange of information within the individual systems and with third countries. This to mitigate, not only the increasing impact that terrorism has through the use of technology, but also to try to reform the police and intelligence staff, in order to dismantle that counterproductive culture of parochialism.

FUTURE RESEARCH DIRECTIONS

This study could represent an interesting starting point for future researches dealing with the development of a common counter-terrorism policy at European level. By carrying out PESTLE analyses for each EU's Member States, it could emerge some common and important implications useful to elaborate a valid Communitarian counterterrorism strategy.

Figure 1. Summary of the causes of radicalization and proposed remedies

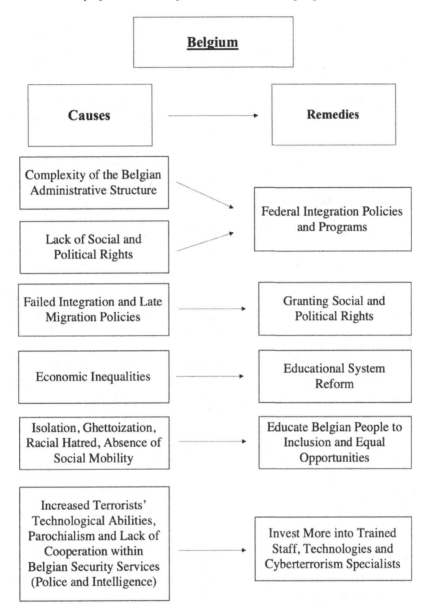

REFERENCES

Baudet, M. B. (2019, March 26). Perché il Belgio è il focolaio del jihadismo europeo. *Internazionale.* Retrieved November 25, 2019 from https://www.internazionale.it/notizie/2016/03/23/belgio-jihadismo-europeo

BBC News. (2015, November 16). *Why is this Belgian suburb linked to so many terrorist attacks?* Retrieved November 27, 2019 from https://www.bbc.co.uk/programmes/p0385tzj

BBC News. (2016, April 9). *Brussels explosions: What we know about airport and metro attacks.* Retrieved November 30, 2019 from https://www.bbc.com/news/world-europe-35869985

Borum, R. (2003). Understanding the terrorist mindset. *FBI Law Enforcement Bulletin, 72*(7), 7-10. Retrieved November 30, 2019 from https://www.ncjrs.gov/pdffiles1/nij/grants/201462.pdf

Cruickshank, P. (2017, October 30). The inside story of the Paris and Brussels attacks. *CNN.* Retrieved November 25, 2019 from https://edition.cnn.com/2016/03/30/europe/inside-paris-brussels-terror-attacks/index.html

Dalgaard-Nielsen, A. (2010). Violent radicalization in Europe: What we know and what we do not know. *Studies in Conflict and Terrorism, 33*(9), 797–814. Retrieved November 27, 2019, from. doi:10.1080/1057610X.2010.501423

Ealing, M. (2018). *PEST analysis identifying "big picture" opportunities and threats.* London: University of Westminster. Retrieved November 30, 2019 from https://www.academia.edu/37754145/PEST_Analysis

Elnakhala, D. (n.d.). *Ct overview: Belgium, 4TU Center for Ethics and Technology.* Retrieved November 20, 2019 from http://counterterrorismethics.com/the-belgian-counter-terrorism-landscape/

European Council, Council of the European Union. (n.d.). *EU counter-terrorism strategy.* Retrieved November 21, 2019 from https://www.consilium.europa.eu/en/policies/fight-against-terrorism/eu-strategy/

European Council, Council of the European Union. (n.d.). *Response to the terrorist threat and recent terrorist attacks in Europe.* Retrieved November 21, 2019 from https://www.consilium.europa.eu/en/policies/fight-against-terrorism/foreign-fighters/

Europol. (2018). *European Union terrorism situation and trend*. Report. Retrieved November 20, 2019 from https://www.europol.europa.eu/activities-services/main-reports/european-union-terrorism-situation-and-trend-report-2018-tesat-2018

Greisman, H. C. (1979). Terrorism and the closure of society: A social-impact projection. *Technological Forecasting and Social Change*, *14*(2), 135–146. doi:10.1016/0040-1625(79)90100-8

Grieger, T. (2006). Psychiatric and societal impacts of terrorism. *The Psychiatric Times*, *23*(7), 1–2. Retrieved December 10, 2019, from https://www.psychiatrictimes.com/disaster-psychiatry/psychiatric-and-societal-impacts-terrorism

Ha, H., & Coghill, K. (2008). E-Government in Singapore a SWOT and PEST Analysis. *Asia-Pacific Social Science Review, 6*(2), 103-130. Retrieved April 13, 2020 from https://www.researchgate.net/publication/242314776_E-Government_in_Singapore_a_SWOT_and_PEST_Analysis

INFOSEC. (2018, February 3). *The role of technology in modern terrorism*. Retrieved November 22, 2019 from https://resources.infosecinstitute.com/the-role-of-technology-in-modern-terrorism/

Kroet, C. (2016, January 1). Belgium has most foreign fighters per head: Anti-terror report says most radicalized fighters come from Just 4 EU countries. *Politico*. Retrieved November 25, 2019 from https://www.politico.eu/article/a-third-of-isil-foreign-fighters-return-to-europe-report/

Lasoen, K. L. (2017). For Belgian eyes only: Intelligence cooperation in Belgium. *International Journal of Intelligence and CounterIntelligence*, *30*(3), 464–490. doi:10.1080/08850607.2017.1297110

Lasoen, K. L. (2018). Plan B(ruxellles): Belgian intelligence and the terrorist attacks of 2015-16. *Terrorism and Political Violence*, 1–19. doi:10.1080/09546553.2018.1464445

Lee, J. K., & Rao, H. R. (2005). *Risk of Terrorism, Trust in Government, and e-Government Services: An Exploratory Study of Citizens' Intention to use e-Government Services in a Turbulent Environment*. YCISS Working Paper Number 30, pp.1-27. Retrieved April 13, 2020 from https://yorkspace.library.yorku.ca/xmlui/bitstream/handle/10315/1348/YCI0020.pdf?

Mandin, J. (2014). *An overview of integration policies in Belgium.* INTERACT RR 2014/20, Robert Schuman Centre for Advanced Studies, San Domenico di Fiesole (FI): European University Institute. Retrieved November 21, 2019 from http://diana-n.iue.it:8080/bitstream/handle/1814/33133/INTERACT-RR-2014%20-%20 20.pdf?sequence=1&isAllowed=y

Martiniello, M. (2003). Belgium's immigration policy. *The International Migration Review, 37*(1), 225–232. doi:10.1111/j.1747-7379.2003.tb00135.x

Moghaddam, F. M. (2005). The staircase to terrorism: A psychological exploration. *American Psychological Association, 60*(2), 161–169. Retrieved December 2, 2019 from https://www.academia.edu/3450594/The_staircase_to_terrorism_a_ psychological_on

Muslims in Belgium. (2008). *Insights, 1*(2), 119-144. Retrieved November 19, 2019 from http://www.euro-islam.info/spip/article.php3?id_article=2168

Nelson, R., & Sanderson, T. M. (2011). *A threat transformed: Al Qaeda and associated movements in 2011.* Center for Strategic and International Studies. Retrieved December 10, 2019 from https://csis-prod.s3.amazonaws.com/s3fs-public/legacy_files/files/ publication/110203_Nelson_AThreatTransformed_web.pdf

OECD. (2002). Economic consequences of terrorism. *Economic Outlook, 71,* 117–140. Retrieved November 23, 2019, from https://www.oecd.org/economy/ outlook/1935314.pdf

OHCHR. (2018, May 23). *France: UN expert says new terrorism laws may undermine fundamental rights and freedoms.* Retrieved November 22, 2019 from https://www. ohchr.org/EN/NewsEvents/Pages/DisplayNews.aspx?NewsID=23130&LangID=E

Ross, S. (2019, May 20). *Top 5 ways terrorism impacts the economy.* Investopedia. Retrieved December 10, 2019 from https://www.investopedia.com/articles/ markets/080216/top-5-ways-terrorism-impacts-economy.asp

Sageman, M. (2008). A strategy for fighting international islamist terrorists. *The Annals of the American Academy of Political and Social Science, 618*(1), 223–231. doi:10.1177/0002716208317051

Samata, S. (2016). Language, exclusion and violent jihad: Are they related? *International Journal of Bilingual Education and Bilingualism,* 1–10. Retrieved November 23, 2019, from. doi:10.1080/13670050.2016.1208143

Schreuer, M. (2019, January 5). Belgium bans religious slaughtering practices, drawing praise and protest. *The New York Times.* Retrieved November 27, 2019 from https://www.nytimes.com/2019/01/05/world/europe/belgium-ban-jewish-muslim-animal-slaughter.html

Silber, M. D., & Bhatt, A. (2007). *Radicalization in the West: The homegrown threat.* The New York City Police Department.

Team, F. M. E. (2013). *PESTLE analysis: Strategy skills. Electronic Publication: Free Management Ebooks.* Retrieved December 10, 2019 from https://docplayer. net/9768722-Pestle-analysis-strategy-skills team-fme-www-free-management ebooks-com-isbn-978-1-62620-998-5.html

Terzi, M. (2019). E-Government and Cyber Terrorism: Conceptual Framework, Theoretical Discussion and Possible Solutions. *TESAM Akademi Dergisi - Turkish Journal of TESAM Academy, 6*(1), 213-247. Retrieved April 13, 2020 from https:// dergipark.org.tr/en/pub/tesamakademi/article/528011

The National Interest. (2019, February 22). *Technology is making terrorists more effective and harder to thwart.* Retrieved November 22, 2019 from https:// nationalinterest.org/feature/technology-making-terrorists-more-effective—and-harder-thwart-45452

Timmerman, C., Vanderwaeren, E., & Crul, M. (2003). The second generation in Belgium. *The International Migration Review, 37*(4), 1065–1090. doi:10.1111/j.1747-7379.2003.tb00170.x

Traynor, I. (2015, November 15). Molenbeek: The Brussels borough becoming known as Europe's jihadi central. *The Guardian.* Retrieved November 26, 2019 from https://www.theguardian.com/world/2015/nov/15/molenbeek-the-brussels-borough-in-the spotlight-after-paris-attacks

Trump, D. J. (2018). *National strategy for counterterrorism of the United States of America.* Washington, DC: The White House. Retrieved 28 November 2019 from https://www.whitehouse.gov/wp-content/uploads/2018/10/NSCT.pdf

Van Ostaeyen, P. (2016). Belgian radical networks and the road to the Brussels attacks. *CTC Sentinel, 9*(613), 7-12. Retrieved December 2, 2019 from https://ctc. usma.edu/belgian-radical-networks-and-the-road-to-the-brussels-attacks/

Waterfield, B. (2011, December 6). Belgium to have new government after world record 541 days. *The Telegraph.* Retrieved November 27, 2019 from https://www. telegraph.co.uk/news/worldnews/europe/belgium/8936857/Belgium-to-have-new-government-after-world-record-541-days.html

Weimann, G. (2004). Cyberterrorism. How Real Is the Threat? *United State Institute of Peace*. Retrieved April 13, 2020 from https://www.usip.org/sites/default/files/sr119.pdf

Wiktorowicz, Q. (2004). *Joining the cause: Al-Muhajiroun and radical Islam*. Paper: Department of International Studies, Rhodes College. Retrieved November 26, 2019 from https://securitypolicylaw.syr.edu/wp-content/uploads/2013/03/Wiktorowicz.Joining-the-Cause.pdf

Williams, L. K., Koch, T. M., & Smith, J. M. (2013). The political consequences of terrorism: Terror events, casualties, and government duration. *International Studies Perspectives*, *14*(3), 343–361. doi:10.1111/j.1528-3585.2012.00498.x

Wilner, A. S., & Dubouloz, C. J. (2010). Homegrown terrorism and transformative learning: An interdisciplinary approach to understanding radicalization. *Global Change, Peace & Security*, *22*(1), 33–51. doi:10.1080/14781150903487956

Wonderful Wanderings. (2015, May 19). *Belgium explained: Language and political structure*. YouTube Video. Retrieved December 2, 2019 from https://www.youtube.com/watch?v=2ehWO-f_6uk

ADDITIONAL READING

Argomaniz, J., Bures, O., & Kaunert, C. (2017). EU counter-terrorism and intelligence: A critical assessment. Abingdon-on-Thames, UK: Routledge. doi:10.4324/9781315674360

Crone, M., & Harrow, M. (2011). Homegrown terrorism in the West. *Terrorism and Political Violence*, *23*(4), 521–536. Retrieved November 21, 2019, from. doi:10.1080/09546553.2011.571556

Ersen, U. M., & Kibaroğlu, M. (2011). *Analysis and strategies to counter the terrorism threat*. IOS Press.

Forest, J. F. (2015). *Essentials of counterterrorism*. Praeger Publishers.

Giusto, H. (2015). *Daesh and the terrorist threat: From the Middle East to Europe*. Foundation for European Progressive Studies and Fondazione Italianieuropei.

King, M., & Taylor, D. (2011). The radicalization of homegrown jihadists: A review of theoretical models and social psychological evidence. *Terrorism and Political Violence*, *23*(4), 602–622. Retrieved November 22, 2019, from. doi:10.1080/09546553.2011.587064

Mitts, T. (2019). From isolation to radicalization: Anti-Muslim hostility and support for ISIS in the West. *The American Political Science Review*, *113*(1), 173–194. Retrieved November 28, 2019, from. doi:10.1017/S0003055418000618

OECD. (2003). *The e-Government Imperative*. OECD Publication Service.

Stevenson, J. (2016). After Brussels: Understanding and countering ISIS's strategy. *Strategic Comments*, *22*(2), iii–v. Retrieved November 30, 2019, from. doi:10.108 0/13567888.2016.1174433

Wade, M., & Maljević, A. (2010). *A War on Terror? The European Stance on a New Threat, Changing Laws and Human Rights Implications*. Springer.

KEY TERMS AND DEFINITIONS

Counterterrorism: Set of strategies and security measures implemented by a government to protect the country from terrorist attacks and to prevent terrorists from using their resources.

Cyberterrorism: Particular type of terrorism which uses the Internet as the main means of attack. It can cause economic losses, damage infrastructure or cause people's death through the use, for example, of malware and viruses.

Discrimination: It is a differentiated and disparaging treatment on the basis of physical details, age, gender or race.

Homegrown Terrorist: It is a person of Middle Eastern origin but born or lived since childhood in the West who, suddenly, decides to commit a terrorist act against his country.

Jihad: It is the term used by terrorist groups and organizations to denote the holy war the faithful Muslim extremist must carry out against the infidel Westerns.

Jihadist Propaganda: Series of documents, videos, images, and files posted online and translated into various languages that serve as a means for terrorist organizations to recruit followers and foreign fighters around the world.

Parochialism: It is the practice adopted by public organizations and institutions which consist in not exchanging information and working on their own. This tendency creates state's functioning problems. In fact, it works more slowly, with incorrect or incomplete communications and in an uneven way.

Radicalization: Process by which an individual, following a personal crisis, rejects the system of Western values and adopts an extremist view of world which culminates in the acceptance of violence as a form of expression towards the contemptuous West.

Second-Generation Children: Children of immigrants. They are born, raised and citizens of the host country of their parents.

ENDNOTES

[1] Protection pillar. To learn more about the PNR Directive see: https://www.consilium.europa.eu/en/policies/fight-against-terrorism/passenger-name-record/ (Retrieved November 21, 2019)

[2] Porsecution pillar.

[3] Response pillar.

[4] It should be noted, however, that recruiting and finding new people to radicalize is a cornerstone of any terrorist organization. For further information on the recruiting topic, see: Spechard, A. (2009). The militant jihad in Europe: Fighting home-grown terrorism. In Pick T.M. et al. (ed.), *Home-Grown Terrorism* (pp.151-155). Amsterdam: IOS Press.

[5] It is also called PEST, STEEPLE, STEP, PESTLIED.

[6] Especially when the counterterrorism measures taken don't address people's discomfort and malaise, exacerbated by low wages, high levels of corruption and low financial resources. It is in this context then that people legitimize terrorism as form of expression.

[7] In this regard, in 2018, the International Institute for Counterterrorism warned about "the possibility of terrorist organizations to acquire offensive capabilities on the Internet by hiring hackers or receiving assistance from terror- sponsoring countries."

[8] It is very probable that, in the future, terrorist organizations will be able to improve their hacking skills in order to penetrate the systems of health, administrations, transportations and communications, production and power plants.

[9] In this context, according to the OHCHR, French antiterrorism laws seem to undermine Muslim community's fundamental rights and freedoms. However, to avoid misunderstandings, it should be stress that there are some cases defined by law in which may be allowed the temporary limitation of these rights.

[10] The Moroccan district of Molenbeek is the center of European Islamic activity. From Molenbeek came several homegrown terrorists who, during the 2000's, conducted attacks in Europe. This neighborhood is characterized by high unemployment and poverty rates and, until 2014, there it was active the Zerkani's recruitment terrorist network which sent to Syria at least 60 foreign fighters (among them we find 2 Paris bombers and 2 Brussels bombers).

11   The analysis considers Political, Economic, Social, Technological and Legal variables, leaving out environmental variables.

12   Among the non-European nationalities in Belgium, Turkish and Moroccan are the most widely represented with respectively 2% and 3.7% of the total population.

13   The "doctrine of zero immigration" provided for the regulation of the illegal immigration and recognized the right of family reunification, asylum and study permits.

14   The Flanders adopt a multicultural approach; they recognize ethnic minorities and pay particular attention to the economic and social aspects of migrants in the development of integration policies. Wallonia and Brussels-Capital Region don't recognize minorities and opt for anti-exclusion policies which are more similar to assimilation rather than integration approach.

15   This term characterizes the Belgian integration programs. They provide for language, socio-cultural and work-related courses and encourage cultural assimilation and conformity in order to try to eliminate the characteristic features of every minority present within the territory.

16   The only possibility the Muslim community has to be politically represented is up to a few Muslim candidates from the Socialist Party.

17   The extremist parties also are discredited and recently, on September 2018, some parties tabled a proposal to the Belgian parliament for a constitutional amendment to prevent the participation in elections to "Islam", the Islamist party born in 2012.

18   Islam was recognized as religion with the law of July 19, 1974. The principle of State's neutrality towards religion until it does not damage the society is contained in the art.19 of the Belgian Constitution: *"Freedom of worship, its public practice and freedom to demonstrate one's opinions on all matters are guaranteed, but offences committed when this freedom is used may be punished."*

19   The most striking case is that of the Moroccan majority district of Molenbeek where, during the period 2012-2014, it was active Zerkani's terrorist and recruitment network.

20   The VSSE is the most affected intelligence body by this resource deficit. Over times, it has suffered extensive budget cuts and this fact, especially with the emergence of the threat of foreign fighters, caused it many problems: lack of personnel, neglecting operations and weakening of other important areas of their competence, such as counter-espionage and proliferation.

21   Despite everything, in fact, in a country where 4% of the population is Muslim, the facilitated opening of places of worship, gathering points and the constitution of political parties must be supervised and monitored periodically to prevent

radicalization and dismantle recruitment networks hidden in Belgium's social fabric.

Chapter 3

Exploring Cognitive Biases, Groupthink, and Polythink Syndrome in Security Decisions and Business Outcomes

Luisa Dall'Acqua
University of Bologna, Italy & LS TCO, Italy

ABSTRACT

Cognitive bias among workers can undermine security work and lead to critical misinterpretations of data. Understanding cognitive biases can improve understanding of how employees make decisions. This work analyzes key factors to better understand, predict, and obviate the detrimental bias symptoms, focusing on groupthink and polythink phenomena occurring in security and business decisions. It intends to provide support for the strategic versus tactical hypothesis in a strategic group decision-making, confirming how even in a clear-cut decision, following a groupthink or polythink dynamic, implementation becomes difficult due to a group dynamics at the other end of the decision-making continuum.

DOI: 10.4018/978-1-7998-4339-9.ch003

INTRODUCTION

Cognitive Biases

The human brain is capable of 1016 processes per second, which makes it far more powerful than any computer currently in existence.

But that doesn't mean our brains don't have major limitations. Some decisions are made after careful calculation whereas others are more intuitive. Cognitive limitations can often distort information processing.

When evidence is lacking or ambiguous, analysts evaluate hypotheses by applying their general background knowledge concerning the nature of systems and behavior.

Firstly, it's important to distinguish between cognitive biases and logical fallacies. A logical fallacy is an error in logical argumentation.

A cognitive bias, on the other hand, is a genuine deficiency or limitation in our thinking. It is a flaw in judgment that arises from (i.e.) errors of memory, social attribution, and miscalculations (such as statistical errors or a false sense of probability).

Paradoxically, some social psychologists believe our cognitive biases can help us process information more efficiently, especially in dangerous situations. But they lead us to make grave mistakes, more of the times. We may be prone to such errors in judgment, but at least we can be aware of them.

Cognitive biases are mental errors caused by our simplified information processing strategies.

- Cultural, emotional or intellectual predisposition toward a certain judgment
- Distinction: cultural bias, organizational bias, and bias that results from one's own self-interest

Cognitive biases are similar to optical illusions in that the error remains compelling even when one is fully aware of its nature, but the awareness of the bias, by itself, does not produce a more accurate perception.

In short, these tendencies usually arise from:

- Information processing shortcuts
- The limited processing ability of the brain
- Emotional and moral motivations
- Distortions in storing and retrieving memories
- Social influence
- Preferences and beliefs regardless of contrary information

Figure 1. Most relevant biases groups

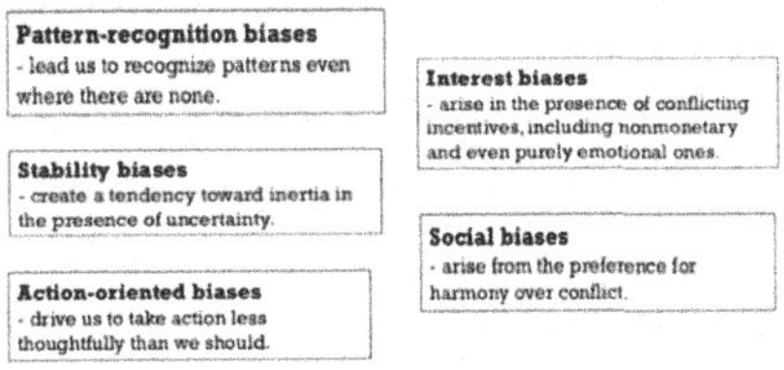

Pattern-recognition biases
- lead us to recognize patterns even where there are none.

Stability biases
- create a tendency toward inertia in the presence of uncertainty.

Action-oriented biases
- drive us to take action less thoughtfully than we should.

Interest biases
- arise in the presence of conflicting incentives, including nonmonetary and even purely emotional ones.

Social biases
- arise from the preference for harmony over conflict.

What happens when these dynamics apply to the social dimension, where members of a group have to make shared decisions, evaluating decision strategies, with possible conditioning of cognitive prejudices.

Specifically, a group decision-making dynamic is based on different members in a decision-making unit espouse a plurality of opinions and offer divergent group policy prescriptions. They can result in intragroup conflict, a disjointed decision-making process, and decision paralysis, as each group member pushes for his or her preferred policy action.

In a group dynamic, the "risky shift" phenomenon as well as the opposite, a "cautious shift" (Stoner, 1961) can occur: individuals tend to take more or fewer risks after a group discussion.

Possible explanations can be a group polarization phenomenon (Moskovici & Zavaloni, 1969)):

- The extreme majority alternative gets more discussion time
- Responsibility is shared among individual members
- Extreme individuals become more extreme when they discover that their opinion is not as extreme as viewed
- The extreme alternative is valued higher due to group effect
- Groups are risk-neutral while members are risk-averse

How could a Government and policy-making team, including foreign policy and national security experts, make policy decisions that lead to possible cognitive biases and negative outcomes? There are similar factors at play?

This chapter intends to provide support for the strategic versus tactical hypothesis in a strategic group decision-making, confirming how even in a clear-cut decision. It is the result of two very different, but similarly destructive, types of sub-optimal group decision-making processes at the elite level, such as the result of the phenomenon called Groupthink or of the opposite dynamic Polythink. Furthermore, their possible implementation in Foreign Policy Decision Making is analyzed. It is difficult due to a group dynamic at the other end of the decision-making continuum.

Table 1. Examples of group decision making

VARIABLES	DESCRIPTION
Context	• High stress from external threats with low hope of a better solution than the leader's ; • Low self-esteem temporarily induced by: a. Recent failures; b. Excessive difficulties on current decision-making task that lowers members' self-efficacy; c. Moral dilemmas: Apparent loss of feasible alternatives except ones that violate ethical standards;
Advantages	• Multiple views and types of expertise • Social facilitation due to directed open discussion • Brainstorming might lead to creative solutions
Disadvantages	• Often fails to equal the best individual solution • Conformity bias (e.g., the Asch (1951-1956) 3 lines experiments) • Groupthink (overconfidence, ignorance of facts) • Polarization effect (e.g., "risky shift" phenomenon) • Social loafing (pool, elevator experiments) • In general: No optimal decision rule exists for more than 2 options
Defective Individual Decision-Making	• Incomplete survey of alternatives; • Incomplete survey of objectives; • Failure to examine risks of preferred choice; • Failure to reappraise initially rejected alternatives; • Poor information search; • Selective bias in processing information at hand; • Failure to work out contingency plans;
Structural Faults of the Organization	• Insulation of the group; • Lack of tradition of impartial leadership; • Lack of norms requiring methodical procedures; • Homogeneity of members' social background and ideology

Groupthink

What is Groupthink?

Irving Janis (1972) used the term 'groupthink' as a quick and easy way to refer to a mode of thinking that people engage in when they are deeply involved in a cohesive in-group, when the members' strivings for unanimity override their motivation to realistically appraise alternative courses of action.

Groupthink refers to a deterioration of mental efficiency, reality testing and moral judgment.

Other possible synthetic definitions:

• a way of deliberating that group members use when their desire for unanimity overrides their motivation to assess all available plans of action (Janis, 1972)

- A deterioration of mental efficiency, reality testing and moral judgment that results from in-group pressures (Janice, 1982)
- a mode of thinking that people engage in when they are deeply involved in a cohesive in-group, when the members' strivings for unanimity override their motivation to realistically appraise alternative courses of action. (Griffin, 1991)

Groupthink is a type of thought exhibited by group members who try to minimize conflict and reach consensus without critically testing, analyzing, and evaluating ideas. It occurs when a group makes faulty decisions because group pressures lead to a deterioration of "mental efficiency, reality testing, and moral judgment" (Janis, 1972, p. 9).

Janis thinks that the high cohesiveness of a policy making group endangers independent and critical thinking. Members of a small cohesive group tend to maintain the spirit of the body by unconsciously developing a series of shared illusions and relative norms that interfere with critical thinking and verification of reality. (Janis, 1982: 35).

Groups sometimes fall into a style of thinking where the maintenance of the group's cohesion and togetherness becomes all-important and results in very bad decision-making.

Individual creativity, uniqueness, and independent thinking are lost in the pursuit of group cohesiveness, as are the advantages of reasonable balance in choice and thought that might normally be obtained by making decisions as a group.

Groupthink happens most often when the group is already cohesive, is isolated from conflicting opinions and where the leader is open and directive.

The lack of a formal decision process is also common. Problem-solving and task-oriented groups are particularly susceptible. Occurs when groups are cohesive and insulated from the outside, while inside pressures for group loyalty and conformity lead to muddled thinking. Resulting decisions are often based on incomplete information and fail to consider alternatives and risks.

Groupthink theory maintains that groupthink can occur in any group where members consider loyalty to the group more important than the action it decides to take. Not all cohesive groups end up succumbing to groupthink. Cohesiveness is a necessary but not sufficient condition for excessive concurrence seeking.

Since the groupthink is considered a social-cognitive syndrome, it is possible to identify some symptoms that forewarn (Paul Hart, 1991).

Janis wanted to understand how a blue-ribbon group could make such a terrible decision. He believed that group dynamics were responsible for the poor decision making in synthesis, he called it groupthink. According to Janis thought, groupthink famous examples are: Bay of Pigs invasion; Challenger space shuttle launch; Israel

Table 2. Symptoms of groupthink according to Mintz and Wayne (2016)

TYPE	MEANING
Invulnerability	It is the shared conviction about the success of a decision. Overconfidence that leads to irrational decisions. The collective belief that "we are too powerful or the best"
Rationale	It occurs when there is a collective tendency to discredit warnings and negative feedback. E.g. Pearl Harbor rationale If Japan attacks USA it will trigger an all-out war that Japan will lose.
Morality	The group believes that their path is morally the right path. Thus, they don't consider the moral and ethical results of their actions. This is a war between good and evil. Hence we can do any means necessary.
Stereotypes	It is a stereotypical view on opponents Underestimating the enemy
Pressure	It occurs with a group pressure to "domesticate dissenters". Any critical stance is downgraded and avoided. Belittling dissenters through nicknames «Here comes Mr. Stop-the-bombing!»
Self-censorship	It occurs when group members do not voice their concerns to keep the group integrity. They are also afraid of standing against the group leader
Unanimity	It is the illusion that everybody shares the same view when there was no dissenting opinion raised. Belief that unanimous view is the correct view. Sense of unanimity makes the group confident about their decisions. Therefore, the group does not need to check the validity of their decision
Mindguards	It occurs when certain group members act as the protector of the group leader's decision sidelining criticisms. We must be united in these dark times. Don't criticize..

before the October 1973 war, as well as the Challenger Launch; Pearl Harbor; invasion of North Korea; Vietnam war; Watergate coverup. Janis' position is that the consensus-seeking tendency of close-knit groups can cause them to make inferior decisions.

A perfect functional depiction of groupthink in action can be Hans Christian Andersen's story The Emperor's New Clothes. When the emperor parades through the streets in what he has been talked into imagining is a dazzling new suit, all his deferential subjects acclaim it as handsome beyond compare. Only the little boy points out that the emperor is not wearing any clothes at all, and is stark naked. And, of course, those caught up in the 'consensus' all viciously turn on him for pointing out the truth. In the epilogue I shall refer briefly to other instances of groupthink that have become only too familiar in our present-day world. But before we apply Janis's three rules to the 'non-debate' over global warming, we must also add one more very important aspect of the way groupthink operates which he didn't touch on, because it wasn't relevant to the particular examples he was analyzing (Janis, 1982).

Since the introduction of Groupthink in the 1970s (Mintz&Wayne, 2016), much emphasis has been placed in national security and foreign policy decision-making circles on the procedures, processes, methods, and techniques that can be utilized to

Table 3: The three rules of groupthink (Booker. 2018)

Roles	Descriptions
ROLE 1 The creation of a belief-system	is that a group of people come to share a common view or belief that in some way is not properly based on reality. They may believe they have all sorts of evidence that confirms that their opinion is right, but their belief cannot ultimately be tested in a way that confirms this beyond doubt. In essence, therefore, it is no more than a shared belief.
ROLE 2 Creating the illusion of a 'consensus'	is that, precisely because their shared view cannot be subjected to external proof, they then feel the need to reinforce its authority by elevating it into a 'consensus', a word Janis himself emphasised. To those who subscribe to the 'consensus', the common belief seems intellectually and morally so self-evident that all right-thinking people must agree with it. The one thing they cannot afford to allow is that anyone, either within their group or outside it, should question or challenge it.
ROLE 3 Putting 'non-believers' beyond the pale	in some ways the most revealing of all, is a consequence of that insistence that everyone must support the 'consensus'. The views of anyone who fails to share it become wholly unacceptable. There cannot be any possibility of dialogue with them. They must be excluded from any further discussion. At best they may just be marginalised and ignored, atworst they must be openly attacked and discredited. Dissent cannot be tolerated.

prevent Groupthink from occurring, such as a leader remaining impartial rather than stating a particular view; dividing the group into subgroups to hammer out differences; bringing in outside experts to challenge policymakers' views; and assigning specific members of the group to play the role of "devil's advocate" (Janis, 1981).

Janis (1982) proposed a possible way to avoid groupthink. Going outside the group thinking "outside the box." One member should always play the devil's advocate. Leaders should refrain from declaring opinion at the beginning of the meeting. Multiple advocacy. No decisions are made without an open internal bargaining process.

Changes can be made in:

- Insulation of the group;
- Impartial leadership;
- Procedural methods (e.g., encourage dissent);

Groupthink can severely undermine the value of a group's work and, at its worst, it can cost people their lives (AA.VV. 2019). On a lesser scale, it can stifle teamwork, and leave all but the most vocal team members disillusioned and dissatisfied. If you're on a team that makes a decision you don't really support but you feel you can't say or do anything about it, your enthusiasm will quickly fade.

Teams are capable of being much more effective than individuals but, when Groupthink sets in, the opposite can be true. By creating a healthy group-working

Table 4. business group techniques that help to avoid groupthink (Source: AA:VV. 2019)

Type	focus
Brainstorming	Helps ideas flow freely without criticism.
Modified Borda Count	Allows each group member to contribute individually, so mitigating the risk that stronger and more persuasive group members dominate the decision making process
Six Thinking Hats	Helps the team look at a problem from many different perspectives, allowing people to play "Devil's Advocate".
The Delphi Technique	Allows team members to contribute individually, with no knowledge of a group view, and with little penalty for disagreement.

environment, you can help ensure that the group makes good decisions, and manages any associated risks appropriately.

Historical Examples

Since the 9/n attacks, the U.S., and the world, have never been the same. Following the attacks, the U.S. entered the costly War on Terror, launching two wars in Afghanistan and Iraq. Today, ongoing unrest in Iraq, Syria, and Afghanistan, the ISIS threat, and other terrorist attacks around the globe continue, with offensive operations by the U.S. in Iraq, Syria, and other countries in the region occurring as well (Mintz&Wayne, 2016).

Examples of groupthink include the US government's failure to anticipate Pearl Harbor, the Vietnam War escalation and the Second Gulf War. In US Invasion of Iraq, predetermined Policy Decision about Iraq and Saddam Hussein. Reasonably, discount warnings and do not reconsider their assumptions even as other countries challenge them. Possible dealing with dissenters was a pressure not to express arguments against any of the administration's actions. Imminent Danger from Weapons of Mass Destruction could be a selective bias in processing information at hand, instead, a limited Examination of Risks of Actions could have conducted to a possible failure to work out contingency plans (Mintz & Schneiderman, 2018).

According to Jack Eaton thought (2001), UK companies Marks & Spencer and British Airways. In the 1990s, both companies introduced globalization strategies in which, according to Eaton, all eight symptoms of groupthink were present. The illusion of invulnerability led both companies to underestimate the elements leading to their failure.

The Flying Bank is one of the prime entrepreneurial examples of groupthink in business. This refers to the collapse of Swissair, a Swiss airline company that believed itself to be so financially stable that it became known as the Flying Bank. Authors Aaron Hermann and Hussain Rammal described two symptoms of groupthink in their article "The Grounding of the 'Flying Bank.'" These symptoms were the belief that the group was invulnerable and its morality superior. Before its collapse, Swissair reduced its company board, losing much of its industrial expertise in the process. Experts attribute the resizing as a factor in groupthink (Kilhefner, 2019).

Another possible example can be the recent Swissair situation: it took a surprising nose dive which many put down to organizational groupthink. The airline was once so financially secure it was referred to as the "Flying Bank". However, the airline eventually went bankrupt as board members began to believe they were invulnerable and failed to question poor decisions and mismanagement. They made ill-advised acquisitions and failed to respond to up-and-coming budget airline competitors like Ryanair and Easy Jet. They were bailed out by the Swiss Federal Government in 2002 but eventually all operations collapsed.

Polythink

In a Groupthink scenario, the overarching tendency to strive for consensus and unanimity rather than carefully reviewing a set of diverse pol-icy options and the risks and benefits that accompany each leads to sub-optimal decision-making processes that in turn result in the many policy "fiascoes" with which we are all too familiar, such as the attack on Pearl Harbor (Janis 1982).

The leading concept of group dynamics, groupthink, offers one explanation: policy-making groups make sub-optimal decisions due to their desire for conformity and uniformity over dissent, leading to a failure to consider other relevant possibilities. But presidential advisory groups are often fragmented and divisive.

Janis and others have also recognized that many of these policy prescriptions could have detrimental effects if they are poorly managed. These strategies could lead to prolonged debates that could be costly when a crisis requires immediate action, or they might damage good relations between group members. Thus, oftentimes the prescriptions provided by theorists and practitioners for addressing Groupthink leave decision makers at risk of swinging too far in the other direction and contributing to the advent of a very different, but no less detrimental phenomenon that we term Polythink (Mintz&Wayne, 2016)

Polythink is a group dynamic whereby different members in a decision-making unit espouse a plurality of opinions and offer divergent policy prescriptions, and even dissent, which can result in intragroup conflict and a fragmented, disjointed decision-making process.

Polythink is the opposite of Groupthink. It means a plurality of opinions and views that leads to; deep disagreements and a conflict among group members divergent and disjointed foreign policy decision-making process. The polythink, although it is defined by characteristics opposite to those of the groupthink, can be categorized as a distortion of the decision-making process.

Members of a Polythink decision-making unit, by virtue of their disparate worldviews, institutional and political affiliations, and decision-making styles, typically have deep disagreements over the same decision problem.

Mintz and Wayne (2016) analyzed eleven key national security and foreign policy decisions:

1. The national security policy designed prior to the terrorist attacks of 9/n;
2. The decision to enter into Afghanistan;
3. The decision to with-draw from Afghanistan;
4. The Iraq War entry decision;
5. The decision on the Surge in Iraq;
6. The decision to withdraw from Iraq;
7. And (8) the crisis over the Iranian nuclear program (analyzed from both the American and the
8. Israeli perspectives);
9. The 2012 UN Security Council decision on the Syrian Civil War;
10. The 2013-14 Kerry peace negotiations between the Israelis and Palestinians;
11. The 2014 decision by the U.S. to engage in targeted strikes against the emergent ISIS threat.

Through the analysis of these decisions, they conclude that many of these national security and foreign policy decisions of the U.S. indeed exhibited a number of important symptoms to Polythink, due to the wide-ranging chorus of viewpoints and policy prescriptions that members of the group espouse.

The presence of these symptoms in decisions taken by a decision-making unit can be utilized to diagnose whether the group indeed suffers from a Polythink syndrome as compared to Groupthink

Causes of Polythink

The reasons for Polythink at the national level boil down to a few key factors (Mintz&Wayne, 2016)

First, the pluralism of views by different units and sub-units often means that diverse sets of decision makers must work together to develop cohesive policies for the nation while at the same time effectively representing their various constituencies, political parties, governmental branches, and institutions.

Table 5. Symptoms of polythink, according to Mintz and Wayne (2016)

Type	Meaning
Intragroup Conflict	competing viewpoints, chronic rivalry, distrust, Turf battles
Fear of Leaks	Reluctance to share information due to the fear that someone might leak critical information to media or else…
Lack of Communication	inability to establish healthy communication between governmental agencies; Reluctance to share information
Group disunity limits policy options	Military action is inherently risky; Policymakers often hesitate to use military force unless there is a strong consensus on its strategic necessity and probability of success. Decision paralysis
Greater likelihood	• of group conflict and turf battles • of leaks • of confusion and lack of communication 4. Greater likelihood of framing and counter-framing
Limited review	• of policy options (similar to Groupthink) • of previously rejected policy options (similar to Groupthink)

Second, individuals in decision-making groups bring with them vastly different types of decision-making styles, experiences, and roles within the group. These diverse perspectives hinder the ability of individual group members to see eye to eye on important issues.

Finally, the vast scale and number of different agencies and decision-making units at the federal level often lead to a lack of communication flow that severely impedes the timely, uniform information processing necessary in order to make informed decisions at the national level.

The key explanations of Polythink are (Mintz, Wayne, 2014):

- Institutional "turf war" battles
- Political considerations
- Normative differences
- Expert-novice divides
- Leader-followers relationship

These factors can drastically affect the judgment of key decision makers, leading to conflicting viewpoints, policy prescriptions, and interpretations of the situation or threat at hand—often leaving decision-making groups hopelessly paralyzed or relegated to taking only non-controversial "lowest-common-denominator" stances that are not in the best interests of the country as a whole.

Table 6 Decision support tools that help to groupthink as well as Polythink phenomenon (Source: AA:VV, 2019)

Type	focus
Risk Analysis	Helps team members explore and manage risk
Impact Analysis	Ensures that the consequences of a decision are thoroughly explored.
	Helps people check and validate the individual steps of a decision-making process.

Examples

According to Mintz and Wayne (2016), the starting point is the 9/11 commission report made in 2004 that stated that the attacks were made possible because of the communication failures between different parts of the government and security agencies. The authors state that the 9/11 attacks have a lot of symptoms that are unique to the Polythink syndrome. First of all, there were large disagreements between the most important parts of the advisory group. Secondly, there were also leaks and the fear of leaks. The information could not be given to others, because of a fear that the information would be leaked. A third reason for Polythink was the confusion and a lack of communication.

Another case. Speaking of the Gulf War, Marrin (2013) emphasized the reasons why the intelligence did not work. First, the intelligence was not able to provide correct and accurate information; in fact shortly before the outbreak of the war analysts were convinced that the war would not break out because the Iraqis knew of a possible retaliation from the United States and this was not a risk they were willing to run. Secondly, as Paul Wolfowitz says, policymakers were aware of the risk of a possible war between Iraq and Kuwait and had already drawn up action plans for future US intervention, bypassing the intelligence reports they considered the war as unlikely. This was one of the most obvious facilitators of Polythink. The political concerns were very high at 9/11, security decisions are most of the time not popular with the electorate. Next to political concerns, there were also normative differences, the national behavior is according to the authors a sum of beliefs of actors, which can differ from each other. The experts and novices had a different way of decision-making. Military personnel was against a military action while the civilian advisors were pro a military action.

CONCLUSION: THE GROUPTHINK-POLYTHINK CONTINUUM

Polythink is essentially the opposite of Groupthink on a continuum of decision making from "completely cohesive" (Groupthink) to "completely fragmented" (Polythink) (Mintz&Wayne, 2016)

While Polythink is defined as a plurality of opinions, views, and perceptions among group members, Groupthink tends toward overwhelming conformity and unanimity. .

The divergence of opinions present in Polythink groups will often lead to myriad interpretations of reality, and policy prescriptions, making it difficult to formulate cohesive policies.

Polythink can thus be seen as a mode of thinking that results from a highly disjointed group rather than a highly cohesive one. For example, some of the symptoms of Polythink are intragroup conflict and the existence of contradictory interests among group members (Mintz $ Wayne, 2014), which may lead to a situation where it becomes virtually impossible for group members to reach a com-mon interpretation of reality and common policy goals. In the context of decision-unit dynamics, it is important to distinguish Polythink from the concept of "multiple advocacy," in which decision makers harness diversity of views and interests in the interest of rational policy making.

Both Polythink and Groupthink should also be considered as "pure" types. In real-world decision-making situations, there is rarely a case of pure or extreme Polythink or Groupthink. It is therefore more useful to think of these two concepts as extremes on a continuum in which "good" decision-making processes typically lie toward the middle and defective decision-making processes fall closer to one of two extremes—the group conformity of Groupthink or the group disunity of Polythink. The case of September 11 provides an illustration of this continuum (Mintz&Wayne, 2016).

Analyzing such key foreign policy decisions will enable us to better understand, predict, and obviate the detrimental symptoms of Polythink that can contribute to defective decision making. Our book utilizes a diverse array of primary and secondary sources, primarily memoirs of former administration officials and advisors, published interviews, government reports, and scholarly analysis.

Because Polythink and Groupthink are two extremes on a continuum of group decision making, this approach is sufficient to distinguish between these two dynamics. The groupthink driving both that belief itself and the political response to it has always essentially been centered on those countries of the Western world, which not only originated the panic over global in the first place, but have remained its main drivers ever since. Indeed, it is precisely this fact which is now turning out to be the crux of the whole story.

Future research should pay more attention to the architecture of building decision units capable of making critical decisions, i.e. how leaders can move from Destructive Polythink to Constructive Polythink.

REFERENCES

Avoiding Groupthink. Avoiding Fatal Flaws in Group Decision Making. (2019). *Mindtools*. Available in https://www.mindtools.com/pages/article/newLDR_82.htm

Booker, C. (2018). *GLOBALWARMING. A case study in groupthink. How science can shed new light on the most important 'non-debate' of our time*. The Global Warming Policy Foundation GWPF Report 28.

Eaton, J. (2001). Management communication: The threat of groupthink. *Corporate Communications*, *6*(4), 183–192. doi:10.1108/13563280110409791

Griffin, R. (1991). Introduction. *Journal of Management, 17*(4), 787-787.

Janis, I.L. (1972). Victims of Groupthink. *Political Psychology, 12*(2), 247-278.

Janis, I. L. (1982). *Groupthink: Psychological studies of policy decisions and fiascoes*. Houghton Mifflin.

Kilhefner, J. (2019). *Groupthink Examples in Business*. Available in: https://work.chron.com/groupthink-examples-business-21692.html

Marrin, S. (2013). Revisiting Intelligence and Policy: Problems with Politicization and Receptivity. In Intelligence and National Security. Routledge.

Mintz, A., & Schneiderman, I. (2018). From groupthink to polythink in the yom kippur war decisions of 1973. *European Review of International Studies.*, *5*(1), 48–66. doi:10.3224/eris.v5i1.03

Mintz, A., & Wayne, C. (2014). Group decision making in conflict: From groupthink to polythink in the war in Iraq. In P. T. Coleman, M. Deutsch, & E. C. Marcus (Eds.), *The handbook of conflict resolution: Theory and practice* (pp. 331–352). Jossey-Bass.

Mintz A., Wayne C. (2016). *The Polythink Syndrome: U.S. Foreign Policy Decisions on 9/11, Afghanistan, Iraq, Iran, Syria, and ISIS*. Stanford University Press.

Moscovici, S., & Zavalloni, M. (1969). The group as a polarizer of attitudes. *Journal of Personality and Social Psychology*, *12*(2), 125–135. doi:10.1037/h0027568

Stoner, J. (1968, October). Risky and cautious shifts in group decisions: The influence of widely held values. *Journal of Experimental Social Psychology*, *4*(4), 442–459. doi:10.1016/0022-1031(68)90069-3

KEY TERMS AND DEFINITIONS

Cognitive Bias: It is a systematic pattern of deviation from the norm or from rationality in judgment The bias is a form of distortion of the evaluation caused by the injury. A person's mind map presents bias where it is conditioned by pre-existing concepts not necessarily connected to one another by logical and validities.

Groupthink: The term indicates a way of thinking that people adopt when they are deeply involved in a highly cohesive group, where the tendency to reach unanimity prevails over the motivation to realistically evaluate more functional alternatives for action (Janis, 1982, p. 9).

Polythink: It is a group decision-making dynamic whereby different members in a decision-making unit espouse a plurality of opinions and divergent policy prescriptions, resulting in a disjointed decision-making process or even decision paralysis.

Chapter 4
Intel Cycle for Private Professionals:
Acquisition, Management, and Dissemination of Information

Aldo Montanari

https://orcid.org/0000-0002-5440-3492

IT Army, Forli, Italy

ABSTRACT

This work focused on the method of analysis, to be understood in general terms and following the intelligence cycle as developed by various international realities, with possible variations. This method was exposed, also graphically, before going further into the details of the different phases or the acquisition, processing of data, and news for subsequent dissemination. These procedures have been described in practical terms and from a distinctly private perspective, also providing the necessary connections with the figures responsible for their development up to the description and requirements that the information product must satisfy, also in this case from a customer's perspective.

INTRODUCTION

Enterprises and companies have an important need of intelligence because of the huge amount of information requested for quite every type of purpose in their business. Intel cycle applied in private professionals framework could have some differences with the one aimed at government's concerns.

DOI: 10.4018/978-1-7998-4339-9.ch004

The process starts from an organization (i.e. a person or a decision-making group) that needs one or more information to make some decisions. Once the information request has been received and the price of the finished product has been agreed, the intelligence operator (the self-employed professional or the company representative) will use a few days if not a few weeks to get to know the customer. This delicate phase is necessary to study the client's current activities with a sort of identification with his decision-making bodies, managing to define in the 'cleanest' way possible from where the information need derives, what is the purpose that the organization aims to achieve, which business to carry out (or which function in the case of government organizations), when to carry out its activities and where to do it. Defined these premises with precision and simplicity, which in case of new customers can mean up to a month of activity, the operator can start the information collection phase to collect as much data as possible and above all by isolating the so-called news from these.

In this regard, the sources of this news are mentioned, with which a specific type of intelligence is associated.

It is evident that only a part of the whole spectrum will be necessary for the production of the analysis and moreover it is particularly difficult for a company to develop the suitable skills to carry out any type of intelligence. For these reasons, it is desirable and economic to develop only some of these skills in order to be able to entrust any need for news acquisition to third parties, perhaps for instrumental needs that involve expensive investments in associated technologies and skills.

ACQUISITION

The acquisition represents the first step aimed at producing intelligence. It includes the definition of objectives and information research.

After having carried out adequate adherence with the customer, the questionnaire will be elaborated, ideally broken down into increasingly refined details aimed at clearly identifying the objectives that will connote the final product. This questionnaire will originate from the client's needs which will not necessarily be translated into objectives directly related to information research. The level of detail of the questionnaire is related to the customer's needs but also to the time available and the contingencies of the activity (risks, legal constraints, budget, etc.) (Carter, 2009).

Acquisition is made up by different sources which are linked to intel disciplines. Anyway, this means using many approaches to acquire data and information that need to be collected and analyzed. Some approaches are based on useful tools that scan the web in order to set links and visualize different pattern of data related to a particular theme. These softwares could be free or very expensive, their aim is to provide open source intel on your PC. This is the same for software that are focused on geo-processing data found elsewhere from every kind of sources. It's very important to pay attention on how easy could be to acquire information with these tools and some interviews done with fake identities. Just with the collaboration of an ICT technician, a skilled analyst is capable of doing acquisition with very low costs.

INTEL DISCIPLINES

The information search makes use of different sources which represent the disciplines of intelligence.

OSINT represents the widest and most valuable activity to define the contours and create a fertile ground on which to cultivate other intel activities. The essential requirement is certainly to adequately identify the quality of the news acquired through Open Source or by making adequate use of the source/information content matrix. The Open is also a very valid starting point because by definition it does not require security authorizations or to provide information access.

The natural follow-up to an information search through open sources is that carried out through photo-interpretation, geo-localizing the data collected on the GIS software and collecting all the soil representations that will be useful in the management phase. Satellite photographs play the leading role and it is clear that since these are now accessible to anyone, the geolocation of the data collected actually represents the added value to research. Geolocation with commercial software that allows you to take advantage of very sophisticated algorithms still requires time and meticulousness.

Moving on we find the research carried out by means of HUMINT or from a human source, being able to distinguish the same as clandestine activity or as a result of recognition. This apparently doctrinal distinction must take into account the fact that part of the HUMINT activity is carried out in purely military contexts and therefore in foreign operating theaters, often at high intensity, where it is necessary to employ militarily trained forces to perform reconnaissance that targets the acquisition information from human sources. In the government context, this task is often devolved to the Special Forces. By clandestine activity, on the other hand, is meant an information acquisition activity carried out without revealing one's work or to the source itself or to the opponent.

The SIGINT or electromagnetic source is in fact the first intel activity that requires specific technical equipment, devolved in particular to crypto-analysis. We can distinguish two activities within the acquisition from electromagnetic source. The COMINT or the interception of communications and the ELINT or the information acquisition from sensors such as radars. It is clear that this type of activity could be outsourced for valid reasons, requiring important technological equipment and above all, being contingencies that require the involvement of governmental entities and therefore of lesser interest for independent professionals.

TECHINT or the acquisition of data and news regarding armament and equipment used by the enemy. Of clear military interest, "technical" intelligence can provide important indicators for the performance of information activities in crisis areas and therefore in a context probably devoted to customer security. This type of acquisition is typically related to political interests but could be carried out in a private framework because of the need of obtaining data regarding just parts of development or production of military armament and equipment. TECHINT is anyway applied as a way of reaching a strategic or operational aim.

CYBINT or the information acquisition from ICT overlooks an extremely vast and differentiated panorama, never as of today of primary importance for the security of an organization, being able to understand the future of intelligence closely connected to the acquisition of data and news in the cyber sector, even more than in the present where it has already been fully protagonist for some time. CYBINT branches into DININT or the direct interception of data within network connected equipment. Like the electromagnetic spectrum, the cyber environment also requires the presence of extremely sophisticated tools as well as high technical skills. In this, in addition to the acquisition alone, it could also be profitable to outsource the evaluation of the data collected to the enabler, such as for example a company with investigation skills in the so-called deep web.

MASINT or the acquisition derived from the collection of quantitative data (such as measurements) and qualitative data (such as distinctive signs in certain disciplines). Difficult to associate with a given context or source, this type of acquisition can lead to extremely productive consequences and also, depending on the type of analysis carried out, may involve outsourcing the activity given the high quality of the equipment and skills necessary techniques.

The listed intelligence disciplines, associated with different sources, represent in fact the heart of the analyst's skills and certainly this can only go to connote the subsequent processing, certainly influenced by the operator's technical skills. For these reasons, the analyst should always keep in mind, at this stage, his role as collector and coordinator of data from extremely different sources. This will subsequently help to maintain an appropriate mental openness and logical flexibility when processing the news.

COLLECTION

Collection is the processing of the news, summarized in the previous paragraph, with specific procedures of transforming the news into information. By remaining intellectually neutral yet strongly adhering to the customer's needs, the operator will first assign to each collected data the assessment of reliability of the source and validity of the news. More or less it will be a matter of assigning to each collected piece, an alphanumeric value deriving from a scheme of this type,

Table 1. Reliability of the source and validity of the data matrix

RELIABILITY		VALIDITY	
A ABSOLUTELY RELIABLE	No doubts, competence, always positive previous collaboration.	1 CONFIRMED	Logic, confirmed by independent, consistent with other news.
B GENERALLY RELIABLE	Doubts present, not completely competent, previous collaboration, however positive.	2 PROBABLY TRUE	Logic, not confirmed by third parties, consistent with other news.
C PRETTY RELIABLE	Widespread doubts, uncertain competence, previous collaboration only sometimes positive.	3 MAYBE TRUE	Quite logical, not confirmed by third parties, consistent only in some aspects with other news.
D GENERALLY NOT RELIABLE	Consistent doubts, incompetence on some aspects, previous collaboration in a less positive part.	4 DIFFICULTLY TRUE	Not entirely logical, not confirmed by third parties, inconsistent with other news but possible.
E UNRELIABLE	Overall doubts, ascertained incompetence, previous negative collaboration.	5 UNLIKELY	Illogical, confirmed its contrary, contradicted by other news.
F NOT ASSESSABLE	Not judgmental, no news to evaluate.	6 NOT ASSESSABLE	Not judgmental, no news to evaluate.

The resulting alphanumeric value is thus extremely useful for the professional who will subsequently have to manage the data because it represents an additional aid to avoid incurring errors or logical biases that prevent any news from being treated consistently with the whole investigation. In the discussion, moreover, it will be appropriate to begin the assignment of reliability/truthfulness, ideally starting from A1 level data beacause, as we have seen, each news item could be influenced by another in the formation of the deductive logical framework. Not assessable news or F6 will probably be discarded unless subsequent investigations occur. Obviously even these latest news could be extremely valuable in the future therefore they will still be archived. Circular intelligence, that is, the unfounded presumption of reliability/truthfulness dictated by the sharing of another operator. This "pathology" misleads the two operators who believe that a news item is usable because it is mutually encountered with the other (Prunckun, 2013).

After carrying out this first assessment, it will be necessary to proceed to create categories, logical containers within which the various data collected will be inserted. Depending on the investigation carried out, there will be very different categories in terms of number and type. Throughout the analysis, this process will allow you to easily dispose of the necessary data and to deepen it, if necessary, together with data similar by type. It is not possible to define how to create the different categories, it is certainly necessary to use categories recognizable by the analyst with ease and immediacy, according to one's personal method. It should also be noted that the processing of these data, without prejudice to the provisions of the privacy law, must take place with special precautions.

First of all, the principle of need to know applies, so that the analyst will keep all information confidential without prejudice to the real need for treatment by external experts (for example in the case of outsourcing/insourcing as seen previously). These data will be kept within a delimited and protected area such as to allow access only to the operator who needs it. In particular, physical data (such as documents for example) must be kept in locked containers, including their reproductions. It is advisable to maintain a list (or register, if you like) of all the data collected, with the attached index of reliability/validity, sorted by category. If it becomes necessary to destroy some of this data, obviously it will be necessary to crush the documents or crush the other supports. Any shipment of this material will take place by protecting the indication of the content on documentation/packs. In the particular case of data and digital news, they must be processed on devices without network connections, wireless or wired, with password-protected BIOS. The use of an antivirus is essential. Some "trivialities" regarding the password to choose: at least #11 characters with the presence of lowercase, uppercase, special and numeric characters. The computer screen itself will have to go out after two or three minutes of inactivity. The use of these devices must take place in delimited and protected environments as described above. Area monitoring is necessary, for example through continuous visual recording. Any destruction of digital data/news must take place taking into account that the same can obviously remain within the device. The complete recovery of the device can take place, for example, by formatting the relative disks, with at least # 4 write/delete cycles, reinstalling the operating system and changing all passwords (and user names). Same procedures must be implemented for any peripherals.

ANALYSIS

Following the categorization, the actual analysis process must begin. Each analyst has the possibility of using different IT schemes and supports, the requirements to be met however are the same. It is a matter of plotting, graphically and in relation to the data collected, the connections between the people involved, the activities that these people carry out, the activities that produced the data and the events related to the data and news. These three types of graphs (people, activities and events) correspond precisely to the three types of nodes that will graphically allow you to view the logical connections between them (the so-called links). The logical connection between the various nodes can take place subsequently in the form of a matrix or through the definition not only of the observed link but also through a label applicable to this link. What kind of bond is it? Is it a real link or is there the possibility that it is not true? The matrix will allow you to read the different relationships between what has been collected, perhaps with reusable labels as part of the investigation. Once the links have been observed and positioned in the matrix, the first hypotheses can be developed and subsequently tested. These assumptions must first of all agree with each other within the overall framework. If the hypothesis, for example, is attributable to statistical information, it will be possible to compare it with the evidence of previously collected data. What has been shown so far is extremely generic and reflects the general principles of analysis that are proposed through various models. In fact, there are real tools and training programs that allow you to learn and implement analysis models depending on the context and the training received. A reference point in this regard is certainly Globalytica which has created a business to offer training in critical analysis thinking and has developed structured analytical techniques since 2010. Among its most successful products, to give an idea of the tools available to an intel analyst, we find

Multiple Hypotheses Generator®, or a process to create different sets of alternative hypotheses.

Indicators Validator®, or a web-base tool that allows the analyst to manage data effectively to evaluate it on the basis of hypothesis sets, perhaps as a result of applying the MHG. -Quadrant Crunching®, a technique for generating a set of adverse options and application scenarios.

These tools are extremely useful for the activities described above and belong to the suite produced by Globalytica called Th!nk Suite®, within which we also find programs dedicated to learning analytical techniques, therefore usable in academic environments. It is in all respects software that allows you to enter the data and news collected to be analyzed through guided procedures that allow to apply the principles described in this paragraph. The International Association for Intelligence Education (IAFIE), founded in 2004, is an international institute that deals, among other things, with developing the study of intelligence at an international level with certified programs that guarantee the possession of adequate logical tools for manage the analysis. It is not uncommon for specific training programs to be requested in favor of organizations where the analysis is intrinsic to their vital interests and therefore it is essential to install these specific software to implement the related methodologies in favor of their reality or, more often, to offer a competitive analytical product (Fisher, 2018).

In any case, after formulating the hypotheses that have passed the tests submitted by the analyst, it will be possible to start defining the information product, the final output or the conclusions reached by the analysis. These conclusions will take two forms depending on the type of analysis required, it will in fact either provide the evaluation of a particular event already concluded or provide forecasts on events that will occur. The report produced must comply with the characteristics and requirements that can be summarized in the following diagram.

Figure 1.

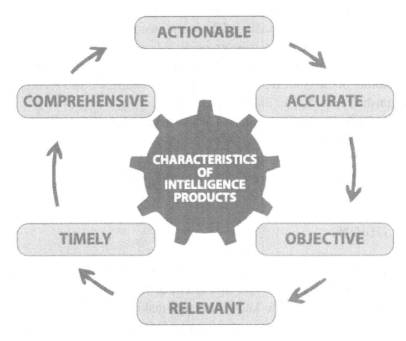

DISSEMINATION

Dissemination begins when the report is practically usable by the customer meaning that it must be effective within its decision-making process through the prior adherence work carried out before carrying out the analysis. It must then be accurate and precise in the information, ideally providing the level of in-depth analysis suitable to be used without further additions. The report will be objective, without being influenced by the analyst's perspective but by exclusively providing the information that best describes the reality of things (possibly also a perception of the same, but real). The information product must be delivered on time, according to what the customer needs because a report delivered late loses completely meaning since the conditions that characterize it have changed. Only data and news can maintain the same utility over time. The information report must be integrated into the customer's overall picture and must be developed on all dimensions relating to the information, it cannot be limited to answering one or more specific questions, it must also include elements of interest that contribute to fulfilling the information need . The result of the analysis, depending on the type of risk connected (or threat if a military, security context occurs), can be distinguished in tactical, operational or strategic output. On a qualitatively increasing scale, depending on the customer and the reality in which it operates, the information may concern recurring or otherwise ordinary (tactics), particularly delicate and extraordinary conditions, up to questioning the existence of the customer in the context in which it operates (strategic). The report can still be distinguished according to its periodic nature in

An alert in the event of monitoring which resulted in the observation of an unusual phenomenon.

A periodic bulletin, always in case of monitoring.

An evaluation in case of request without monitoring activity.

CONCLUSION

The final product is thus ready to be distributed and delivered to the customer, in people who physically need information. Thus we distinguish the right to know (role, responsibility) and the need to know (decision-making process, relevance). The delivery of this product closes the cycle described in the previous paragraph which, however, could immediately start again due to changed environmental conditions or to changes in customer needs, especially in particularly dynamic sectors such as could occur in the case of evaluations for investments or in the management of reality security located in crisis areas.

REFERENCES

Carter, D. (2009). *Law Enforcement Intelligence: A Guide for State, Local, and Tribal Law Enforcement Agencies*. Office of Community Oriented Policing Services.

Fisher, R. (2018). *Introduction to Security*. Butterworth-Heinemann.

Prunckun, H. (2013). *Intelligence and Private Investigation: Developing Sophisticated Methods for Conducting Inquiries*. Charles Thomas.

Chapter 5
Tactical Art of Risk Management in the History of Ninja

Maria Luisa Nardi
Independent Researcher, Italy

ABSTRACT

The notion of the innovation system is connected to the role of leaders and decision makers in the management of the scientific and technological environment. Innovative frameworks of analysis, by approaching science and technology systemically (i.e., in relation to the economy, politics, and society), adapt stress for success. Any research and innovation policy must take account of a complex set of problems. The focus of this work is to analyze the application of tactical strategies in the risk management, looking at the historical ninja training. Their worldview, the "way of the warrior" as an art of war but also as a path of inner knowledge, has also had great importance in artistic production, culture, and the construction of social relations.

INTRODUCTION

The notion of the innovation system is connected to the role of leaders and decision-makers in the management of the business, scientific and technological environment. Any research and innovation policy must take account of a complex set of problems. Innovative frameworks of analysis occur by approaching science and technology systemically (i.e. about the economy, politics, and society), by stress adaptation, at glocal (global and local) level.

DOI: 10.4018/978-1-7998-4339-9.ch005

Generally, managerial decision-making involves problem-solving skills, certainty and uncertainty management, programmed and unprogrammed decision-making, intuitive and rational approach making decisions, finally, group decision making management (with benefits as well drawbacks) (dall'Acqua, 2018). A complex problem does not have a unified solution, it cannot be addressed by breaking it into its elementary parts, because it is not their summation, but their link and interaction.

According to Cristoferri thought (Cristoferri, 2016), managerial intelligence comes from a combination of three factors:

- Critical thinking and the ability to turn it into action:
- Ability to grasp the complexity of interpersonal relationships, working with and through people (social intelligence)
- Continuous assessment of themselves to adapt thinking and action to the context in which it is being operated (introspective intelligence)

Line managers, staff managers, functional managers as well general managers need to improve "managerial intelligence" in a global updating mindset.

In the presence of extraordinary conditions of uncertainty, typical in turbulent times for the economy, especially in a context of innovation and proactive business management, with objectives clearly defined by the company and adequately set in operational terms, risk management becomes an indispensable tool to support decision-making processes at a tactical and strategic level, substantially contributing to the choice of actions aimed at containing potential future liabilities. Risk Management acquires value as a solution for a rapid general rationalization of the company in terms of costs and economic and operational efficiency, such as strategies aimed at limiting any losses, protecting the brand, through adequate levels of internal control, highlighting, and significantly reducing unnecessary operating costs.

The focus of this work is to explore strategies of business management by the application of tactics of the historical ninja training.

History of Ninjas

Ninjas are, and always have been, intrinsically linked with the long and multifaceted history of Japan. Whilst the world inherently understands ninjas as part of the culture of the past and a big part of pop-culture worldwide today, only extreme enthusiasts really delve into the background of their mystery

Ethimologically, The word "ninjutsu" is composed of:

- Nin (忍 patience, endurance), in the meaning of "waiting for the right moment to act without being seen".

- Jutsu (術 art, technique)

A possible translation of the term is: "stealth technique". According to the reading Kun, the word changes in "Shin or Shino (bu)", that is **Shinobi**. The meaning of the verb Shinobu which means "to hide, to hide", something not at all foreign to a ninja who, as we all know very well, used to act in the dark and acting in anonymity was his main characteristic.

The word Shinobi was actually the most used word to indicate this category of "secret agents", the word ninja, although of equally ancient connotation, begins to be used much more frequently than the word Shinobi only after the Second World War as it was much simpler and easier in pronunciation for a Westerner who was getting to know for the first time typical figures of the Japanese tradition.

They were mysterious warriors or mercenaries widespread in the period of feudal Japan. The ninja was a figure known for espionage, sabotage, secret infiltration, or even assassinations depending on the situation in which they found themselves.

According to the Ninja Museum of Igaryu: "The roots are found in the "art of warfare" that began around 4000 B.C. in Indian culture, was passed to the Chinese mainland, and around the 6th century, passed through the Korean peninsula and crossed over to Japan." Sun Tzu, the great Chinese military theoretician, talked about the importance and necessity of deception if you want to win in a war in the 5th century B.C. It is thought from this belief that the ninja made its way to Japan

In the Asuka Period, it is said a man name Otomono Sahito, who was used by ruler Shotoku Taishi, gave birth to the first ninjas. This continental military strategy, involving mountain training, and adapted to Japan's extremely hilly, narrow geography, becoming unique Japanese strategy. From this body of strategy emerged **Ninjutsu** (Ninja Museum, 2019).

Although Ninjas too can be called warriors for their, however, combative training, they differed far from the samurai, mainly for their furtive and hidden almost invisible way of operating. The samurai, unlike the ninja also observed strict and harsh rules of combat and honor, which is not contemplated by the ninja.

The shinobi (or ninja) were actually a specialized group specially trained to be spies and mercenaries, very famous in the Sengoku era, a historical period known for the bloody "wars between states". In the chaos period that was in fact the Sengoku period, mercenaries and spies were very active among the provinces, many ninja were even hired by the clans. After the unification of Japan in the Tokugawa era, the ninja figure disappeared along with the clans and their group was replaced by a body of secret agents called **Oniwabanshu.**

With the arrival of the Meiji Restoration (1868), shinobi had become part of popular tradition, a pure fantasy topic that filled stories and folklore with mystery.

Throughout history, the Shinobi mainly known for their use of secrecy and deception were assassins, explorers and spies hired mostly by territorial lords.

Many different schools have taught their unique versions of Ninjutsu. An example of these is the Togakure-ryū, a school developed by a defeated samurai warrior called Daisuke Togakure who fled to the Iga region. The samurai later came into contact with the warrior-monk Kain Doshi, who taught him a new way of seeing life and the means of survival (ninjutsu).

John Man, author of "Ninja: 1,000 Years of the Shadow Warrior", told Time magazine: "The height of the ninja was in the 16th century. They'd been evolving. As Japan descended into warlord-ism in the early Middle Ages, the areas where the ninja lived became more and more isolated. As the warlords scrapped over the rest of Japan, Iga and Koka developed their own commune system and self-defense and worked toward sort of a peak of ninja-ism toward the end of the 16th century, at which point their skills had been admired by everyone else, so they were finding employment in the rest of Japan as mercenaries (Tharoor, 2013)

In some ways the history of the Ninja begins with Minamoto no Yoshitsune, a formidable warrior whose qualities reside in the in-depth study of the book "The Art of War", a military treatise written in the 6th century BC by the Chinese general Sun Tzu.

Probably, the first martial techniques that would determine the birth of Ninjutsu, developed during the Nara period (710 - 784 AD) when a training style aimed at Satori - illumination -, typical of Buddhists, which was practiced in isolated villages of which it was difficult to know, so much so that legends of mysterious rituals and magic ended up circulating around them: probably they were ceremonies that were based on Mikkyo, an esoteric school of Buddhism.

These places were called Shinobi no Sato, that is "villages inhabited by Shinobi", and it is perhaps in them that in the Heian period (784 -1185 AD) the Koga-Ryu and Iga-Ryu, together with the Fuma-Ryu, were born. the most important Ninjitsu styles.

After the Heian period, the techniques underwent substantial changes: in the face of the ancient approach based on the number of soldiers, the value of the leaders and the availability of weapons, many generals in the Kamakura period introduced war tactics based on surprise and intelligence: a collection of information and use of infiltrators.

In the following period - Muromachi (1336 - 1573 AD) -, under the Shogunate of Yoshihira Ashikaga characterized by relative tranquility, the leaders created more refined war strategies and in the long period of civil war that goes from the XV to the XVII century, called Sengoku, the Ninja were used very often as spies: the Shogun himself, the absolute military leader of the Empire, asked for help and in doing so entire provinces ended up under their control.

The first specialized espionage training seems to have emerged in the mid-fifteenth century: the shinobi began training at a very young age and learned survival and surveillance techniques, the use of poisons and explosives and physical skills such as climbing, running over long distances and swimming.

We also know that some ninjas, such as the shinobi Iga reported in a historical account of Ii Naomasa, had useful medical knowledge in battle; to minimize their body odor, they tended to have a vegetarian diet in preparation for a mission.

The most famous group of Iga ninja is Hattori, Momochi, and Fujibayashi. Hattori Hanzo, Momochi Tambanokami, and Fujibayashi Nagatonokami are the three Iga Ninja Grandmasters. Hattori controlled western Iga. Momochi controlled southern Iga. Fujibayashi controlled northeastern Iga. Fujibayashi Yasutake, the author of traditional Ninjutsu text "Mansen Shukai" was of this group.

Figure 1. Bansenshukai: Japanese book containing a collection of knowledge of the clans of the regions of Iga and Kōga, who had dedicated themselves to training ninja (Source: http://factsanddetails.com/japan/cat16/sub107/item498.html)

NINJA ESPIONAGE TRAINING

Skills

Ninjutsu is not a martial art. Ninjutsu is an independent art of warfare that developed. The jobs of a ninja are divided into the two main categories of performing espionage and strategy. The methodology for performing espionage and strategy is Ninjutsu. Espionage is similar to the job of modern spies, wherein one carefully gathers intelligence about the enemy and analyzes its military strength. Ninja who thought rationally thought of war by intellect as great, and war by military strength (weapons) as foolish.

Ninjutsu was developed as a collection of fundamental survivalist techniques in the warlike state of feudal Japan. Ninja used their art to ensure survival in a time of violent political unrest.

Yuji Yamada, an expert on ninjas at Mie University, told the Yomiuri Shimbun. "The most important role of ninja is to collect intelligence. They tried to avoid fighting as much as possible. They were required to have good memories and communication skills first and foremost, rather than physical strength. Ninja insisted on having an existence like a shadow. They accomplished their duties behind the scenes and through unofficial negotiations. They share those characteristics in common with Japanese today (Hays, 2009).

School of Koga is an ancient school of ninjutsu, according to Japanese legend. It originated from the region of Koga (modern Koka City in Shiga Prefecture). Members of the Koga school of shinobi (ninja) are trained in disguise, escape, concealment, explosives, medicines, and poison; moreover, they are experts in techniques of unarmed combat and in the use of various weapons. They studied the techniques of non-detection, avoidance and deception, training in free running, disguise, escape, concealment, archery and medicine.

The shinobi began to organize themselves into guilds made up of different families of shinobi and to develop a system of degrees: the join were the ninja of the highest rank. Although of low rank, the genins carried out fundamental activities such as the collection of sensitive information, sabotage, and infiltration.

The shinobi must necessarily also have knowledge of various professions in order to infiltrate the enemy in disguise. They often disguised themselves as priests, monks, beggars, merchants, and entertainers: disguising themselves as a minstrel made it possible to infiltrate inside enemy buildings, while the dress of the komuso monks allowed to completely mask the face through the typical basket.

Some Ninja Techniques

Strategic activities are skills that reduce the enemy's military power. Ninja did not fight strong enemies by themselves. Ninja fought enemies after they had reduced the enemies' military power. In times of peace, Ninjutsu was called the art of "entering from afar", while in times of war, Ninjutsu was called the art of "entering from "nearby", wherein ninja would constantly gather intelligence concerning the enemy, thinking of ways to beat the enemy, but not fighting the enemy directly.

Espionage, infiltration and "stealth" techniques were loosely grouped into five groups: fire, water, wood and earth.

CORE OF NINJA TECHNIQUES IN STRATEGIC MANAGEMENT

Fire - Or distracting technique

The primordial element of social control is the strategy of distraction which consists in diverting the attention of the public from important problems and changes decided

Table 1. Strategies used for espionage

Name	Description
FIRE - Hitsuke Or distracting technique	distracting the guards by setting fires away from the shinobi entry point, the practice of distraction by setting a fire in the distance from the actual point where a ninja had to break. Hitsuke is known as a fire technique however in reality is used to distract guards or any foes who stood in the way of the ninjas. They would start a small fire in the opposite directions of their destination to lure away the guards away so that they could slip by without being noticed. In fantasy these fire techniques would include using energy that radiates from the body to wield fire attacks.
WATER - Ukigusa-gakure Or submerged movement technique	use of aquatic plants to hide underwater movements; Ukigusa-gakure is known as water techniques and teaches how to counsel underwater movement. Although this isn't seen much in media, it is an important skill to possess if one is to come a shinobi.
WOOD - Tanuki-gakure Or visual camouflage technique	climbing on trees and camouflage among the foliage. It is one of the "wood techniques", the practice of climbing a tree or camouflage among the foliage to hide. Tanuki-gakure teaches the use of climbing trees and camouflaging and is known as wood techniques. When Tanuki-gakure is compared to ninjas from shows and video games it's easy to see that these wood techniques relate into the typical high jumping and running from tree to tree that you see within ninjas in media.
EARTH - Uzura-gakure Or technique of standing still	curl up like a ball and stand still to look like a rock, the practice of standing still like stone in order to hide by pretending to be part of the surrounding environment.

by political and economic elites, through the flood technique or floods of continuous distractions and insignificant information .

According to Chomsky (2017), the most recurring of **mass manipulation strategies** is distraction. It consists in directing the attention of the public towards irrelevant or trivial topics that keep them busy. This can be one of the strategies of mass manipulation for making unpopular decisions. For example, when they want to privatize a public company and intentionally make their service worse. In the end, this justifies its sale. To distract people, they are overloaded with information. Excessive importance is given, for example, to sporting events, theater, curiosities, etc. This causes people to lose sight of the real problems. Sometimes power deliberately stops dealing with certain realities or does it inefficiently. This is shown to citizens as a problem that requires an external solution. They themselves propose the solution. This is one of the strategies of mass manipulation for making unpopular decisions. For example, when they want to privatize a public company and intentionally make their service worse. In the end, this justifies its sale.

It is another of the strategies of mass manipulation to introduce measures that people would not normally accept. It consists in applying them gradually, so as to make them practically imperceptible. This is what happened, for example, with the reduction of workers' rights. Measures or ways of working have been implemented in several companies which have ended up showing as normal the fact that a worker has no guarantee regarding social protection. This strategy consists in making citizens believe that a measure is used which is temporarily harmful, but which in the future will be able to offer great benefits to the whole of society and, obviously, to individuals.

Water - Or Submerged Movement Technique

Neuromarketing is the application of neuroscientific knowledge and practices to marketing, in order to analyze the unconscious processes that take place in the consumer's mind and that influence purchasing decisions or emotional involvement with a brand. According to Gerald Zaltman (2008), 95% of consumer decisions are influenced by processes that involve the unconscious and are therefore irrational. Over the course of a day, we are continuously exposed to countless sensorial inputs such as advertisements, commercials, road signs, product designs and consumer experiences which, if considered relevant, are kept in memory, allowing new memories to be connected to other purchases made previously. Neuromarketing has had the advantage of scientifically deepening the study of the decision-making process, going beyond the simple declaration of the target groups. This has undoubtedly contributed to improving communication, business marketing strategies and sales techniques.

An alternative technical method can be **the eye tracking**. The **eye tracker** is the tool that allows you to measure the movements of the gaze, it is possible to obtain some data on the visual processes (even the unaware ones), related to the points of fixation of the gaze and to the saccades, that is the movements that take place between a fixation and the other one. Eye tracking is essentially a method of analyzing visual attention that, although dating back to the 1920s, has recently spread in the marketing sector, because it allows you to identify the elements that attract the consumer's attention when watching a commercial., a printed advertisement, a packaging or a website.

Wood - or Visual Camouflage Technique

Visual Marketing is a fundamental sector of marketing based on the visual aspect of communication, i.e. visual language and everything related to it. It therefore refers to a type of non-verbal communication made up of images, photos, infographics, drawings, symbols, videos. Visual marketing is the discipline that studies the relationship between object, context in which it is inserted and image. It is mainly applied in the fashion and design sectors, and represents an interdisciplinary point of contact between economics, laws of visual perception and cognitive psychology. A fundamental element of modern marketing, visual marketing places the ability of an object to be the "protagonist" of visual communication at the center of study and critical analysis. The product and its visual communication thus become inseparable and their fusion is the component that reaches the public, influencing and determining their choices (in a communicative mechanism of persuasion). Everything we see puts in place a series of associations and connections on a mental level that refer us to things or concepts already known and thanks to which we are able to give us an opinion.

Earth - or Technique of Standing Still

When the temptation to do another activity comes from what is planned and which is better to complete the decision is to do nothing. Using own time does not mean doing as much as possible, but in doing the things you need to achieve your goal. It's not about learning how to do more in less time, but about doing it differently to get more done. The right thing, at the right time, in the right way because the right thing,

REFERENCES

Chomsky, N. (2017). *"10 Strategies of Manipulation" by the Media*. Retrieved in: https://politics1660.wordpress.com/2017/01/05/noam-chomsky-10-strategies-of-manipulation-by-the-media/

Cristoferri, G. (2016). *Elan: "Le figure più richieste e meno reperibili"*. Retrieved in: https://www.repubblica.it/economia/affari-e-finanza/2016/02/01/news/elan_le_figure_pi_richieste_e_meno_reperibili-132532463/

Dall'Acqua, L. (2018). Risk Taxnomoy and Strategic Rationality in Enterprise Decision-Making Process. A Metacognitive Analysis. In *Improving Business Performance*. IGI Global.

Hays, J. (2009). *Ninjas in Japan and their history*. Retrieved in: http://factsanddetails.com/japan/cat16/sub107/item498.html

Ninja Museum of Igaryu Igaueno. (2019). Retrieved in: https://www.iganinja.jp/en/museum/index.html

Zaltman, G., & Zaltman, L. (2008). *Marketing Metaphoria: What Deep Metaphors Reveal about the Minds of Consumers.* Harvard Business School Press.

ADDITIONAL READING

ZonWu. (2019). *Ninja: gli shinobi tra verità storica e mito*. Retrieved in: https://www.vitantica.net/2019/03/18/ninja-shinobi-verita-storica-e-mito/#Ninjutsu_le_arti_dello_spionaggio

KEY TERMS AND DEFINITIONS

Mass Manipulation Strategies: Consists in directing the attention of the public towards irrelevant or trivial topics that keep them busy.

Neuromarketing: Is the application of neuroscientific knowledge and practices to marketing, in order to analyze the unconscious processes that take place in the consumer's mind and that influence purchasing decisions or emotional involvement with a brand.

Shinobi: Means to hide something not at all foreign to a ninja who, as we all know very well, used to act in the dark and acting in anonymity was his main characteristic.

Chapter 6
Private Intel for Corporate Protection

Aldo Montanari

(iD) https://orcid.org/0000-0002-5440-3492

IT Army, Forli, Italy

ABSTRACT

The private information analysis is strictly inherent to the protection of corporate interests. This generally means protecting the company from fraud, theft of industrial secrets, and intellectual capital as well as protecting its cyber architecture. The tasks are delicate and suited to the various corporate interests. This information work would usefully be placed in the national intelligence context by providing a precious link between the national security services and the company itself, to which such an adhesion would be difficult to guarantee in any other way.

INTRODUCTION

The private information analysis is strictly inherent to the protection of corporate interests.

These interests are always related to strategic affairs that come up with reaching every business target during specific periods of time.

This generally means nowadays to protect the company from fraud, theft of industrial secrets and intellectual capital as well as protect its cyber architecture. The tasks-related are delicate and suited to the various corporate interests.

These particular aspects of companies' organization are as a matter of fact some targets of governments' secret services in order to safeguard national interests abroad.

DOI: 10.4018/978-1-7998-4339-9.ch006

But this are in particular some specific areas that could be greatly investigated by private agencies that support business clients outside national borders.

From the information point of view, the salient aspect certainly concerns the analysis of corporate vulnerabilities dictated by local crime but above all the ability of the service provider to be able to effectively coordinate any additional specific service providers to be included in the framework of corporate risk management . In practical terms, moreover, the analysis activity can be understood as a continuous and intelligent coordination of various professional skills capable of bringing out data of a different nature which are linked together to create the final product that can be sold to the customer. This synergy is more realistic than ever for the elaboration of highly valuable information.

An essential aspect, the initial awareness report, will be described in a dedicated paragraph.

INITIAL AWARENESS REPORT

The initial awareness report is the basis of the work to investigate any eventuality described in the following paragraphs and any coordination activity with the company that is being protected. There are steps that must be carried out in close contact with the customer while adhering to his organization, for about a month, in order to understand the corporate culture (Shorrock, 2008).

First of all, it will be necessary to obtain a sort of chronology of the main activities of the client company. The key moments that led to symbolic or significant changes in the corporate organization often also determine physical or policy changes that can affect security. Subsequently, the external perception of the company's activity must be defined. It will thus be clearer to identify the origin of any targeted attacks or in any case of threats or any actors who have reason to harm the company. From the chronology of company activities and from the sentiment resulting from the analysis of the press, the media, social networks or interviews, the first logical connections allow to bring clarity on events that have occurred or to highlight threats previously considered irrelevant.

The next steps involve processing all the cartography of interest with any mapping of the physical locations to obtain full awareness of the physical vulnerabilities and the ways that the company has put in place to mitigate them. Follow the data, statistical or determined, which may derive from the surveys, company forecasts, financial statements or can be produced by the analyst on topics strictly related to the business activity. At that point, investment trends, growth factors and the use of corporate capital can be highlighted more clearly.

Now, the forms of contact or collaboration of the company with local or national institutions follow with consequent relief about peculiarities or sensitivity of legal nature that may emerge from the company's sector experts. Only with this awareness are we finally ready to catalog any criminal or harmful activities carried out in the past against the customer.

The report will be completed with logical deductions deriving from the current resources of the company, on considerations relating to the future media exposure or in public events and finally describing analogies that emerge from the analyst's previous experience in other contexts or with other customers (Butti, 2016).

From this generic basic analysis, carried out in collaboration with the customer, it will be possible to address any aspect of interest that is the subject of the contract for the supply of services.

FRAUDS

The occurrence of having to face fraud protection, one of the greatest threats to a company, with unpredictable economic consequences, is not uncommon. At international level there is a real convention in this regard, the Budapest Convention which aims to prevent breaches of network security, computer fraud and other computer infringements. The Fraud Act, on the other hand, is a British regulation which punishes the same activities and not only on an IT level. The American legal system is also very sensitive to this type of offense. The same companies can place themselves variously as victims of these activities or as subjects who perpetrate fraud against other private subjects. It is also not uncommon for the threat to come from within the corporate organization. This last aspect is very important because the resolution of such affairs requires a strict coordination with the headquarter, imposing usually a long period of adaptation with personnel working inside the organization (Saccone, 2014).

Despite being a difficult phenomenon to circumscribe, fraud governance represents one of the main protagonists of the information analysis. In this case, the analyst will have to deal with delimiting the risk of fraud by acquiring in-depth knowledge of the company organization, then producing a first fraud risk assessment (perhaps detecting related events) and assisting the creation of a fraud prevention system following the delivery of the information product. It should be noted that in these cases the information product could be determined precisely by continuous company monitoring to issue alerts or bulletins to safety managers or directly to top management. Given the legal implications of any illegal behavior towards protected corporate rights, part of the analysis work could be devolved to a private investigator. It remains to be understood, however, that fraud currently is composed of many nuances.

Linked to fraud analysis is certainly the legal aspect. The prevention of disputes, the drafting of contracts that present detailed information requirements to avoid future economic damage, are today a constant of the most varied international commercial realities. Indeed, the contracts relating to the supply of information analysis products is a particular case of trade discipline which very often takes the international form. Above all, there are differences and similarities depending on the use that should be made of the contractual instrument based on the size of the activity, the object of analysis and the countries involved (Keefe, 2010).

In the end, fraud prevention requires investigative abilities mixed with application of various intel disciplines that rely on HUMINT for the core collection.

CYBER SECURITY

Another well-known intel-related issue that is part of the future of information analysis and which has long been part of our present, is that of cyber security. One of the main references in this regard certainly goes to the legislation on personal data, even if we must immediately say that, as emerged from present researches, it is substantially impossible to provide a general policy a priori that is suitable for any company. Surely it will be appropriate to focus your attention on the processing phases rather than on the data itself, being the manipulation of these to dictate the critical issues related to the technologies implemented in the company. This manipulation and in particular communications represent an incredible opportunity for anyone who wants to commit crimes. It is no coincidence that cyber security is nowadays a very hot topic at the government level. It is evident that such risks are in fact related to the existence of the networks, being the communicative aspect between the various nodes the real nerve center of the vulnerabilities (it is known that the home user is also at risk precisely because of the possible compromise of the home network with consequent data theft, identity, liquidity, etc.). There are many IT companies providing useful products that prevent government and private business from receiving undesired attacks. These products are integrated in the IT architecture of the business, detecting intrusions and performing analysis that research threats with open source techniques based on the activities of clients and links of different objects (Mele, 2014).

Among the inherent and highly topical issues, we point out the introduction of 5G technology which raises particular concerns alongside the undoubted potential that it offers. The NIS Cooperation Group of the European Union took care of producing a report on the issue, on 9 October 2019, which describes the security risks of the technology, clearly highlighting that the use of 5G requires having to rely on private structures and managers that may need state and/or federal control. The report describes practical risks, for example related to the management and maintenance of equipment that is in fact completely in the hands of corporate bodies. Although the concern is more than founded, it is clear that the risks will be greater than the current technology and integration with the private analysis sector could be a strengthening tool of control at federal level. In any case, the analyst who has the high technical skills, will have to implement a series of actions aimed at containing the risks or preventing them also through monitoring activities. Cyber security is fundamentally focused on prevention, unless the information product consists of an alert that goes to detect a compromise that has already occurred, thus proceeding to evaluate the consequences for recreating a safe environment (the latter phases make use of the skills of technicians or specialized firms). Another use of the analyst with suitable skills could be to create a protocol tailored to the company to achieve the cyber security objectives set by the management. This would allow the creation of internal standards (updated to the threats of the moment) to which the networks must conform, thus creating the first corporate prevention tool. It would basically be a real system, called Intrusion Detection System, which through its technology would be able both to prevent and identify the threat through an alert and then proceed to its resolution. As we compare ourselves with the material, it becomes increasingly evident that the presence of a technician represents an essential feature of the cyber discipline, the particular case of constant use of an enabler like the logistical support. Entering into the merits of the functioning of the IDS systems, they are based on the presence of a series of data that allow to constantly assess the situation of the corporate network, therefore keeping the requirements associated with the data (correctness of communications, performance of the operation) at the same quality level. Very interesting, and extremely technical in nature, is the ability of these systems to learn new possibilities of action thanks to the dataset inside which could allow you to perform new tasks on the basis of them (your knowledge). It is clear that these competences go beyond those, however equally technical, of analysis. Before moving on to further examples of corporate protection, I want to emphasize that cyber security is currently (and probably will also be in the future) the field of greatest collaboration between public and private. Already the European cyber strategy of 2013 reported a complex and holistic protection plan that did not exclude close collaboration and synergistic development of policies with private companies. The same cooperation highlighted at European level is also formalized in almost all member states of the European Union. There are no similar cases in relation to other risk sectors where there is such an explicit collaboration, confirming both the vital importance of cyber protection and the provision of public/private collaboration if the risk is of national strategic importance (Morano, 2015).

INDUSTRIAL SECRET

Another extremely typical business risk, although much more traditional than the above, is that dictated by the revelation of the secrets related to its production, its economy. This is valid more than ever in today's highly globalized contexts where the defense the know-how is of fundamental importance. For example, the task of an analyst is not only the defense of the secrecy of the entire knowledge base of the company, but also the protection (also to contractual level) of key knowledge, or of those elements that allow to correctly order the skills that are perhaps exported. It will thus be possible to copy the individual skills but not to insert them in the production framework capable of creating the expected output. Sometimes voluntarily disinteresting in the export of particular skills can in fact represent a significant saving of liquidity and energy. A very different case is represented by the permanent loss of the holders of some of the key knowledge, i.e. the employees who cease their working relationship and represent a potential threat to the protection of industrial secrecy, in fact a danger to corporate power. The context appears extremely varied, affirming the corporate culture, the awareness of employees and top management, aspects of a physical, contractual, legal and organizational nature. All this may concern company assets invisible to the eye such as internal practices and processes. In fact, if it is clear that it is necessary to physically protect all that pertains to corporate knowledge (documents and archives for example), the analyst's real challenge lies in identifying the knowledge to be protected in terms of ideas, past solutions, purely business interpretations to common problems, past experiences, lesson-learned, reflections. They are distributed variously among employees, collaborators, consultants who can insist either within the company organization or at other places. How do the owners of this knowledge relate to each other? Which of these, as reported above, must actually be protected? The answer is the output of the information analysis, carried out for qualitative and quantitative criteria and using technical or organizational precautions keeping in mind the legal protection against this capital (Van Puyvelde, 2019). This information report will obviously only take into account the causes of the risks for the protection of this knowledge. As for physical media, you can easily think of thefts, damage, fire, system failure/interruption, alteration, explosion or meteorological/environmental event. Non-physical media are instead subject to other risks such as ineffective communications, eavesdropping, copying. Furthermore, at organizational level, deficiencies in controls, procedures and regulation may occur. The same employees (in the necessary number) should be adequately selected, managed, monitored, and trained with specific behavioral models. It is in fact the personnel, without prejudice to the case of internal fraud analyzed above, which can follow up on errors capable of compromising the corporate intellectual property. These errors can be innumerable: communication, processing and data loading, in the use of systems or documentation, in the design, implementation and management of all the technology in use by the company. The possibility of backup in these cases can stem the error and allow recovery. Each company is a reality in itself to be evaluated in the analyst's preliminary work. Also not to be underestimated is the potential subtraction of the knowledge base through interviews with employees of other competitive realities, visits of false identities, in-depth due diligence that have not followed. Whatever the result of the intelligence work to protect this precious heritage, it will be subject to a natural deadline due to natural variations that will inevitably occur. The forecast of these variations is also to be taken into account in the drafting of contracts, for which the legal advisor, in harmony with the analyst, will be able to provide the elements most resistant to these variations over time. And obviously, the foregoing also requires considerable attention paid to the compliance of the business with the legislation in force in the operating environment, to the assessment of investments, to purely financial aspects and to disputes in which the institutional or economic entity may be involved (Costanzo, 2014).

ABROAD

A last fundamental case of intel application for corporate protection is of an extremely classic and recurrent nature, i.e. the protection of secondary offices abroad and of the employees/assets that insist on it. Ingrained in crisis areas, the need to protect your company presence abroad is fundamental as can also be seen from recent reports that have seen example of seizing company assets or employees. The company is in fact responsible for the protection of its employees who work in risky contexts having to use all the necessary measures to achieve the purpose. Physical security is an area of extreme delicacy. It is important, in this regard, to underline that this is one of the very few risks that easily intersects with the public interest for the legal aspects and for the skills to be applied (Britovšek, 2018). Also in this case, a holistic approach is of fundamental importance, especially when physical security must be guaranteed even in areas of crisis or along elaborate logistic chains. The distinctly military connotation is also an important detail to be taken into consideration when it is necessary to guarantee the protection of private interests very distant from the headquarters of the business (Saccone, 2015).

The events related to the abduction of employees of national production companies, has repeatedly brought to the attention the contribution of national intelligence to the protection of the national presence abroad, to be understood in a broad sense and therefore also aimed at companies. Making use of private intelligence entities would therefore appear perfectly in line with the same needs.

Those listed are just some of the specific sectors of corporate protection that appear naturally connected to the potential of private intelligence institutions and which are equally in line with the recent needs of protection and safeguarding the interests of companies operating abroad. This information work would usefully be placed in the national intelligence context by providing a precious link between the national security services and the company itself, to which such an adhesion would be difficult to guarantee in any other way.

REFERENCES

Britovšek, J., Tičar, B., & Sotlar, A. (2018). Private intelligence in the Republic of Slovenia: Theoretical, legal, and practical aspects. *Security Journal, 31*(2), 410–427. doi:10.105741284-017-0107-0

Butti, G. (2016). *La tutela del capitale intellettuale*. http://www.sicurezzanazionale. gov.it

Costanzo, B. (2014). *La protezione del segreto industriale*. http://www. sicurezzanazionale.gov.it

Keefe, P. (2010). *Privatized spying: the emerging intelligence industry*. Loch Johnson.

Mele, S. (2014). *Le best practice in materia di cyber-security per le PMI*. http:// www.sicurezzanazionale.gov.it

Morano, C. P. (2015). *Cyber security, intrusion detection systems e intelligenza artificiale*. http://www.sicurezzanazionale.gov.it

NIS Cooperation Group. (2019). *EU coordinated risk assessment of the cybersecurity of 5G networks*.

Puyvelde, V. (2019). *Outsourcing US Intelligence*. Edinburgh University Press. doi:10.3366/edinburgh/9781474450225.001.0001

Saccone, U. (2014). *Lo sviluppo di un sistema antifrode: considerazioni programmatiche e ruolo della Security*. http://www.sicurezzanazionale.gov.it

Saccone, U. (2015). *Security aziendale e protezione dei lavoratori all'estero*. http:// www.sicurezzanazionale.gov.it

Shorrock, T. (2008). *Spies for hire: the secret world of intelligence outsourcing*. Simon & Schuster.

Section 2
Technologies

Chapter 7
Agent–Based Approach for Monitoring Risks in Software Development Projects

Jirapun Daengdej
Assumption University, Thailand

ABSTRACT

According to various surveys conducted, regardless of how many studies in software development projects have been done, the chance that software development projects may fail remains very high. A relatively new approach to the problem of failure is using the concept of artificial intelligence (AI) to help automate a certain part(s) of the projects in order to minimize the issue. Unfortunately, most of the works proposed to date use AI as a standalone system, which leads to limiting the degree of automation that the overall system can benefit from the technology. This chapter discusses a preliminary work on a novel risk monitoring, which utilizes a number of agent-based systems that cooperate with each other in minimizing risks for the projects. The proposed model not only leads to a high degree of automation in risk management, but this extensible model also allows additional tasks in risk monitoring to be easily added and automated if required.

INTRODUCTION

Issues of software development project failure has long been recognized long time ago. In 1994, one of the most talk about reports by Standish Group called "Chaos Report" rises the issue that only around 16% of software development projects success worldwide (Clancy, 1994). Almost a decade after that, in 2012, a research

DOI: 10.4018/978-1-7998-4339-9.ch007

team of McKinsey Digital in collaboration with University of Oxford found that only around 50% of projects, which cost more than $15 million, completed projects within their budgets. In fact, they report that large IT projects usually spend 45% over budget, while delivering only around 56% less value than what originally planned (Bloch, et. al., 2012). Regardless of how much resources and researches have been put in area of Software Project Management, chance of software project failure still remains very high. According to the latest survey by KPMG, 70% of organizations has at least one project failure in the past 12 months (Krystal, 2019).

One of the reasons of such a high rate of failure is because there are a large number of risks can occur during project lifecycle. As a result, these risks have to be closely and efficiently monitored in order to minimize issues that may occur. Risk monitoring is considered to be one of the most crucial areas in project management in general. Unfortunately, the necessity and difficult in monitoring these risks can easily be magnified when comes to software development projects. The risks are higher in software development projects than other kind of projects because software is intangible in nature. Successfulness of the projects, in many cases, cannot be easily seen and judge explicitly. Progress of the software projects is also very difficult to measure. This is the reason why agile concept, which focus on final products rather than what happen during the project, has been recently introduced and rapidly accepted and adopted by industry (Burger, 2018)(Wolpers and West, 2019).

The goal of this research is to investigate how agent-based approach proposed by Artificial Intelligence (AI) community, which has already been applied in various areas, can be used in risk monitoring of software project management. This chapter provides a preliminary discussion on how the agent-based approach can be used in performing the task and layout issues that require further investigations for those who are interested.

BACKGROUND

The following discusses three main concepts related to focus of the paper. These concepts include project management, risk management, and agent-based approach.

Software Project Management

Project management has been considered as one of the most mature fields as far as industry is concerned (Spalek, 2005). However, regardless of the success of the field in helping projects to meet their expected results, a large number of software development projects are still considered as challenges or even fails (Coronado and Jaén, 2002). According to Anantatmula and Anantatmula, M. (2008), regardless of the success and failures occurred until today, in general, software project management consist of the following steps:

1. Initiation
2. Project Planning
3. Project Execution
4. Project Monitoring and Controlling
5. Project Termination

As far as the failure or challenges is concerned, according to Arnuphaptrairong (2011), example of issues that can occur during the projects include:

- Misunderstanding of requirements
- Lack of top management commitment and support
- Lack of adequate user involvement
- Failure to gain user commitment
- Failure to manage end user expectation
- Changes to requirements
- Lack of an effective project management methodology

With regard to the steps in project management, the project monitoring and controlling is considered to be the most crucial activities in managing the projects (Rozenes, et. al., 2006)(Clayton, 2019).

Risk Management

In most cases, risks in Distributed Software Development (DSD) can include issues such as trust, communication, difference in time zone and culture (Jiménez, et. al., 2009). The issues can occur in both general software development projects, and where agile approach is used in managing the projects (Bosnić, et. al. 2019) (Nadeem and Lee, 2019).

According to result of a research done by Enfei (2015), **risk factors** in software development projects can be classified into 6 groups. Table 1 depicts some of examples of the risks.

Similarly, from practitioner's perspective, according to an article by Cast Software Inc., Risk Management in Software Development and Software Engineering Projects includes:

1. **New, unproven technologies**. New technologies often lead to project failure due to unfamiliarity and uncertainty in applying the technologies the projects.

Table 1. Six groups of risk factors

Risks	Examples
Personnel	- Lack of effective "people skills" - Insufficient responsibilities
User	- Lack of cooperation and support from users - Users resistance to change
Requirements	- Users are not clear about requirements - Continually changing requirements
Technology	- Introduction of new technology - Change of development tools
Organization/Environment	- Lack of effective development process/methodology - Lack of top management commitment to the project - Change in organizational management
Planning/Control	- No planning or inadequate planning - Inadequate estimation of required resources - Project progress not monitored closely enough

Source: (Enfei, 2015)

2. **User and functional requirements**. Similar to most of the discussions found in literature about requirements from users, in most case, requirements from users are unclear, complex, and, in many cases, lengthy, which increase the chance of failure of the projects.

3. **Application and system architecture**. Unlike most of the discussions about risk existed in software development projects, this particular article also includes the fact that ability to clearly to architecture of the system has a direct impact to the successful of software development projects.

4. **Performance**. Expectations of users and all stakeholders on performance of the system being developed is critical for the success of projects. Therefore, it is important to ensure that risk management also take into consideration on how the system can achieve the expected performance.

5. **Organizational**. Ensuring that adequate resources are acquired into a project and they are properly organized in order to meet with expectations of all stakeholders are crucial for the success of the projects.

With regard to risks that can occur with software development project in particular, according to Test Institute, a well-known certification body in the area of software testing, software risk management is specifically about risk quantification of risk, which includes:

1. Giving a precise description of risk event that can occur in the project

2. Defining risk probability that would explain what are the chances for that risk to occur
3. Defining how much loss a particular risk can cause
4. Defining the liability potential of risk

Monitoring Project Risks

According to the Project Management Institute (PMI), a worldwide institute specializes in project management, as far as risks monitoring is concerned, PMBOK 5th Edition, the document includes a process called "Control Risks" which is defined as:

The process of implementing risk response plans, tracking identified risks, monitoring residual risks, identifying new risks, and evaluating risk process effectiveness throughout the project.

However, small change has been in the 6th edition of the document. In the 6th Edition of PMBOK, the "Control Risks" process is changed to "Monitor Risks". The process is described as:

"Monitor Risks is the process of monitoring the implementation of agreed-upon risk response plans, tracking identified risks, identifying and analyzing new risks, and evaluating risk process effectiveness throughout the project." (PMBOK Guide, 2017).

Furthermore, Hall of Project Risk Coach describes that there are four steps to monitoring project risks

1. **Monitor Agreed-Upon Risk Response Plans**: Upon identifying possible risks within a project, a response must be planned in order to ensure that proper actions are taken, if the risk occurs.
2. **Track Identified Risks:** In general, a project tracking tools is used to track all identified risks of the project. In this case, triggers are defined in order to ensure that all risks are notified, if occurs.
3. **Identify and Analyze New Risks:** Regardless of how much efforts are given in planning the project, new risks can always arise. Identifying new risks and rechecking existing risks are recommended to be done periodically. The following events are suggested with regard to when to identifying new risks:
   a. Major changes to the project or its environment
   b. Key milestones reached
   c. Occurrence of a major risk
   d. Unexpected risks

    e.   Changes in key team members or stakeholders
4.   **Evaluate Risk Process Effectiveness**. A plan or process usually must be monitored and revised regularly. The risk management process is the same. There are seven main activities involved in the process:
    a.   Plan for risk management
    b.   Identify risks
    c.   Perform qualitative risk analysis
    d.   Perform quantitative risk analysis
    e.   Plan risk responses
    f.   Implement risk responses
    g.   Monitor risks

Evaluation must be carried out periodically to ensure that the process can still efficiently and effectively lead to expected result.

Agent-Based Approach

Artificial Intelligence (AI) is a concept that currently has been applied in almost every area. According to one of the latest reports by PWC "2019 AI Predictions: Six AI Priorities You Can't Afford to Ignore":

Most executives know that artificial intelligence (AI) has the power to change almost everything about the way they do business—and could contribute up to $15.7 trillion to the global economy by 2030.

In addition, a number of recent articles well-known entities such as Forbes, PWC, Harvard Business Review suggests that, regardless of the size of businesses, every business must think very carefully how can they utilize the concept in their organizations before they are left behind (Marr, 2019)(Rao, et. al., 2019)(Chui, et. al.,2018). According to Marr (2019), regardless of the size of companies, examples of AI applications in organizations include:

- Developing more intelligent products
- Developing more intelligent services
- Making business processes smarter
- Automating repetitive business tasks
- Automating manufacturing processes

For small business, in particular, an AI system can be used to monitor inventory and sales recording databases and inform owners of the business that certain supplies are needed. The AI can even be programmed to place an order, if the business owner allows (Mills, 2019).

The fundamental of AI is to build a system that can mimic how human think and perform our tasks (Daugherty and Wilson, 2019)(Pesheva and Menting, 2020). In general, since the systems will work in the same way that human do things, understanding how human think and solve problems are the key to the concept. Unfortunately, one of the most difficult issues in building an intelligent system is ability acquire knowledge that cover all possible situations that the system may face in its operation.

One of the solutions to this knowledge acquisition issue is to, rather than trying to develop one very large system, develop a number of small systems that and allow them to interact with each other in solving problems. This idea of system development lead to an approach called agent-based software development (Schlesinger and Parisi, 2001). The approach is heavily influenced by the way human experts work together in solving problems (Bonabeau, 2002).

As far as the goal of development is concerned, the main focus of this agent-based approach is to get all small programs or agents to work together, learn how to deal with problems at hand, and finally make decision (DeAngelis and Diaz, 2019). In general, agents have to be designed and developed specifically for each type of problems. As a result, various architectures of agents, which are suitable for different kinds of tasks, have been proposed in literature. This includes logic-based architecture, reactive architecture, BDI architecture, hybrid architecture, cognitive architecture, and semantic architecture (Chin, et. al., 2014)(Girardi and Leite, 2013). However, despite the maturity of all the concepts proposed, note that the issues related to acquiring proper environment and information for the agents are still open-issues that require further investigations. These issues are detailed in research directions at the end of the chapter.

Agent-based approach has been applied in various areas. Ronal, Sterling, and Kirley (2007) use the approach to model pedestrian behavior. Kirer and çırpıcı (2016) discuss and compare a number of agent-based approach for complex networks, which especially focus on modeling of complex networks. With the approach ability to deal with highly dynamic situations, Carter, Levin, Barlow, and Grimm (2015) use the approach to model tiger population and territory dynamics.

Agent-Based Approach in Risk Monitoring

As mentioned earlier, agents are usually designed and developed specifically for a certain task. For monitoring risk in software development projects, each of the agents have to be quite flexible in dealing various input that can occur during the projects. As a result, the current research focuses on using Belief-Desire-Intension or BDI architecture as the blueprint for the agent development. The architecture is known to be a well suite architecture for complex task like what existed in software development projects (Chin, et. al., 2014). In fact, one of the recent works by Microsoft also utilize the BDI architecture in building their Travel Assistant Agent (TAA) (Perez, 2019). Figure 1 shows overview of the BDI architecture by Perez (2019).

Figure 1. BDI Agent Architecture
Source: Perez, 2019

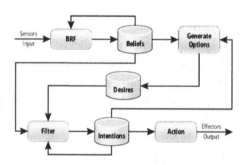

According to Caillou, Gaudou, Grignard, Truong and Taillandier (2015), the followings describe details of the architecture and how each of its components help in monitoring risks in software development activities.

- **Perception**: According to Figure 1, Belief-Revision-Function (BRF) receives or perceive input from sensors. This input is can be one or a number of events that occurs in the environment. The BRF accept the input then pass it to the "Beliefs".
- **Plan and Action**: In Figure 1, plan and action are what the agents will do before they act or output back to the environment.
- **Filter**: The filter function is used to filter previously obtained desires in order to turn them to intentions.

In addition, the BDI can be described as:

- **Belief:**. It is the internal knowledge existed in the agents about the world. Depending on what happened in the word surrounding the agents, which are perceived by the BRF, this belief is regularly updated according to its environment. The belief can be seen as knowledge that is responsible for "What the agents think?".

- **Desires**: It is the objectives that the agents would like to achieve. Desires are usually equipped with priority values, but, similar to what happen to beliefs, these values can be dynamically changed during agent's executions because what happen in the environment can influence these priority. In general, the desire can be seen "What the agents want?".
- **Intensions**: Intensions are what the agents choose to do according to what happen to desire that input to the filter. Output from the intensions are the plans and actions that will be carried out to the environment.

  The following model is used to develop an agent-based system for risk monitoring.

```
FOR each type of the risk identified{
agent = createAnAgent();
agent.setGoal();
agent.setBelief();
agent.getCurrentStatusOfEnvironment();
WHILE project is still on{
agent.updateBelief();
agent.updateDesire();
agent.createPlan();
agent.createActions(plan);
agent.executeAction();
}
}
```

FUTURE RESEARCH DIRECTIONS

Despite the fact that the proposed solutions can deal with complex risk monitoring tasks, this research is only considered to be a preliminary work, a number of issues still require further researches. The two most important issues are:

- **Providing Environmental Input that are Suitable (and Sufficient) for Agent to Perceive**: While the BDI is considered by industry to be one of the most practical agent-based architectures available today, designing environmental data that can be efficiently perceived by the agents is not at all simple. The reason is because there are large amount of crucial information related to activities in software development projects that can heavily influence the chance of projects' success. In addition, in many cases, quantifying this information is a very difficult task. Example of the information include attitude of project members during the project (Edwards, 2010), strategies used by management of the projects with regard to managing project members, processes and resources (Discenza and Forman, 2007), and level of quality of works relative to expectation of stakeholders of the projects (Pawlak and Poniszewska-Marańda, 2018).

- **Setting up Values Used by BDI Agent**: The three components: beliefs, desires, and intensions, have to be able to efficiently interact with each other in order for the agents to efficiently act toward its goal. Wrongly processing and using wrong values can directly make the agents misbehave or unable to achieve the goal (Ring and Orseau, 2011). Unfortunately, computerized systems can only best process or compare quantitative values. This is the reason why issue of having proper data is one of the 3 most important issues in one of the latest reports commissioned by IBM (Aslett and Curtis, 2019). Reasoning with symbolic values and images are still a major challenge even with today technology (Matheson, 2019a)(Matheson, 2019b). In addition, misbehaving of AI systems is a major concern today for both academic and industry (Behzadan, et. al., 2018). With regard to the values of beliefs, desires, and intensions, similar to most of the systems that require setup, to our knowledge, there is no systematic approach toward the questions what values should be used and how to best represent all these values in such a way that the all agents can most benefits from them.

CONCLUSION

Issues in risk management, especially risk monitoring, within project management is considered to be one of the most difficult tasks in software project management. Keeping track of all possible risks required large amount of efforts for the project team. This chapter explains a preliminary work on using agent-based approach. With the nature of the approach that allows multiple agents, which are responsible for different tasks to run simultaneously, can result in increasing efficiency of the overall picture of monitoring process. Since the agents can also autonomously update their own knowledge and necessary information about the project and its environment, the approach requires less efforts (manual works) in doing the task.

On the other hand, while the overview picture of how the approach can be applied in risk monitor of the software development projects, regardless of the fact there are a number of agent-based tools and platforms currently available, a number of issues related to preparing input from environment and information that the agents used internally still require further investigations.

REFERENCES

A Guide to the Project Management Body of Knowledge. (2017). (6th ed.). PMBOK® Guide. Project Management Institute.

Anantatmula, V. S., & Anantatmula, M. (2008). *Use of Agile Methodology for IT Consulting Projects*. Paper presented at PMI® Research Conference: Defining the Future of Project Management, Warsaw, Poland.

Arnuphaptrairong, T. (2011). Top Ten Lists of Software Project Risks: Evidence from the Literature Survey. *Proceedings of the International Multi Conference of Engineering and Computer Scientists*.

Aslett, M. & Curtis, J. (2019). *Accelerating AI with Data Management; Accelerating Data Management with AI*. Pathfinder Report. 451 Research.

Behzadan, V., Munir, A., & Yampolskiy, R. V. (2018). A Psychopathological Approach to Safety Engineering in AI and AGI. *Proceedings of International Conference on Computer Safety, Reliability, and Security*. 10.1007/978-3-319-99229-7_46

Bloch, M., Blumberg, S., & Laartz, J. (2012). *Delivering Large-Scale IT Projects on Time, on Budget, and on Value*. Retrieved from https://www.mckinsey.com/business-functions/mckinsey-digital/our-insights/delivering-large-scale-it-projects-on-time-on-budget-and-on-value#

Bonabeau, E. (2002). Agent-Based Modeling: Methods and Techniques for Simulating Human Systems. *Proceedings of the National Academy of Sciences*.

Bosnić, I., Čavrak, I. & Žagar, M. (2019) Assessing the Impact of the Distributed Software Development Course on the Careers of Young Software Engineers. *ACM Transactions on Computing Education (TOCE)*, *19*(2).

Caillou, P., Gaudou, B., Grignard, A., Truong, C. Q., & Taillandier, P. (2015). A Simple-to-Use BDI Architecture for Agent-based Modelling and Simulation. *Proceedings of the Eleventh Conference of the European Social Simulation Association (ESSA 2015)*.

Carter, N., Levin, S., Barlow, A. & Grimm, V. (2015). *Modelling Tiger Population and Territory Dynamics Using an Agent-Based Approach*. Ecol. Model.

Chin, K. O., Gan, K. S., Alfred, R., Anthony, P. & Lukose, D. (2014). Agent Architecture: An Overview. *Transactions on Science and Technology*, *1*(1).

Chui, M., Henke, N., & Miremadi, M. (2018, July). Most of AI's Business Uses Will Be in Two Areas. *Harvard Business Review*, 20.

Clancy, T. (1994). *The Chaos Report*. The Standish Group.

Clayton, M. (2019). *7 Uncomfortable Truths for Project Managers. Project Management Update*. Retrieved from https://www.projectmanagementupdate.com/estimate/monitoring/?open-article-id= 9629696&article-title=7-uncomfortable-truths-for-project-managers &blog-domain=projectmanager.com&blog-title=projectmanager-com

Coronado, S., & Jaén, J. A. (2002). *A Software Project Management Method: A3*. Paper presented at PMI® Research Conference 2002: Frontiers of Project Management Research and Applications, Seattle, WA.

Daugherty, P. R., & Wilson, H. J. (2019, Apr.). Using AI to Make Knowledge Workers More Effective. *Harvard Business Review*, 19.

DeAngelis, D. L. & Diaz, S. G. (2019). Decision-Making in Agent-Based Modelling: A Current Review and Future Prospectus. *Journal of Frontiers in Ecology and Evolution*, 6.

Discenza, R., & Forman, J. B. (2007). *Seven Causes of Project Failure: How to Recognize Them and How to Initiate Project Recovery*. Paper presented at PMI® Global Congress 2007.

Edwards, J. (2010). A Process View of Knowledge Management: It ain't What You Do, It's the Way That You Do It. *Proceedings of the 11th European Conference on Knowledge Management*.

Enfei, L. (2015). *Risk Factors of Software Development Projects in Chinese IT Small and Medium Sized Enterprises*. KTH Royal Institute of Technology.

Girardi, R., & Leite, A. (2013). A Survey on Software Agent Architectures. *IEEE Intelligent Informatics Bulletin, 14*(1).

Hall, H. (n.d.). *What Project Managers Should Know About Monitoring Project Risks*. Project Risk Coach. Retrieved from https://projectriskcoach.com/monitoring-project-risks/

Jiménez, M., Piattini, M. & Vizcaíno, A. (2009). Challenges and Improvements in Distributed Software Development: A Systematic Review. *Advance in Software Engineering*.

Kirer Silva Lecuna, H. (2016). A Survey of Agent-Based Approach of Complex Networks. *Ekonomik Yaklasim., 27*(98), 1. doi:10.5455/ey.35900

Krystal. (2019). *Top 8 Causes of Project Failure in 2020*. Retrieved from https://www.softwaresuggest.com/blog/top-causes-project-failure/

Marr, B. (2019). *Why Every Company Needs An Artificial Intelligence (AI) Strategy For 2019*. Forbes. Retrieved from https://www.forbes.com/sites/bernardmarr/2019/03/21/why-every-company-needs-an-artificial-intelligence-ai-strategy-for-2019/#18da0fd468ea

Matheson, R. (2019a, Nov. 2). *Better Autonomous "Reasoning" At Tricky Intersections: Model Alerts Driverless Cars When It's Safest to Merge into Traffic at Intersections with Obstructed Views*. MIT News.

Matheson, R. (2019b, May 22). *Bringing Human-Like Reasoning to Driverless Car Navigation: Autonomous Control System 'Learns' to Use Simple Maps and Image Data to Navigate New, Complex Routes*. MIT News.

Mills, K. (2019, June). How AI Could Help Small Businesses. *Harvard Business Review*, 3.

Nadeem, M. A. & Lee, S. U-J. (2019). Dynamic Agile Distributed Development Method. *Mathematics, 7*(10).

Pawlak, M., & Poniszewska-Marańda, A. (2018). Software Test Management Approach for Agile Environments. *Information Systems Management, 7*(1).

Perez, A. (2019, Jan.). Leveraging the Beliefs-Desires-Intentions Agent Architecture. *MSDN Magazine*.

Pesheva, E. & Menting, A. M. (2020, Winter). One Giant Step: Researchers are Building an Artificial Intelligence System that can Mimic Human Clinical Decision Making. *Harvard Medicine*.

Rao, A., Likens, S., Baccala, M., & Shehab, M. (2019). *AI Predictions Six AI priorities you can't afford to ignore*. PWC. Retrieved from https://www.pwc.com/us/en/services/consulting/library/artificial-intelligence-predictions-2019.html

Ring, M., & Orseau, L. (2011). Delusion, Survival, and Intelligent Agents. *Proceedings of the 4th International Conference, AGI 2011*.

Ronald, N., Sterling, L., & Kirley, M. (2007). An agent-based approach to modelling pedestrian behaviour. *Simulation, 8*(1), 1473–8031.

Rozenes, S., Vitner, G., & Spraggett, S. (2006). Project Control: Literature Review. *Project Management Journal, 37*(4), 5–14. doi:10.1177/875697280603700402

Schlesinger, M. & Parisi, D. (2001). The Agent-Based Approach: A New Direction for Computational Models of Development. Developmental Review. *Science Direct, 21*(1).

Spalek, S. (2005). *Critical Success Factors in Project Management: To Fail or Not to Fail, That is the Question!* Paper presented at PMI® Global Congress 2005—EMEA, Edinburgh, UK.

Test Institute. (n.d.). *What is Software Risk and Software Risk Management?* Retrieved from https://www.test-institute.org/What_Is_Software_Risk_And_Software_Risk_Management.php

Chapter 8
State of the Art of Extended Reality Tools and Applications in Business

Irene Maria Gironacci
Swinburne University of Technology, Australia

ABSTRACT

Over the past years, extended reality (XR) technologies, such as virtual, augmented, and mixed reality, have become more popular in business. Through immersive extended reality experiences, businesses of all shapes and sizes are waking up to the possibilities of using this emerging technology to create new opportunities and support their digital transformation. The aim of this chapter is to present the state of the art of extended reality devices, tools, and applications currently available.

INTRODUCTION

Over the past years, Extended Reality (XR) technologies, such as Virtual, Augmented and Mixed Reality has become more and more popular in business. Through immersive extended reality experiences, businesses of all shapes and sizes are waking up to the possibilities of using this emerging technology to create new opportunities and support their digital transformation. The aim of this chapter is to present the state of the art of Extended Reality devices, tools and applications currently available.

DOI: 10.4018/978-1-7998-4339-9.ch008

Virtual Reality

Virtual Reality (VR) is the use of computer technology to create a simulated environment. Virtual Reality is currently used in several fields.

It can be categorized in three main types, based on the level of immersion that the user can perceive:

1. Non-immersive
2. Semi-immersive
3. Fully immersive

Non-immersive VR refers to those VR experiences in which only one of the user's senses is stimulated, allowing for peripheral awareness of the reality outside the VR simulation. For example, user can see and/or interact with the virtual experience through conventional desktop workstations (or laptop), smartphone, or projections.

In a semi immersive simulation, the user is partially immersed into the virtual environment. An example of semi immersive VR applications are flight simulators.

In a fully immersive simulation, the user wears a head-mounted display to see the virtual experience and motion detecting devices able to stimulate senses. This kind of experience is very realistic and lets the user feel totally immersed into the environment.

State of Art Devices and Tools

Currently, the most popular VR headsets are: HTC Vive, HTC Vive Pro, Oculus Quest, Oculus Rift S, HP Mixed Reality, Oculus GO, Valve Index.

The evaluation of Virtual Reality headsets in terms of performance and capabilities is due to several parameters. The main parameters are: Field of View, Resolution, Refresh Rate, Storage. VR headsets can be either PC -Empowered (in case the headset needs to be tethered to a computer to run the experience), or Standalone VR (in case the headset can run the experience independently). PC-Empowered VR headsets' performance highly depends on the computer specifications: a powerful computer will lead to a better VR experience. In case the virtual reality headset is Standalone VR, additional parameters are considered, such as processor, RAM, integrated graphics and internal storage – these headsets have the advantage of portability, as no wires are necessary during the experience, but they are limited by these hardware parameters in terms of performance.

Applications in Industry and Education

It can be used to explore a museum remotely, as demonstrated by The Kremer Collection VR Museum (Brooks, 2018), a Virtual Reality museum experience containing more than 70 classic works of Old Masters rendered in stunning details, and accompanied by both text and audio.

In Space Exploration, as demonstrated by BBC's Home: a VR Spacewalk: Inspired by real-life NASA training simulations and commissioned by the BBC, Home: A VR Spacewalk allows users to experience a space walk in first-person as they float 250 miles above Earth. After opening the airlock, players must traverse the exterior of the space station - with an accompanying view of Earth below - to a radiator panel. Home won the Audience award at the Sheffield film festival in 2016 and is available now on HTC Vive and Oculus (BBC, 2018).

Another example of Virtual Reality application is the navigation within the virtual environment of a robotic laboratory, with the possibility of interacting with some elements, as shown in the Figure below (Gironacci, 2012).

Figure 1. Virtual environment in Unity3D (Gironacci, 2012)

AUGMENTED REALITY

Augmented Reality (AR) can be defined as a technology used to "augment" the visual field of the user with some information. Augmented Reality can be categorized in:

- Marker-based
- Markerless
- Projection-based
- Outlining

- Superimposition-based

Marker-Based (e.g. Image recognition)

Marker-based AR uses a camera and some types of visual markers as reference, for overlaying virtual contents. In this case, the AR application is able to recognize the marker from any other real world object when the marker is under the focus of the camera, and then render the virtual content in overlay to the marker. The technology behind Marker-based AR is Image Recognition. The complexity of the marker can vary from the simplest pattern available. An example of Marker-based AR is the display of a virtual content of a violin when the application scan and recognize the poster of a concert, as shown in the Figure below (Gironacci, 2012).

Figure 2. Marker-based AR (Gironacci, 2015)

Markerless (e.g. Location-Based)

Markerless AR Uses GPS, digital compass, velocity meter or accelerometer of a device to provide data based on the current user's position. The technology behind Markerless AR is Simultaneous localization and mapping technology (SLAM). It is most commonly used for mapping directions, finding nearby business etc.

Projection-Based

Projection-based AR projects the virtual image (represented by artificial light) onto physical objects. Detecting the user's interaction is done by differentiating between an expected (or known) projection and the altered projection (caused by the user's interaction). Another interesting application of projection based AR utilizes laser plasma technology to project holograms.

Outlining

Outlining AR detects the outline of a real world object (e.g. the road or the main features of your face, such as mouth, nose, eyes etc.), uses these positions as reference points, and then overlay virtual contents in real-time with the actual movement of the real world object.

Superimposition-Based

Superimposition-based AR either partially or fully replaces the original view of an object with a newly augmented view of that same object. The technology behind superimposition-based AR is Object Recognition, a technology that let the application recognize the real world object that should be augmented by the virtual object. It is commonly used for architecture and engineering.

State of Art Devices and Tools

The most popular AR libraries nowadays are: ARKit, ARCore, Vuforia, and Wikitude. These libraries are described below, and a comparison between these is illustrated at the end of the paragraph.

ARKit

ARKit is a framework by Apple for creating AR applications. ARkit uses your iOS device's cameras to map out your environment, recognize where the walls and floor are, establishing the basic geometry of the space. Afterwards, ARKit lets you drop objects inside this environment, and manipulate them using the touchscreen. The main focus of ARKit is to keep track of objects as the iOS device is moved, rather than recognizing real-world objects. ARKit is commonly used for interior design (e.g. placing an augmented chair in your living room), games, education (e.g. showing some information when a portrait is scanned), etc.

The main features of ARKit are: Marker-less AR, Light Estimation, environment understanding, Face Tracking, 3D Tracking, Image Recognition

Although ARKit present a high potential in terms of possibilities, some limitations are available as well, such as:

- It's fairly processor intensive, making the iOS device warm
- It's only available for iOS devices
- It's not designed to cope with very fast motion
- Real-world objects are not recognized
- Common limitation of AR libraries: place should be big enough in some cases (e.g. room space consisting of a bedroom that only just fits in a double bed is not enough), because the environment mapping relies on identifying planes like floor, walls and ceiling.

Wikitude

Wikitude is a framework that allows for augmented reality applications to be built. Available features: image recognition, object recognition, 3D markless tracking, scene recognition (augment large objects for outdoor gaming, construction, etc.), New extended recording and tracking of objects (scan and see augmented objects beyond markers), Instant targets (save and share instant augmentations), Unity live preview (AR-view feature into Unity editor to test the SDK features), ARKit and ARCore support, Windows OS support.

ARCore

ARCore is a software development kit developed by Google that allows for augmented reality applications to be built. ARCore uses three key capabilities to integrate virtual content with the real world as seen through your phone's camera:

- Motion tracking allows the phone to understand and track its position relative to the world. This allows users to walk around a virtual 3D object.
- Environmental Understanding: It allows the phone to detect the size and location of all type of surfaces: horizontal, vertical and angled surfaces like the ground, a coffee table or walls. For example, you can place an object on a table and appear to rest on it.
- Light estimation allows the phone to estimate the environment's current lighting conditions. This allows a virtual object's lighting will reflect the lighting in the environment.

Disadvantages:

- ARCore requires a device with a back-facing camera, an accelerometer, and a gyroscope. While nearly all phones have the required camera and accelerometer, the gyroscope requirement removes compatibility with a large portion of low-end Android devices typically purchased by cost-conscious consumers and especially those in the developing world.
- ARKit experiences significantly less positional lag than ARCore. (For example, when "placing" an inanimate AR object in the middle of a room, walking around the house, and returning with the expectation of finding the AR object at the same coordinates as it was placed, ARKit significantly outperformed our tests of ARCore on two different Android devices).
- Available only on Android devices.

Vuforia

Vuforia is a software library developed by PTC Inc.

- **Features:** Image Recognition, Object Recognition, VuMarks, MultiTarget recognition, Occlusion management.
- **Advantages of Vuforia:** It's multiplatform: the developers can build an AR experience whatever platform are they using (iOS, Android, windows), it's highly accessible (free licence), it can work with a wide variety of phones, it's integrated in Unity.
- **Disadvantages:** No light estimation, no face tracking, sometimes there is some kind of jittering in the AR experience, no environmental understanding or motion tracking.

Feature-Based Comparison

Table 1. Feature-Based comparison between AR libraries

Feature	ARKit	Wikitude	ARCore	Vuforia
Image Recognition	✓	✓	✓	✓
Object Recognition (small objects)	✓	✓	✗	✓
Location-based (markerless tracking)	✗	✓	✗	✗
Environmental Understanding	✓	✓	✓	✗
Motion Tracking	✗	✗	✓	✗
Light estimation	✓	✗	✓	✗
Face tracking	✓	✗	✗	✗

Applications in Business and Education

AR is a technology used in many sectors such as military, medicine, engineering, tourism and advertisement (Wu, 2014). In 2017 IKEA developed an augmented reality application to virtually "place" IKEA products around the room the user is currently in (Wired, 2017). Cosmetic company Sephora uses AR technology to augment eye, lips, and cheek products on the face of potential customers (The Verge, 2017). Augmented Reality technology can also be used in healthcare: to evaluate fundamental features of dental arches (Procházka et al., 2019), to promote wellbeing in older adults (Lee, 2019), In education, AR can be used to augment books (Billinghurst, 2012), One of the most famous examples in entertainment industry is Pokémon Go (Niantic, 2019).

Mixed Reality

Mixed Reality can be defined as a technology used to "mix" the real world and the artificial world.

State of Art devices and Tools

The most popular Mixed Reality headsets available today are: Microsoft Hololens, Acer Mixed Reality, Lenovo Mixed Reality, Samsung Odyssey+, Magic Leap.

Hololens

HoloLens is a fully untethered, see-through holographic computer. Below are described features, advantages and disadvantages of the first version of Hololens.
Features:

- Several kind of inputs (gaze, gestures, voice)
- Spatial sound
- Voice recognition
- Holographic UI
- Spatial anchors
- Spatial mapping
- Spatial understanding

All these features are accessible using a library called HoloToolkit, that lets the user create amazing mixed reality experiences and have the feeling that holograms are almost real.
Limitations:

- Limited field of view (35^0 degrees)
- Indoor usage only (in bright environments
- Holograms don't appear clearly defined)
- Missing geo-location feature
- Holograms are not high poly (there is a limitation on the amount of polygons possible).

Some improvements will be available in the next generation of HoloLens, such as the integration of AI and wider field of view.

Acer Mixed Reality

Advantages:

- Easy to setup
- Spatial Audio
- Better field of view compared to HoloLens and Magic Leap
- Cheaper price compared to HoloLens and Magic Leap
- 6DOF: The headset allow for six degrees of freedom, which allows the user to move in all directions and orientations within a three-dimensional space
- Wireless controllers

Disadvantages:

- No Graphic Processing Unit, like HoloLens
- Tracking can be off at times
- Limited content right now

Samsung Odyssey+

Advantages:

- 6DOF: The headset allow for six degrees of freedom, which allows the user to move in all directions and orientations within a three-dimensional space
- Good resolution
- Easy setup
- Good sound
- Good field of view, compared to HoloLens

Disadvantages

- No spatial audio available
- No Graphic Processing Unit, like HoloLens

Magic Leap One

Advantages:

- 6DOF: The headset allow for six degrees of freedom, which allows the user to move in all directions and orientations within a three-dimensional space
- Eye Tracking
- Hand Tracking

Disadvantages:

- Expensive, compared to Acer MR, Lenovo explorer and Samsung Odyssey+
- No spatial audio available

Hardware-Based Comparison

Table 2. Hardware-Based comparison between MR devices

Features	HoloLens	Acer MR	Odyssey+	Magic Leap 1
Resolution	1268 x 720	2880 x 1440	2880 x 1440	1280 x 960
Refresh	240 Hz	90 Hz	90 Hz	120 Hz
Field of View	35^0	100^0	95^0	40^0
Motion tracking	6 DOF	6 DOF	6 DOF	6 DOF
OS	Win10	Win10	Win10	Lumin OS
RAM	2 GB	16 GB	8 GB	8 GB
Storage	64 GB	10 GB	10 GB	128 GB
CPU	Intel 32 bit	AMD Radeon RX 480	Intel	ARM 64-bit cores
Tracking	Gyroscope, Magnet. Acceler.	Gyroscope, Magnet. Acceler. Proximity	Gyro, IPD, Magnet., Acceler., Proximity	Gyroscope, Accelerometers
Input	Controller, Gaze Gestures, Voice Clicker, Keyboard, Mouse	Controller Keyboard Mouse Haptic	Controller	Controller Voice
Wi-Fi	Yes	No	Yes	Yes
Bluetooth	Yes	Yes	Yes	Yes

REFERENCES

BBC. (2018). Home – A VR Spacewalk. Retrieved from https://www.bbc.co.uk/taster/pilots/home-a-vr-spacewalk

Best VR headsets for 2020. (n.d.). Retrieved from https://www.gamespot.com/articles/best-vr-headsets-for-2020-half-life-alyx-compatibi/1100-6473057

Best VR headsets Review. (n.d.). Retrieved from https://www.tomsguide.com/us/best-vr-headsets,review-3550.html

Billinghurst, M., & Dünser, A. (2012). Augmented Reality in the Classroom. *Comput. (Long Beach Calif.)*, *45*, 56–63.

Brooks, J. (2018). Promises of the virtual museum. *XRDS*, *25*(2), 46–50. doi:10.1145/3301483

Gironacci, I. (2012). *Virtual Environment modelling and development with Unity3D game engine*. Academic Press.

Gironacci, I. (2015). *Interactive Augmented Reality Mobile Applications*. Academic Press.

Lee, L. N., Kim, M. J., & Hwang, W. J. (2019). Potential of Augmented Reality and Virtual Reality Technologies to Promote Wellbeing in Older Adults. Applied Sciences (Basel, Switzerland), 2019(9), 3556. doi:10.3390/app9173556

Lenovo Mirage Solo Specs. (n.d.). Retrieved from https://www.lenovo.com/ca/en/virtual-reality-and-smart-devices/virtual-and-augmented-reality/lenovo-mirage-solo/Mirage-Solo/p/ZZIRZRHVR01

Lenovo Mirage Solo with Daydream Review. (n.d.). Retrieved from https://www.theverge.com/2018/5/4/17318648/lenovo-mirage-solo-google-daydream-standalone-vr-headset-review

Mixed Reality Specs. (n.d.). Retrieved from https://www.tomshardware.com/reviews/hp-windows-mixed-reality-headset,5665.html

Niantic, I. (n.d.). Pokémon GO Plus System Requirements and Compatibility–Pokémon Support. Available online: https://support.pokemon.com/hc/en-us/articles/360000938393-Pokémon-GO-Plus-system-requirements-and-compatibility

Oculus Go Specs. (n.d.). Retrieved from https://www.theverge.com/2018/5/1/17306458/oculus-go-standalone-vr-headset-review

Oculus Quest. (n.d.). Retrieved from https://www.forbes.com/sites/solrogers/2019/05/03/oculus-quest-the-best-standalone-vr-headset/#64d6e4e08ed8

Oculus Quest Pro and Cons. (n.d.). Retrieved from https://www.engadget.com/2019/04/30/oculus-quest-review-wireless-vr

Oculus Rift. (n.d.). Specifications. Retrieved from https://www.tomshardware.com/reviews/oculus-rift-s-vr-headset,6148.html

Oculus Rift S Specs by RoadVR. (n.d.). Retrieved from https://www.roadtovr.com/palmer-luckey-oculus-founder-rift-s-optimal-70-population-ipd/

Oculus Rift S vs HTC Vive. (n.d.). Retrieved from https://versus.com/en/htc-vive-vs-oculus-rift-s

Oculus Rift S vs Oculus Quest. (n.d.). Retrieved from https://www.windowscentral.com/oculus-rift-s-vs-oculus-quest

Procházka, A., Dostálová, T., Kašparová, M., Vyšata, O., Charvátová, H., Sanei, S., & Mařík, V. (2019). Augmented Reality Implementations in Stomatology. Applied Sciences (Basel, Switzerland), 9(14), 2929. doi:10.3390/app9142929

The Verge. (2017). Sephora's latest app updated lets you try virtual makeup on at home with AR. Retrieved from https://www.theverge.com/2017/3/16/14946086/sephora-virtual-assistant-ios-app-update-ar-makeup

Valve Index Official Website. (n.d.). Retrieved from https://www.valvesoftware.com/en/index

Valve Index Review. (n.d.). Retrieved from https://www.tomshardware.com/reviews/valve-index-vr-headset-controllers,6205.html

Vive Pro Features. (n.d.). Retrieved from https://www.vive.com/us/product/vive-pro/

Vive Std Features. (n.d.). Retrieved from https://www.vive.com/

Which VR headsets can you actually buy? (n.d.). Retrieved from https://www.theverge.com/2019/5/16/18625238/vr-virtual-reality-headsets-oculus-quest-valve-index-htc-vive-nintendo-labo-vr-2019

Wired. (2017). Ikea's new app flaunts what you'll love more about AR. Retrieved from: https://www.wired.com/story/ikea-place-ar-kit-augmented-reality/

Wu, H.-K., Lee, S. W.-Y., Chang, H.-Y., & Liang, J.-C. (2013). Current status, opportunities and challenges of augmented reality in education. *Computers & Education*, *62*, 41–49. doi:10.1016/j.compedu.2012.10.024

Wu, L. (2014). The browsemaps: Collaborative filtering at LinkedIn. *CEUR Workshop Proceedings*, ●●●, 1271.

Yen, J.-C., Tsai, C.-H., & Wu, M. (2013). Augmented reality in the higher education: Students' science concept learning and academic achievement in astronomy. *Procedia: Social and Behavioral Sciences*, *103*, 165–173. doi:10.1016/j.sbspro.2013.10.322

KEY TERMS AND DEFINITIONS

Augmented Reality: Augmented reality (AR) can be defined as a technology used to "augment" the visual field of the user with some information. Here the environment is real, and the contents are virtual: the user can see the real world with some virtual elements in overlay.

Extended Reality: Extended reality (XR) is a term referring to all real-and-virtual combined environments and human-machine interactions generated by computer technology and wearables.

Virtual Reality: Virtual reality (VR) can be defined as a technology in which both environment and contents are virtual (artificial). Users are immersed in a virtual world and can't see the real world around them.

Chapter 9
Literature Review of Recommendation Systems

Irene Maria Gironacci
Swinburne University of Technology, Australia

ABSTRACT

Artificial intelligence technologies are currently at the core of many sectors and industries—from cyber security to healthcare—and also have the power to influence the governance of domestic industry, the security and privacy citizens. In particular, the rise of new machine learning methods, such as those used in recommendation systems, provides many opportunities in terms of personalization. Big players like YouTube, Amazon, Netflix, Spotify, and many others are currently using recommendation systems to improve their business. Recommender systems are critical in some industries as they can generate income and provide a way to stand out from competitors. In this chapter, a literature review of recommendation systems is presented, as well as the application of recommendation systems in industry.

INTRODUCTION

Artificial Intelligence (AI) can be defined as the study of programmed systems that can simulate human intelligence and activities, such as perceiving, thinking, learning, and acting. Examples of these tasks are visual perception, speech recognition, decision-making, and translation between languages. Artificial intelligence is already part of our everyday lives: self driving cars, navigation systems, chatbots, smart non-player characters. AI has developed as a field of research but also as a technology that expands across a wide range of applications. What differentiates AI

DOI: 10.4018/978-1-7998-4339-9.ch009

from other digital technologies is that AIs are set to learn from their environments in order to take autonomous decisions.

From a business perspective, AI systems have the potential to deliver several advantages that lead to increased productivity. In particular, the most common benefits of AI reside in forecasting, empirical decision-making, operations automation, personalized customer services, enhanced user experiences, process and product optimization, new business models, greater access to services.

Overall venture capital funding for start-ups specializing in AI applications grew by a compound annual growth rate of 85% between 2012 and 2017. Funding tripled between 2016 and 2017, reaching over 11 billion euro (Venture Scanner, 2017). Regardless of the approach pursued, it emerges that countries are engaged in a sort of AI race that aims at achieving AI leadership, and the demand of AI is exponentially growing.

Many companies are currently using Artificial Intelligence to boost their businesses, such as Google (DeepMind's deep learning technology), Microsoft (Cortana, Azure AI), Disney (Disneyland wristbands), Netflix, and others. Google is one of the pioneers of deep learning since Google Brain project in 2011. Google use deep learning to provide better video recommendation on YouTube, studying viewer's habits and preferences when they stream content, to help self-driving cars. Virtual assistant Cortana helps you to use windows 10 systems and chatbots in Skype can interact with you and give you some suggestions. Furthermore, Microsoft lets other companies use Microsoft AI Platform to create their own intelligent tools (e.g. Microsoft Azure AI). Disney gives wristbands to every visitor. These can be used as ID, hotel room key, ticket, FastPasses and a payment system. The wristbands collect data obtained from the visitor history and predict guest's needs to deliver a personalized experience. Netflix uses AI to recommend you films based on things you watch, actors involved, genre, filming location, etc. Other popular examples of AI that's being used today are: Siri (Apple's pseudo-intelligent digital personal assistant that uses ML to get smarter and better able to predict and understand our natural language questions and requests), Alexa, Tesla, Cogito, Boxever, Amazon. com. American Express uses AI to spot divergence in client's financial behaviour patterns, using rule-based systems able to identify transactions that indicate fraudulent activities. In retail, AI can use natural language tools to search on social media for user preferences and come up with a list of recommended items that users are less likely to discover by themselves.

Recommendation Systems

A particular field of Artificial Intelligence this research project will focus on is Knowledge-Based Artificial Intelligence. More specifically, Recommendation Systems.

A recommender system is a system that predicts the likelihood that a user would prefer an item (e.g., movies, songs, books, jokes, gadgets, applications, websites, travel destinations and e-learning material), based on a set of information acquired by the system (Bodabilla, 2013). This information can be acquired explicitly (e.g. user's ratings) or implicitly (e.g. monitoring user's behaviour, such as seen items) (Lee, 2010), (Choi, 2012), (Valdéz, 2012).

Recommendation systems can be classified in three major types: User based (or collaborative filtering systems), Item-based (or content based) systems, Hybrid systems (Akhil, 2017).

Collaborative Filtering approach makes a recommendation to a user based on other similar users (called "neighbours") whose choices are similar to the target user. Many examples of Collaborative Filtering systems are available in Literature (Jannach and Hegelich 2009; Kirshenbaum et al. 2012; Liu et al. 2010). The similarity of users or items is commonly calculated using the following methods: Pearson correlation, Vector cosine, and Mean-Squared-Differences (Lee et al., 2012). Collaborative Filtering can be further classified into memory-based filtering (or neighbourhood-based, or user-based) and model-based filtering (or item-based) (Lee et al., 2012).

In memory-based collaborative filtering, a subset of users are chosen based on their similarity to the active user, and a weighted combination of their ratings is used to produce predictions for this user (Melville, 2017). This is motivated by the assumption that if two users have similar ratings on some items they will have similar ratings on the remaining items. Or alternatively if two items have similar ratings by a portion of the users, the two items will have similar ratings by the remaining users (Lee et al., 2012). When applied to millions of users and items, conventional memory-based CF algorithms do not scale well, because of the computational complexity of the search for similar users. As an alternative, item-to-item collaborative filtering matches a user's rated items to similar items (Linden, 2003).

In model-based collaborative filtering, a subset of items are chosen based on their similarity to the queried item (e.g. last movie watched, or last product viewed by the target user), and an estimation of the rating is performed as the average of the ratings of these similar chosen items. Model-based CF methods include cluster-based CF (Ungar, 1998; Sarwar, 2002; Xue et. al., 2005), Bayesian classifiers (Miyahara, 2000; Miyahara,2002), and regression-based methods (Vucetic, 2005), matrix factorization – Non negative (Lee and Seung, 1999), Probabilistic Matrix Factorization (Salakhutdinov, 2008), Bayesian PMF (Salakhutdinov, 2008), Non-

Linear PMF (Lawrence, 2009), Maximum Margin Matrix Factorization (Srebro, 2005); Nonlinear Principal Component Analysis (Yu et al., 2009).

Content based approach utilizes a series of discrete characteristics of an item in order to recommend additional items with similar properties. In this system, instead of finding relationship between users, the system make recommendations based on items the target user has browsed or viewed in the past. This recommendation does not involve other users other than the target user (Pazzani, 2007). Based on what we like, the algorithm will simply pick items with similar content to recommend to us. These discrete characteristics (the content) of each item is represented as a set of descriptors or terms, typically the words that occur in a description. The user profile is represented with the same terms and built up by analysing the content of items that have been seen by the user. In collaborative filtering systems, habits of users can be changed. This situation makes hard the recommendation difficult (in some cases). However, unlike users, items do not change. Therefore the recommendation in the content-based approach is easier. In this case there will be less diversity in the recommendations, but this will work either the user rates things or not. Also, comparing users can generate a lot of computations, especially in the case of thousands of users. This approach does not present this problem. Finally, content-based recommenders are capable of recommending items not yet rated by any user, therefore, these recommenders do not present the problem of new items never recommended due to no ratings available – compared to Collaborative Filtering systems (Pasquale, 2011). Although this approach presents the advantage of not depending on user's behaviour (including rating) and does not present the problem of requiring many computations to compare users, it presents the following problems: a) the system will recommend items similar to those already consumed ("over-specialization"); b) no content-based recommendation system can give good recommendations if the content does not contain enough information to distinguish items the user likes from items the user doesn't like (Pazzani, 2007); In recommending some items, there often isn't enough information in the word frequency to model the user's interests - as a consequence, other recommendation technologies, such as collaborative recommenders, should be used in such situations like (Pazzani, 2007). Famous systems in literature include: web recommenders – Letizia (Lieberman, 1995), Personal WebWatcher (Mladenic, 1999), Syskill & Webert (Pazzani, 1996), ifWeb (Asnicar, 1997), Amalthea (Moukas, 1997), WebMate (Chen, 1998).

Hybrid Systems combine both collaborative and content-based approaches (Claypool, 1999), (Melville, 2002), (Su, 2007), (Pazzani, 1999), (Balabanovic, 1997), (Good, 1999), (Basu, 1998), (Soroboff, 1999), (Popescul, 2001), (Hofmann, 1999), (Schein, 2002). One hybrid approach could be to generate a ranked list of recommendations from both content-based and collaborative filtering methods, and then merge the results (Cotter, 2000). Further recommender systems are presented by Burke in his survey (Burke, 2002).

Recommendation Systems Applications in Industry

Presently, many organizations such as Google, Twitter, LinkedIn, Netflix, and Amazon use recommendation systems as a decision maker to either maximize its profits and minimize the risk possibility (Bouneffouf, 2013; Chen, 2008).

For example, Netflix uses recommendation system to suggest to people new movies according to their past activities that are like watching and voting movies (see Figure 1). Amazon uses recommendation systems to recommend products in his e-commerce website (see Figure 2).

In particular, Netflix's recommendation system has been the result of a machine learning and data mining competition, called The Netflix Prize, that aimed to predict movie ratings of users on a 5-star scale (Amatriain, 2015).

Another example is Spotify, developed by Christopher Johnson, who was previously working on a PhD in machine learning: Spotify uses recommendation systems in

Figure 1. Netflix Recommendations (Techcrunch, 2014)

the Discover Weekly playlist, known as Release Radar, to update personal playlists on a weekly basis so that users won't miss newly released music by artists they like (Nam et al, 2019).

Figure 2. Amazon Recommendations (Towards Data Science, 2019)

Recommendation systems can also be highly valuable in the context of training professionals. There is a tremendous variety in the available trainings within an organization (technical, project management, quality, leadership, domain-specific, soft-skills, etc.), and the demand of personalised training becomes more and more important. Recommendation Systems are a powerful tool to achieve this goal. An example is the Recommendation System for industrial training of employees proposed by Srivastava, that make use of the past training-related data within the organization to continually improve the quality and effectiveness of its recommendations (Srivastava, 2018). Recommendation Systems can also be used to secure students industrial work experience schemes placements, as demonstrated by Ogunde et al. (Ogunde et al., 2019). Other applications of recommendation systems include the recommendation of scientific publications (Achakulvisut et al. 2016), YouTube videos (Davidson, 2010), tourists attractions (Wang et al., 2012), restaurants (Chu and Tsai, 2017), e-commerce items (Jing et al, 2015; Zhao et al,2016; Guo et al, 2017).

REFERENCES

Achakulvisut, T., Acuna, D. E., Ruangrong, T., & Kording, K. (2016). Science concierge: A fast content-based recommendation system for scientific publications. *PLoS One, 11*(7), e0158423. doi:10.1371/journal.pone.0158423 PMID:27383424

Akhil, P. V., & Joseph, S. (2017). A survey of recommender system types and its classification. *International Journal of Advanced Research in Computer Science*, *8*(9), 486–491. doi:10.26483/ijarcs.v8i9.5017

Amatriain, X., & Basilico, J. (2015). Recommender Systems in Industry: A Netflix Case Study. In Recommender Systems Handbook. doi:10.1007/978-1-4899-7637-6_11

Asnicar, F., & Tasso, C. (1997). ifWeb: a Prototype of User Model-based Intelligent Agent for Documentation Filtering and Navigation in the Word Wide Web. *Proceedings of the First International Workshop on Adaptive Systems and User Modeling on the World Wide Web, Sixth International Conference on User Modeling*, 3–12.

Balabanovic, M., & Shoham, Y. (1997). Fab: Content-based, collaborative recommendation. *Commun Assoc Comput Mach*, *40*(3), 66–72.

Basu, C., Hirsh, H., & Cohen, W. (1998). Recommendation as classification: using social and content-based information in recommendation. *Proceedings of the fifteenth national conference on artificial intelligence (AAAI-98)*, 714–720.

Bobadilla, J., Ortega, F., Hernando, A., & Gutiérrez, A. (2013). Recommender systems survey. *Knowledge-Based Systems*, *46*, 109–132. doi:10.1016/j.knosys.2013.03.012

Bouneffouf, D., Bouzeghoub, A., & Ganarski, A. L. (2013). Risk-aware recommender systems. In *Neural Information Processing* (pp. 57–65). Springer. doi:10.1007/978-3-642-42054-2_8

Burke, R. (2002). *User Modeling and User-Adapted Interaction.* doi:10.1023/A:1021240730564

Chen, L., & Sycara, K. (1998). WebMate: A Personal Agent for Browsing and Searching. In *Proceedings of the 2nd International Conference on Autonomous Agents*, (pp. 9–13). ACM Press. 10.1145/280765.280789

Chen, L. S., Hsu, F. H., Chen, M. C., & Hsu, Y. C. (2008). Developing recommender systems with the consideration of product profitability for sellers. *Inf. Sci.*, *178*(4), 1032–1048. doi:10.1016/j.ins.2007.09.027

Chois, K. (2012). A hybrid online-product recommendation system: Combining implicit rating-based collaborative filtering and sequential pattern analysis. *Electronic Commerce Research and Applications*, *11*(4), 309–317. doi:10.1016/j.elerap.2012.02.004

Chu, W. T., & Tsai, Y. L. (2017). A hybrid recommendation system considering visual information for predicting favorite restaurants. *World Wide Web (Bussum)*, *20*(6), 1313–1331. doi:10.100711280-017-0437-1

Claypool, M., Gokhale, A., & Miranda, T. (1999). Combining content-based and collaborative filters in an online newspaper. *Proceedings of the SIGIR-99 workshop on recommender systems: algorithms and evaluation*.

Cotter, P., & Smyth, B. (2000). PTV: intelligent personalized TV guides. *Twelfth conference on innovative applications of artificial intelligence*, 957–964.

Davidson, J., Liebald, B., Liu, J., Nandy, P., Van Vleet, T., Gargi, U., Gupta, S., He, Y., Lambert, M., Livingston, B., & Sampath, D. (2010). The YouTube video recommendation system. In *RecSys'10, Proceeding of the fourth ACM Conference Recommender Systems* (pp. 293-296). Academic Press.

Good, N. (1999). Combining collaborative filtering with personal agents for better recommendations. *Proceedings of the sixteenth national conference on artificial intelligence (AAAI-99)*, 439–446.

Guo, Y., Wang, M., & Li, X. (2017). Application of an improved Apriori algorithm in a mobile e-commerce recommendation system. *Industrial Management & Data Systems*, *117*(2), 287–303. doi:10.1108/IMDS-03-2016-0094

Hofmann, T. (1999). Probabilistic latent semantic analysis. In *Proceedings of the fifteenth conference on uncertainty in artificial intelligence*. Morgan Kaufmann.

Jannach, D., & Hegelich, K. (2009). A case study on the effectiveness of recommendations in the mobile internet. *Proceedings of the 3rd ACM Conference on Recommender Systems*, 205–208. 10.1145/1639714.1639749

Jing, Y., Liu, D., Kislyuk, D., Zhai, A., Xu, J., Donahue, J., & Tavel, S. (2015). Visual Search at Pinterest. *KDD'15, Proceedings of the 21th ACM SIGKDD International Conference Knowledge Discovery and Data Mining*, 1889-1898. 10.1145/2783258.2788621

Kirshenbaum, E., Forman, G., & Dugan, M. (2012). A live comparison of methods for personalized article recommendation at Forbes.com. In *Machine Learning and Knowledge Discovery in Databases* (pp. 51–66). Springer. doi:10.1007/978-3-642-33486-3_4

Lawrence, N. D., & Urtasun, R. (2009). Non-linear matrix factorization with gaussian processes. *Proceedings of the 26th Annual International Conference on Machine Learning*. doi:10.1145/1390156.1390267

Lee, D., & Seung, H. (1999). Learning the parts of objects by non-negative matrix factorization. *Nature, 401*(6755), 788–791. doi:10.1038/44565 PMID:10548103

Lee, J., Sun, M., & Lebanon, G. (2012). *A Comparative Study of Collaborative Filtering Algorithms.* ArXiv, abs/1205.3193

Lee, S. K., Cho, Y. H., & Kim, S. H. (2010). Collaborative filtering with ordinal scale-based implicit ratings for mobile music recommendations. *Information Sciences, 180*(11), 2142–2155. doi:10.1016/j.ins.2010.02.004

Lieberman, H. (1995). Letizia: an Agent that Assists Web Browsing. *Proceedings of the International Joint Conference on Artificial Intelligence*, 924–929.

Linden, G., Smith, B., & York, J. (2003). Amazon.com recommendations: Item-to-item collaborative filtering. *IEEE Internet Computing, 7*(1), 76–80. doi:10.1109/MIC.2003.1167344

Liu, J., Dolan, P., & Pedersen, E. R. (2010). Personalized news recommendation based on click behavior. *Proceedings of the 15th International Conference on Intelligent User Interfaces, IUI '10*, 31–40. 10.1145/1719970.1719976

Melville, P., Mooney, R. J., & Nagarajan, R. (2002). Content-boosted collaborative filtering for improved recommendations. *Proceedings of the eighteenth national conference on artificial intelligence (AAAI-02)*, 187–192.

Miyahara, K., & Pazzani, M. J. (2000). Collaborative filtering with the simple bayesian classifier. *Proceedings of the 6th Pacific Rim International Conference on Artificial Intelligence*, 679–689. 10.1007/3-540-44533-1_68

Miyahara, K., & Pazzani, M. J. (2002). *Improvement of collaborative filtering with the simple bayesian classifier.* Academic Press.

Mladenic, D. (1999). Text-learning and Related Intelligent Agents: A Survey. *IEEE Intelligent Systems, 14*(4), 44–54. doi:10.1109/5254.784084

Moukas, A. (1997). Amalthaea Information Discovery and Filtering Using a Multiagent Evolving Ecosystem. *Applied Artificial Intelligence, 11*(5), 437–457. doi:10.1080/088395197118127

Name, J. (2019). Deep Learning for Audio-Based Music Classification and Tagging. IEEE Signal Processing Magazine, 36(1).

Pasquale, L., De Gemmis, M., & Semeraro, G. (2010). *Recommender Systems Handbook. Springer Science Business Media, LLC.* doi:10.1007/978-0-387-85820-3_3

Pazzani, M. J. (1999). A framework for collaborative, content-based and demographic filtering. *Artificial Intelligence Review*, *13*(5–6), 393–408. doi:10.1023/A:1006544522159

Pazzani, M. J., & Billsus, D. (2007). Content-Based Recommendation Systems. In P. Brusilovsky, A. Kobsa, & W. Nejdl (Eds.), Lecture Notes in Computer Science: Vol. 4321. *The Adaptive Web*. Springer. doi:10.1007/978-3-540-72079-9_10

Pazzani, M. J., Muramatsu, J., & Billsus, D. (1996). Syskill and Webert: Identifying Interesting Web Sites. In *Proceedings of the Thirteenth National Conference on Artificial Intelligence and the Eighth Innovative Applications of Artificial Intelligence Conference*, (pp. 54–61). AAAI Press / MIT Press.

Popescul, A., Ungar, L., Pennock, D. M., & Lawrence, S. (2001). Probabilistic models for unified collaborative and content-based recommendation in sparse-data environments. In *Proceedings of the seventeenth conference on uncertainity in artificial intelligence*. University of Washington.

Salakhutdinov, R., & Mnih, A. (2008). Probabilistic matrix factorization. *Advances in Neural Information Processing Systems*.

Salakhutdinov, R., & Mnih, A. (2008). Bayesian probabilistic matrix factorization using markov chain monte carlo. *Proceedings of the International Conference on Machine Learning*.

Sarwar, B. M., Karypis, G., Konstan, J., & Riedl, J. (2002). Recommender systems for largescale e-commerce: Scalable neighborhood formation using clustering. *Proceedings of the 5th International Conference on Computer and Information Technology*.

Schein, A. I., Popescul, A., Ungar, L. H., & Pennock, D. M. (2002). Methods and metrics for cold-start recommendations. In *SIGIR '02: proceedings of the 25th annual international ACM SIGIR conference on research and development in information retrieval*. ACM. 10.1145/564376.564421

Soboroff, I., & Nicholas, C. (2000). Collaborative filtering and the generalized vector space model (poster session). *Proceedings of the 23rd annual international conference on Research and development in information retrieval*, 351–353. 10.1145/345508.345646

Srebro, N., Rennie, J. D. M., & Jaakola, T. S. (2005). *Maximum-margin matrix factorization* (Vol. 17). MIT Press.

Srivastava, R., Palshikar, G. K., Chaurasia, S., & Dixit, A. (2018). What's Next? A Recommendation System for Industrial Training. *Data Sci. Eng., 3*(3), 232–247. doi:10.100741019-018-0076-2

Su, X., Greiner, R., Khoshgoftaar, T. M., & Zhu, X. (2007). Hybrid collaborative filtering algorithms using a mixture of experts. Web Intelligence, 645–649. doi:10.1109/WI.2007.10

Techcrunch. (2014). *Netflix's Neil Hunt Says Personalized Recommendations Will Replace The Navigation Grid.* Retrieved from https://techcrunch.com/2014/05/19/netflix-neil-hunt-internet-week/

Towards Data Science. (2019). *Product Recommender using Amazon Review dataset.* Retrieved from https://towardsdatascience.com/product-recommender-using-amazon-review-dataset-e69d479d81dd

Ungar, L. H., & Foster, D. P. (1998). Clustering methods for collaborative filtering. *AAAI Workshop on Recommendation Systems.*

Valdéz, E. R. (2012). Implicit feedback techniques on recommender systems applied to electronic books. *Computers in Human Behavior, 28*(4), 1186–1193. doi:10.1016/j.chb.2012.02.001

Venture Scanner. (2017). *Artificial Intelligence Startup Highlights.* Author.

Vucetic, S., & Obradovic, Z. (2005). Collaborative filtering using a regression-based approach. *Knowledge and Information Systems, 7*(1), 1–22. doi:10.100710115-003-0123-8

Wang, Y., Chan, C. F., & Ngai, G. (2012). *Applicability of demographic recommender system to tourist attractions: A case study on trip advisor.* Paper Presented at *IEEE/WIC/ACM International Conference on Web Intelligence and Intelligent Agent Technology.* 10.1109/WI-IAT.2012.133

Xue, G. R. (2005). Scalable collaborative filtering using cluster-based smoothing. In *Proceedings of the 28th annual international ACM SIGIR conference on Research and development in information retrieval,* (pp. 114–121). ACM.

Yu, K., Zhu, S., Lafferty, J., & Gong, Y. (2009). Fast nonparametric matrix factorization for large-scale collaborative filtering. *Proc. of the international ACM SIGIR conference on Research and development in information retrieval.* 10.1145/1571941.1571979

Zhao, W. X., Li, S., He, Y., Wang, L., Wen, J.-R., & Li, X. (2016). Exploring demographic information in social media for product recommendation. *Knowledge and Information Systems, 49*(1), 61–89. doi:10.100710115-015-0897-5

Chapter 10
Augmented and Emerging Transformative Interactions With Technology:
Learning in Post Humanism

Maria Antonietta Impedovo
ADEF, Aix-Marseille University, France

ABSTRACT

At this time of digital, social, technological, and economic transformation driven by increasing diversity and inequality in the world, it is worthwhile to question from new theoretical discussion the individual and collective relationship that we have with the technological world around us, going to the roots of our interactions with technology. This chapter questions our capacity to perform individual and collective agentic learning relationship as in an increasingly technological society. Research questions in this chapter are: How do we deal with augmented and emerging interactions with increasingly complex material and virtual objects? What are the learning implications of a posthumanism deeply embedded with technology?

INTRODUCTION

Technologies act '...as active interventions and transformative forces within the world' (Stetsenko, 2017, p. 30). The everyday meaning of the term 'technology' has itself morphed so quickly in recent years that it has become virtually synonymous with the digital technologies that are globally transforming patterns of human life (Pea & Cole, 2019). Gleick (2000) referred to as 'the acceleration of everything':

DOI: 10.4018/978-1-7998-4339-9.ch010

media and devices are now an integral part of daily life for most people in the world (Global Internet Use Report 2019). Emergent and exponential technologies - like Virtual /Augmented /Mixed Reality, Sensory Augmentation Technologies, Artificial Intelligence, Robotics - will soon be widely spread in our daily lives. Part of the community of researchers in psychology currently engages in evaluating and analysing these technologies in people's lives. This is a field of great interest and of considerable scientific, social and commercial impact in which scholars and professionals of human sciences are present. At the same time, the intertwining of psychology and technology is gaining considerable space. Our expressive range and behaviour are increasingly pre-determined by the digital tools, techniques and devices that we use daily, and the interests, experiences, and values of those who create them (Smith, 2019). Consequently, the notion of 'the human' needs urgent redefinition (Ferrando, 2019). Terminology like Transhumanism and Hyperhumanism (Post-humanism) open new challenges (Fiore, 2019; Hayles, 2010; 2012). At this time of digital, social, technological and economic transformation is driven by increasing diversity and inequality in the world (the number of poor increased to 734.5 million people), it is worthwhile to question from new theoretical discussion the individual and collective relationship that we have with the technological world around us, going to the roots of our interactions with technology. This paper questions our capacity to perform individual and collective agentic learning relationship as in an increasingly technological society. Research questions in this paper are: *How do we deal with augmented and emerging interactions with increasingly complex material and virtual objects? What are the learning implications of a posthumanism deeply embedded with technology?* Implications of these reflections willing to contribute to the awareness of our relationship with technology and reduction of present and future kinds of unpowered - inequality (Sticlitz, 2012) linked to the access, exposition, and literacy of the emergent and exponential technology.

Augmented and Emerging Learning Interactions with Technology

Technology is reshaping the micro-ecologies of developing and learning (Pea & Cole, 2019), becoming a part of it, in everyday situations and also giving voices to a sensible target of the population who are not always able to express their perspective. In the following sections, first, the focus is on the materiality and technology side of the interactions; then, on the transformative agentive side in the interaction with technology.

Material and Technological side of the learning interaction

In mainstream psychology, inspired by Descartes and Kant, the 'subject' is first of all in front of an objective world that he/she defines and organises. From Latin *objectum*, the object is primarily 'what is placed in front of', 'which exists independently from the mind' and is conceived in terms of its physical properties, as a result of attribution by the subject. As a consequence, in these positions, the material and object reality is overlooked. The aim of making material culture visible in psychology brings us close to current debates within Material Culture Studies, a field which emerged in the 1980s in the Anglo-Saxon world. In occidental philosophy, the issue of the thing is one of the old questions reflected upon Heidegger, articulating it to that of the Human Being and the Mundaneity of the world. In the most general sense, philosophy treats objects as things towards which consciousness is directed, what is perceived and imagined, in contrast to an active subject, who perceives and imagines (Blackburn, 2008). In mainstream social theory, which studies and makes sense of social phenomena, objects were given little attention as a separate and independent concept. On the contrary, in the philosophy of technology, the object has a central role (Dusek, 2007; Mitcham, 1994). Pitt (2000) points out that the use of the instrument creates technology and emphasizes technology as ''humanity at work'' (p. 11), in slow and cumulative technological development (DiGironimo, 2011).

Since the overall aim of this paper is to understand the emerging interaction with technology, a synthetic and no exhaustive discussion between theoretical frameworks which have similar aims of explaining the role of objects in the process of emerging social and subjective phenomena is open:

- *In Cultural Psychology*, the artefact has a central role in the mediation of the subject with the environment (Vygotsky, 1978). In this perspective, artefacts are the result of a process of communication between the self and other, around which activities are realised. At the same time, artefacts condense the signs of historical and cultural context in which they are created and are continuously recreated through their own use, making the culture as a system of accumulated artefacts of a community (Cole, 1996; Authors). Cultural-historical perspective allows digital practices to be conceptualised as part of the cultural development. Object-orientedness forms the core principle of this approach: human intentions are directed towards an object of activity. The modern conceptualisation of the notion of object in Cultural Historical Activity Theory (CHAT) offers the potential for facilitating an understanding of why people do things, especially in the case of complex objects and the networks of interacting activity systems around objects (Engeström, 2015).

- *The Actor-Network Theory* (Latour, 2012) deals with humans and nonhumans as actor-networks in heterogeneous socio-technical networks. The approach of actor network theory (ANT) responds to the dualism between nature and society, with concepts of generalised symmetry and the production of nature and society. The ANT proposes an active assembling of humans, things, technologies and concepts. Latour (1996) specifically discussed the importance of non-human actors in networks. The role of human and nonhuman actors in the process of constructing a heterogeneous network is also analysed in equal terms. The construction of knowledge and emergence of artefacts is seen as a consequence of the common effort of opposite poles, both human and nonhuman actors. In this way, agency is distributed among the participants of a network, and a human being is determined by the network (Latour, 1991).

- *In a Post-social theory*, Knorr Cetina (2009) aimed at overcoming the dualism between individualisation and objectualisation with notions of post-social relationship and object-centred sociality. Knorr Cetina discussed the process of objectualisation as an increased orientation towards objects as sources of the self, relational intimacy and social integration. She defined this post-social relationship as follows: "new kinds of bonds such as those constructed between humans and objects. Nonhuman objects have an increased presence and relevance in contemporary life. Such forms of binding self and other are what we call 'postsocial' (Knorr Cetina & Bruegger, 2001, p. 162–163). The analytical potential of conceptualisation of objects lies in the notion of sociality with objects, which helps us to understand the role of objects in social life. This notion refers to a situation in which objects act as centres of sociality. Objects act here as the centres of intentionality towards which the subjects' efforts are directed: as a structure of wanting, the subject becomes defined by the object.

Although the three approaches have different philosophical, disciplinary and methodological backgrounds, they all give a contribution (see Vetoshkina, 2018) to open theoretical tensions for a post-humanism perspective and implication for learning. Indeed, considering the increasing complexity of material and virtual objects, the capacity of action on the reality is questioning. And this capacity has to be proposed for all the segments of populations to be active in the society. For this, it is interesting to question our relationship with technology starting to the agentive potential impact in the reality that we have as human. Human agency refers to the subject's willed quest for transformation. The Subjective dimension of Agency is here discussed in the dialogical tension with new technology, Virtual /Augmented /Mixed Reality, Sensory Augmentation Technologies, Artificial Intelligence,

Robotics, as complex concrete material and virtual objects which we deal with in everyday life and will deal with more in the future, and on which we have to learn to be and learn about.

Transformative Agentive side in the learning interaction with technology

The term 'agency' appears very often in contemporary academic writings at the international level, showing the intellectual interest that this concept fuels. The concept of agency has been indicating as key future competences for the new generation to reach and in also often implicated in policies aimed at social policy. Agency indicates the capacity of a person to act on the environment by transforming it, proposing ideas and choices. Despite its current wide use in scientific and political literature, the concept of agency is often applied without explicit definition and requires conceptual clarification as well as a clarified methodological approach (Archer, 2000; Goller & Harteis, 2017; Moore, 2016). Also, the way scholars interpret the concept of agency can be very different when linked to the theoretical background. The roots of this concept are traced in the social sciences, suggesting the ability of individuals (and groups) to act as transformative agents on their environment. In addition, the concept of agency has been applied in a variety of subject. The dialectic of social structure versus personal individuality has generated much debate. Billet and Pavolva (2005) suggested that agency works in relational and social structures, but that it is not necessarily 'subjugated' by them. Considering this rich background, the concept of agency needs a critical reconstruction in relationship to the actuality of human interaction with emergent and exponential technology, open toward a posthuman agency discussion:

- In Psychology, the notion of agency emphasises local social action, micro and individual, constituting the active component of variable social action. In social cognitive theory, agency is tightly related to personal efficacy (Bandura, 2002). From a sociocultural psychology perspective, individual action must be examined in the social context, considering individuals as cultural agents. Subjects actively create personal meanings in relation to a given situation that can be negotiated in social interaction. Gillespie (2010) defines agency as 'the degree to which an agent can act independently of the immediate situation' (p.32), emphasizing the ability to go beyond the immediate situation. Individual agency is a strong prerequisite for the development of social practices. The social dimension of agency is particularly evident in the notion of so-called relational agency (Edwards & Protheroe, 2005), defined as 'a capacity to align one's thoughts and actions with those of others to interpret aspects of one's world and to act on and respond to those interpretations' (p. 294) and involving the capacity to offer and ask support from others. From this perspective, the person becomes an actor and a reflexive agent, developing an increasing autonomy (Valsiner, 2000, 2014).

- In Education, agency is a hot topic (see the Finish group of research led by Kumpulainen, - Kajamaa & Kumpulainen, 2019). Agency plays a central role in the learning process (Clarke, 2016). To develop and promote agency in learning processes means helping the learners to imagine themselves as future practitioners or active citizens in the world (Bruner, 1990). In this sense, agency becomes a learning objective, helping the learner to find a position in the world, transforming it. An active participation in the society means acting in independent and creative ways, considering that agency lies in improvisations that people create in response to particular situations, mediated by these senses and sensitivities (Holland et al., 1998), shaping learners who are able to (re)construct the meaning of concepts and ideas through reflection and social interaction (Kumpulainen, Rajala & Kajamaa, 2019; Matusov & Marjanovic-Shane, 2017). Technology by itself does not create forms of engaged learning and promote forms of agency. However, the design of specific activities may be such as to promote it (Authors; Tchounikine, 2019).

Deep understanding the individual and collective agency that we have and we will have in the future help to shape the potentiality of the interactions with new and emerging technology. In this way, standard and consolidated actions are breaking away to initiate new perspectives and new practices (Haapasaari & Kerosuo, 2015). This agency is pivotal in moving a process of transformation forward, especially in a society that imposes one-way products, solutions and processes, excluding marginal and alternative perspectives. Having considered the both side of interaction between technology and humans action, one from material and the second by subjectivity, in the following section we go close on learning in post humanism. The hybridity of body, tools and materiality, language, space and time features the new dimension in learning, that will be explored in the next session.

Learning in Post Humanism: Knots of new configurations

Learning activities via like Virtual/Augmented/Mixed Reality, Sensory Augmentation Technologies, Artificial Intelligence, Robotics engage participants in a new embodied activation, mobilizing physical and virtual engagement, spaces and resources. The strict connotation between virtual and material is possible to call here metaphorically as "knots", to show the interweaving of the aspects considered: human body versus cyber or robotics; material versus online resources and tool; space and time new configurations. In the following, we explore knots of hybridity.

Hybridity of Body

Today the emerging technology has led to a progressive adaptation of the interfaces to the body, reaching the development of advanced systems able to fully involve the perceptual apparatus to determine a complete sensorial immersion of the individual in the context. So, the body is becoming present in cyberspace space: the device is adapting to the body; the body is adapting to the device. The concept of the embodiment has gained currency in recent years, particularly in light of new forms of interaction and engagement with emergent technology. This perspective offers rich reflections for conceptualizing the relationship between the physical actions of the body and meaning-making processes (e.g., Cheville, 2006; Dourish, 2004). The materiality that co-present and virtual bodies encounter, manipulate, utilize, and transform in the course of their activities promote a new extended multimodal analysis of social interaction (Mondada, 2019). The body is on one side the frame of reference in which all our experiences take place; on the other, it becomes, through the senses, the main link between the mind and the world (Lakoff & Johnson, 1999). Embodied interaction claims that any action is constituted by a complex arrangement of multiple semiotic fields (e.g., gestures, the body, the language) that are deployed simultaneously and influence each other. Goodwin (2000) writes that the notion of embodiment encompasses orientation, gesture, and intonation, among other physical aspects of interaction. The moment-to-moment arrangement of these various semiotic fields is called a contextual configuration (Goodwin, 2000). The contextual configuration changes during the course of action: new semiotic fields can be brought in and old ones treated as irrelevant, adapting with the news proposes. So, human activity can be understood through the contextualized experience of a body-environment system, and not as the result of representations of the world disconnected from a context. With virtual reality, the body becomes central for the interaction. Transportation in virtual reality is an experience of cognitive, emotional, and imagery involvement into a narrative (Green, Brock, & Kaufman, 2004). In such systems, media interface development is aimed at providing users with fully immersive experiences, with the ultimate goal of making natural and pleasant the virtual experience. With the use of different sensor or perceptual devises, the body plays a central role by becoming progressively extended in the virtual reality. Therefore, it is challenging to determine how the body enter into the real and virtual setting contextual configurations and gain their significance in relation to the activity. Also, the body needs to be differently communicated in this 'hybrid' setting of virtual and real, in a multi-activity (Mondada, 2011) struggle to coordinate interaction. Bodies,

136

language, and objects make sense in this respect, meaningfully assembled in the production of actions as well as in their interpretation (Mandada, 2019).

Hybridity of tools and materiality

Generally, the concepts of "mediation" (Beguin & Raparbel, 2000; Roth, 2007; Engeström, 1990), "artefact" (Wartofsky, 1973; Miettinen, 2001), and "ba" (Nonaka & Konno, 1998) help in investigating how aspects of context impact human thinking. According to the socio-constructivist approach, people interactively construct the realities in which they live, developing symbolic, sense-filled "possible worlds," while they act in their physical, social, and cultural environment (Bruner, 1986). Part of this continuous construction process takes place when people negotiate the contexts in and with which they interact while participating in various activities. The construction of the context is in fact "shaped by the activities of the moment" (Duranti & Goodwin 1992), in line with the objectives that people have set themselves and the activities they are involved in. In fact, in accordance with distributed cognition theory, while carrying out an activity, people project structures of intentionality onto the context, which thus becomes an integral part of human thought and action (Hollan et al. 2000).

Materiality with respect to learning and cognition is a relatively new research paradigm, such as the embodied and extended mind (Alač & Coulson, 2004; Clark, 2008; Menary, 2013; Sørensen, 2009). Materiality, in this case, must be understood as a connection to other entities, both physical as well as social (Sørensen, 2009). For example, the material dimension is relevant in the field of social robots, considering that social robots have a physical body (Alač et al, 2011). Social robotics is a fast-growing research field geared toward the design and study of 'autonomous' robots that are expected to engage in social interaction with humans in a different field. This field is oriented to develop practical applications and to model human cognition (see, for example, Dautenhahn, 1995; Brooks et al., 1998; Breazeal, 2002; MacDorman & Ishiguro, 2006; Ishiguro, 2007; Tanaka et al., 2007). At the same time, social robots are conceived as testing platforms for theoretical models of human cognitive abilities, for example, the interdependencies between the mind and the body. The configuration of space changes with the introduction of robotic with the indigenous population of the classroom (Alač, 2009; Alač, Movellan & Tanaka, 2011).

Hybridity of Language

Virtual/Augmented/Mixed Reality, Sensory Augmentation Technologies, Artificial Intelligence, Robotics acts not only among users but also between them and the environment in which they are immersed. The introduction of an extra dimensions puts a new non-linguistic, bodily and visually learning dimension at the centre of users' experience, removing language from the dominant vector of the experience. The term interaction indicates the complex construction of meaning that human beings do in acting in a space and time, be it simulated or not (Cole, 1996; Duranti & Goodwin, 1992). Meaning emerge as a feature of action in situ, within the arrangements of bodies, objects, places, and environments, along silent or talkative practices. So, the physical and virtual boundaries is not definite by the reality or the virtual but co-constructed (Hirst & Vadeboncoeur, 2006). The sense-making in act between the involved participant is the "edutainment context" (Charsky, 2010) of the virtual or augmented reality is not linear but a continue attempts to clarify the activity and the intersubjective understanding between physical and material process, (Kosmas, Ioannou & Zaphiris, 2019).

Hybridity of space and time

The virtual learning, as a form of hybrid, active a new chronotope that concerns both the immaterial, semiotic, worlds of discourse and narratives and patterns of organization of space and time (Hirst & Vadeboncouer, 2006) that are enacted through the movement of bodies, like gestures, and objects (Rosborough, 2016). The semiotic and material into the human-social robotics interactions also incorporates the space-time dimension. The spatiotemporal coordinates of this interaction become essential in defining the "window" of significant context. Suchman (1987) also highlighted how the organization of a situated action is a property that emerges from the interaction's moment by moment, in a new reconfiguration. The space-time of interactions is here conceptualized in terms of heterotopia – i. e., a place in which many layers of material, symbolic, virtual space overlap and alternate (Foucault, 1967) and chronotope – i. e., patterns of organization of space and time (Lemke, 2004). Understanding the social nature of material objects and the situated character of human bodies involved in interaction cannot be complete until we are willing to carefully observe the richness of everyday activities (including our own actions/reactions as we study those of others) in the environments in which the bodies of social actors are designed and enacted (Cicourel, 1974; Lynch, 1993).

The use of different kinds of emerging technology - Virtual /Augmented /Mixed Reality, Sensory Augmentation Technologies, Artificial Intelligence, Robotics - requires a form of adaptation to the available resources, making explicit the reference to them. The interaction with the new technology is lived no longer as an experience in itself, rather based on the frame of social meanings in which each individual is able to place it. In this sense, learning and interactions are extensively transformed when integrating emerging technologies. Learning therefore could be considered a becoming with and through technology.

DISCUSSION AND CONCLUSION

The manuscript shows ideas about the concept of technology from tangible to intangible features and the consequences of interact with both tangible and intangible technologies. The focus is into materiality and technology and transformative agentive. Posthumanism/hyperhumanism allows us to see existence in inter-connected ways (Smith, 2019) exploring new cognition, perception, and awareness developmental implication (Belhassein, et al, 2019). The relationship between humans and technology, and consequently of learning, is shaped by new challenge like: human ways of living in the anthropocene; artificial intelligence, robots and ethical technology; the ethics of human enhancement and biotechnologies; genetic privacy; technological addiction; environmental sustainability; power, equity and the global dynamics of human interactions with the nonhuman world; drones, space, big data and co-existence; spirituality, religions and mindfulness in the posthuman age. Utopian and dystopian, visionary and critical, theoretical and practical approaches including: philosophical, critical and cultural posthumanism, transhumanism, new materialism, antihumanism, object-oriented ontology, metahumanism, panpsychism, and other approaches have to be considered and listened in our relationship with new technology. The deep and strong connection with technology can help to emerge a new being a human-tech hybrid (Duus, Cooray, Page, 2018), with darker sides still to discover.

In conclusion, explore the relationship between humans and technology means to adopt:

1. An interdisciplinary perspective (philosophy, psychology, education, computer science) to understand awareness and the emerging of transformative human agency in interaction with new technology in post humanism;
2. The rehabilitation of the materiality dimension in which we live. The consideration of technical and material objects as decisive determinants of human activity is a relatively new research paradigm (Mercer, Wegerif & Major, 2019; Mirza, et al. 2014), considering recent ideas of materiality with respect to learning and cognition, such as the embodied and extended mind (Clark, 2008; Sørensen, et al. 2009) - see the maker movement. Materiality in this case must be must be understood as a connection to other entities, both physical as well as social (Sørensen, 2009).
3. The inclusion of postmodern theoretical and postmodern methodological perspectives in a non-dual reality, focus on how matter matters as agentic and intra-active (Deleuze & Guattari, 1987; Freitas & Palmer, 2016; Lenz Taguchi, 2011; Ueno et al., 2015; 2017). Understanding how we live with things, and in turn, how things come to live with us calls for methodologies that go beyond a focus on humans only.

4. Development of technological skills make students able to think critically and to make decisions with respect to twenty-first century problems and future challenges. For these reasons, technological literacy is perceived to be a key competency for the future (Feinstein 2010). Consequently "a good understanding of the nature of technical artefact is a relevant part of technological literacy" (Ineke et al. 2010, p. 277). Technology education, focusing on the technical object, promotes a better understanding and intelligibility of the technical environment (Ankiewicz 2015).

5. Development of powerful human-centric hybrid literacy to address issues of cultural diversity and social inequality in post humanism for all, moving from a content-based economy to a context -based economy; where we no longer focus on the mass production of content to be consumed but shift the primary focus to producing context to be experienced (Smith, 2019).

6. Finally, these reflection joins to a collective dream of human flourishing through a healthy relationship between humans and technology, through a conscious approach on how we explore, design and use exponential technologies for contributing to the individual and the collective possibilities of action. Actual research is opening the "pandora's box" about the multiple interfaces of technology and links it to the cognitive possibilities. Considering the multiplicity of resources, information and interfaces that foster the learning, there is space for discussion about ideas as "If there are more senses involved during learning, then there is more learning" or as "Intelligent and Multimodal Environments engage learning", exploring the concept of individual and collective agency as a catalyst for the potentialities of both technology and cognitive possibilities in the learning context. This thinking flow will open (again) the path on the reflection of subject and object relationship; self and structure; the transformation of the internal self and the external environments; the dialogue between nature and culture.

REFERENCES

Alač, M. (2009). Moving android: On social robots and body-in-interaction. *Social Studies of Science*, *39*(4), 491–528. doi:10.1177/0306312709103476 PMID:19848108

Alač, M., Movellan, J., & Tanaka, F. (2011). When a robot is social: Spatial arrangements and multimodal semiotic engagement in the practice of social robotics. *Social Studies of Science*, *41*(6), 893–926. doi:10.1177/0306312711420565 PMID:22400423

Ankiewicz, P. (2015). *The implications of the philosophy of technology for the academic majors of technology student teachers. In PATT 29 conference proceedings.* Presses Universitaires de Provence.

Archer, M. (2000). *Being human: The problem of agency.* Cambridge University Press. doi:10.1017/CBO9780511488733

Bandura, A. (2002). Social cognitive theory in cultural context. *Applied Psychology*, *51*(2), 269–290. doi:10.1111/1464-0597.00092

Belhassein, K., Cochet, H., Clodic, A., Guidetti, M., & Alami, R. (2019). *From Children to Robots: How the parallel with developmental psychology can improve human-robot joint activities.* Academic Press.

Blackburn, S. (2005). *The Oxford dictionary of philosophy.* OUP Oxford.

Bruner, J. S. (1990). *Acts of meaning* (Vol. 3). Harvard University Press.

Charsky, D. (2010). From edutainment to serious games: A change in the use of game characteristics. *Games and Culture*, *5*(2), 177–198. doi:10.1177/1555412009354727

Cheville, J. (2006). The bias of materiality in sociocultural research: Reconceiving embodiment. *Mind, Culture, and Activity*, *13*(1), 25–37. doi:10.120715327884mca1301_3

Clark, A. (2008). *Supersizing the mind: Embodiment, action, and cognitive extension.* OUP USA. doi:10.1093/acprof:oso/9780195333213.001.0001

Clarke, S. N., Howley, I., Resnick, L., & Penstein Rosé, C. (2016). Student agency to participate in dialogic science discussions. *Learning, Culture and Social Interaction*, *10*, 27–39. Advance online publication. doi:10.1016/j.lcsi.2016.01.002

Cole, M. (1996). *Cultural psychology: A once and future discipline.* Harvard University Press.

DiGironimo, N. (2011). What is technology? Investigating student conceptions about the nature of technology. *International Journal of Science Education, 33*(10), 1337–1352. doi:10.1080/09500693.2010.495400

Dourish, P. (2004). *Where the action is: The foundations of embodied interaction.* MIT Press.

Dusek, V. (2007). *Philosophy of technology: An introduction.* Blackwell Publishing.

Duus, R., Cooray, M., & Page, N. C. (2018). Exploring human-tech hybridity at the intersection of extended cognition and distributed agency: A focus on self-tracking devices. *Frontiers in Psychology, 9*, 9. doi:10.3389/fpsyg.2018.01432 PMID:30150957

Edwards, A. (2005). Relational agency: Learning to be a resourceful practitioner. *International Journal of Educational Research, 43*(3), 168–182. doi:10.1016/j.ijer.2006.06.010

Engeström, Y. (2015). *Learning by expanding: An activity-theoretical approach to developmental research* (2nd ed.). Cambridge University Press.

Feinstein, N. (2010). Salvaging science literacy. *Science Education, 95*(1), 168–185. doi:10.1002ce.20414

Ferrando, F. (2019). *Philosophical Posthumanism.* Bloomsbury Publishing. doi:10.5040/9781350059511

Fiore, S. (2019). *Becoming Transhuman: A roadmap for Augmentation Cognition in the 21tst Century.* University of Central Florida.

Gillespie, A. (2010). Position exchange: The social development of agency. *New Ideas in Psychology, 30*(1), 32–46. doi:10.1016/j.newideapsych.2010.03.004

Gleick, J. (2000). *Faster: The acceleration of just about everything.* Little, Brown.

Goller, M., & Harteis, C. (2017). Human Agency at Work: Towards a Clarification and Operationalisation of the Concept. In M. Goller & S. Paloniemi (Eds.), *Agency at Work. Professional and Practice-based Learning, 20.* Springer. doi:10.1007/978-3-319-60943-0_5

Guattari, F. (1987). As creches e a iniciação. In F. Guattari (Ed.), *Revolução molecular: pulsações políticas do desejo* (pp. 50–55). Brasiliense.

Haapasaari, A., & Kerosuo, H. (2015). Transformative agency: The challenges of sustainability in a long chain of double stimulation. *Learning, Culture and Social Interaction, 4*, 37–47. doi:10.1016/j.lcsi.2014.07.006

Hayles, N. K. (2010). How we became posthuman: Ten years on an interview with N. katherine hayles. *Paragraph*, *33*(3), 318–330. doi:10.3366/para.2010.0202

Ineke, F., Sonneveld, W., & de Vries, M. (2010). Teaching and learning the nature of technical artifacts. *International Journal of Technology and Design Education*, *21*, 277–290.

Kajamaa, A., & Kumpulainen, K. (2019). Agency in the making: Analyzing students' transformative agency in a school-based makerspace. *Mind, Culture, and Activity*, *26*(3), 266–281. doi:10.1080/10749039.2019.1647547

Knorr Cetina, K. D. (2001). Objectual practice. In The practice turn in contemporary theory. Routledge.

Knorr Cetina, K. D. (2009). *Epistemic cultures: How the sciences make knowledge.* Harvard University Press. doi:10.2307/j.ctvxw3q7f

Kumpulainen, K., Rajala, A., & Kajamaa, A. (2019). Researching the materiality of communication in an educational makerspace The meaning of social objects. In N. Mercer, R. Wegerif, & L. Major (Eds.), *The Routledge International Handbook of Research on Dialogic Education. Routledge.* doi:10.4324/9780429441677-36

Latour, B. (1991). Technology is society made durable. In J. Law (Ed.), *A sociology of monster: Essays 132*. Routledge.

Latour, B. (1996). On actor-network theory: A few clarifications plus more than a few complications. *Soziale Welt*, *47*, 369–381.

Latour, B. (2012). *We have never been modern.* Harvard University Press.

Lenz Taguchi, H., & Palmer, A. (2014). Reading a Deleuzio-Guattarian cartography of young girls'"school-related" ill-/well-being. *Qualitative Inquiry*, *20*(6), 764–771. doi:10.1177/1077800414530259

Mercer, N., Wegerif, R., & Major, L. (2019). The Routledge International Handbook of Research on Dialogic Education. Taylor & Francis Ltd. doi:10.4324/9780429441677

Mirza, N. M., Grossen, M., de Diesbach-Dolder, S., & Nicollin, L. (2014). Transforming personal experience and emotions through secondarisation in education for cultural diversity: An interplay between unicity and genericity. *Learning, Culture and Social Interaction*, *3*(4), 263–273. doi:10.1016/j.lcsi.2014.02.004

Mitcham, C. (1994). *Thinking through technology.* The University of Chicago Press.

Moore, J. W. (2016). What is the sense of agency and why does it matter? *Frontiers in Psychology*, *7*, 1272. doi:10.3389/fpsyg.2016.01272 PMID:27621713

Pea, R., & Cole, M. (2019). The Living Hand of the Past: The Role of Technology in Development. *Human Development*, *62*(1-2), 14–39. doi:10.1159/000496073

Pitt, J. (2000). *Thinking about technology - Foundations of the philosophy of technology*. Seven Bridges Press.

Smith, C. H. (2019). Reality Hacking as Intelligence Augmentation. Creative Innovation 2019, Melbourne, Australia.

Stetsenko, A. (2017). *The transformative mind: Expanding Vygotsky's approach to development and education*. Cambridge University Press. doi:10.1017/9780511843044

Valsiner, J. (2000). Culture and human development. *Sage (Atlanta, Ga.)*.

Valsiner, J. (2014). *An invitation to cultural psychology*. Sage. doi:10.4135/9781473905986

Vetoshkina, L. (2019). *ANCHORING: CRAFT. The object as an intercultural and intertemporal unifying factor* (PhD Thesis). Helsinki Studies in Education.

Vygotsky, L. S. (1978). *Mind in society* (M. Cole, V. John-Steiner, S. Scribner, & E. Souberman, Eds.). Harvard University Press.

Chapter 11

Origin of Cyber Warfare and How the Espionage Changed:
A Historical Overview

Maria Luisa Nardi
Independent Researcher, Italy

ABSTRACT

International politics is faced with new and vital issues, linked to aspects such as individual rights, the holding of democracy, the effects of worldwide policies, as well as the geopolitics of technology. The intertwining of technology and international relations is now a fact. Exploring the new and different political challenges posed by new technologies is a factor of transformation of the global society that influence on its actors. Today, an application of technological innovation, digital technology, and artificial intelligence is a steady political field. The focus of this work is to describe over time the notion of information warfare, which has matured and manifested into a form that has a colossal impact on how the contemporary wars are fought, but this has also resulted in the downgrading of strategic side of information warfare or cyber warfare to a decisive tactical force multiplier capable of turning the tides in war.

INTRODUCTION

The benefits of the information age are numerous. Cyber-space is a type of communication, indipendent from physical distance. It's an imaginary area without limits where you can meet people and discover information about any subject. It's an electronic medium used to form a global computer network and to facilitate online communication.

DOI: 10.4018/978-1-7998-4339-9.ch011

The threats and risks relating to cybernetic and space domains, the possible responses and strategies by national and international governments, the technological and industrial capacities necessary to support these responses, are analyzed by experts and representatives of public and private subjects involved in the two sectors. Nascent threats like transnational cyber terrorism and information warfare exist alongside the positive aspects of globalization. A new challenge has emerged for free societies: democracies must find ways to strike a balance between allowing Internet freedom on one hand and maintaining adequate early warning and monitoring systems on the other. These systems, combined with expanded cyber-security cooperation across borders, will be integral in detecting suspicious digital activities and countering attempted acts of cyber warfare and cyber terrorism.

A Definition

Cyberspace is a new domain of operations, vital to national security. States are into an increasingly interconnected world with a diverse threat spectrum, with little understanding of how decisions are made within this amorphous domain

In order to analyze the strategic aspect of cyber warfare, Wirtz (2003) criteria of integration of strategic warfare cross all spectrum of affairs right from the tactical to the grand strategic level provide an important criterion for postulating the strategic framework for cyber warfare.

Cyberwarfare is strategic warfare that can be used as a principal means to achieve strategic ends and as required by Luttwak's criterion for strategic warfare, the framework for strategic cyber warfare is to be defined across all spectrum of affairs right from the grand strategic to the tactical level.

Cyberwar and Cyber-Espionage

Cyberwar is not simply stealing information, neither the global great game of nations spying on each other's governments nor the more controversial sort of private-sector economic espionage that the US has long accused China of carrying out. Cybersecurity is the activity of protecting information and information systems (networks, computers, databases, data centers, and applications) with appropriate procedural and technological security measures (Tonge et al, 2013).

Cyber threat intelligence (CTI) is an area of cybersecurity that focuses on the collection and analysis of information about current and potential attacks that threaten the safety of an organization or its assets. The first case of cyber espionage occurred more than a half-century ago, with the arrest of an East German spy in IBM's German by West Germany's police in 1968.

Cyberwar and Cyber-Crime

Cyberwar is not profit-focused hacking like bank fraud or the ransomware attacks that seek to extort millions from victims, that's cybercrime, no matter how cruel and costly its effects may sometimes be. It is possible to distinguish the crimes perpetrated using IT and telematic systems from the crimes committed against the same systems, no longer intended as tools for carrying out illegal acts but as material objects of the latter; and still, a distinction can be made between crimes committed on the Internet from crimes committed via the Internet with the clarification that this latter category includes a heterogeneous set of crimes municipalities provided by the penal code and by some special laws.

In the spring of 2007, an unprecedented series of so-called distributed denial of service, or DDoS, attacks slammed more than a hundred Estonian websites, taking down the country's online banking, digital news media, government sites, and practically anything else that had a web presence. The attacks were a response to the Estonian government's decision to move a Soviet-era statue out of a central location in the capital city of Tallinn, angering the country's Russian-speaking minority and triggering protests on the city's streets and the web.

Cyberwar and Cyberstalking

Telematic harassment represents a very frequent phenomenon worthy of scientific and social interest, closely related to the constant and exponential progress of technology. The development of new communication technologies allows the stalker to find new tools to implement persecutory behaviors since it is much easier for the offender to reach his victim.

However, just as it happened for stalking in general, also for cyberstalking there were problems in finding a correct definition that could include all those intrusive and persecuting behaviors that are constantly evolving, hand in hand with the development of technologies. This is why the definition of cyberstalking is still debated since some consider it a simple variation of offline stalking, and others who instead consider it a new phenomenon, autonomous and separate from the traditional one, even if connected to it. It is therefore not a computer crime but a computer-related crime, that is a traditional crime characterized however by the use of the new action tools provided by the expansion and evolution of information technologies.

In 1997, within the Council of Europe, the Committee of Experts on Crime in Cyberspace (PC-CY: Committee of Experts on Crime in Cyberspace) was created with the task of drafting a draft international convention to combat and repress crime within the IT space, to facilitate international cooperation in investigations and effective prosecution of computer crimes by the Member States. On November 23,

2001, the Convention on Cybercrime was launched in Budapest, which provides for the adoption, at a national level, of regulatory measures that allow the development of a common policy aimed at protecting the various States (De Fazio, Sgarbi 2012).

Janet Reno, at the request of the then US Vice President Al Gore, in the Report on Cyber-stalking, attempted to define it by claiming that the phenomenon in question consisted in "the use of the Internet, e-mail or other devices electronic communication to harass another person through threatening and repeated conduct" J. Reno (1999).

Cyberwar and Information Warfare

The difference between Information Warfare and Cyberwar may be the most debated. Information warfare is any action to deny, exploit, corrupt, or destroy the enemy's information and its functions, protecting ourselves against those actions, and - exploiting our military information functions. Information Operations are actions taken to affect adversary information and information systems while defending one's information and information system. The traditional forms of Information Warfare are Psychological Operations, Electronic Warfare, Physical Destruction, Security Measures Deception, Information Attack.

Psychological operations use the information to affect the enemy's reasoning. "We can be sure that the global battlefield of the 21st century will be over information -- the dissemination or withholding of facts, the interpretation of events, the presentation or distortion of ideas and ideologies, and the communication of messages and symbols carefully prepared to provoke a particular reaction, either conscious or unconscious, from a target audience. The global info-sphere is influenced by events and information from the battlefield ('space').

Electronic Warfare denies accurate information to the enemy to determine, exploit, reduce, or prevent hostile use of the electromagnetic spectrum. It includes electronic countermeasures, electronic counter-countermeasures, electronic warfare support measures (Jiindals, 2016).

Countries which have understood the importance of EW and thereby electronic countermeasures and counter-countermeasures will try to maintain its quick evolution since electronic warfare is progressively poised to become the primary means of warfare to gain an advantage over the enemy in a war scenario whereby its usage will facilitate in gaining impunity for unopposed assault or substantially diminish the resistance of the adversary. Improving electronic warfare modeling and simulation to better prepare for emerging weapons systems is also a key element of the strategy. This can help anticipate or train against future weapons threats that may not exist yet but nevertheless pose an emerging threat.

Deception. All warfare is based on deception. Hence, "when we are able to attack, we must seem unable; when using our forces, we must seem inactive; when we are near, we must make the enemy believe we are far away; when far away, we must make him believe we are near" (Taylor, 2019).

Cyberterrorism

By definition, cyber terrorism means to damage information, computer systems, data, that result in harm against non-combatant targets. The boundaries between acts of cyber terrorism, cyber crime, 'Hacktivism' are often interlinked.

Hacker profiling deals with the analysis and establishment of the personal, socio-demographic, character and psychological profiles of the organizers of a cyber-attack. On the basis of the psychological aspects and the motivations that drive them to act, it is possible to distinguish hackers in 5 categories:

Table 1. Types of hackers and psychological profiles

Categories	Description
Casual attackers	they tend to be motivated by curiosity and gratified by the simple possibility of using the subscriptions of others on paid sites;
Political attackers	they militate in favor of a cause and their attacks, as well as their knowledge and experience, arise from adherence to an ideal. In this category there is a rational as well as an emotional dimension; they act mainly in order to make their ideal public
Organized crime	it is made up of attackers in general, professionals and sector experts who therefore hardly leave traces of their work and whose motivations are substantially of an economic nature having as their goal the profit
Squatters	they are characterized by the impersonality of their attacks because their objectives are often independent of the recipient and the identity of the owner of the attacked system, the reasons that lead to the cyber attack, in fact, tend to became, not necessarily for criminal purposes
Insiders and intruders	the attacks attributable to this type can be carried out either from the inside, that is from the operators or internal users to an organization or to a computer system (insiders), both from the outside, or from external attackers, which are illegally introduced into an organization (intruders).

Counter Intelligence

Counter Intelligence is a phase of intelligence, covering the activity devoted in destroying the effectiveness of hostile foreign activities and the protection of information against espionage, subversion and sabotage.

Table 2. Who could be an attacker?

Categories	Description
Militaries	developing cyber-weapons and robot soldiers to achieve dominance
Governments	attempting to use AI to establish hegemony, control people, or take down other governments.
Corporations	trying to achieve monopoly, destroying the competition through illegal means.
Hackers	attempting to steal information, resources or destroy cyberinfrastructure targets.
Doomsday cults	attempting to bring the end of the world by any means.
Psychopaths	trying to add their name to history books in any way possible.
Criminals	attempting to develop proxy systems to avoid risk and responsibility.

It reduces the risk of a failure in a command, increasing its security, aids in achieving surprise attacks and decreases the enemy ability to create information about the forces

Categories of Counter-Intelligence Operations are:

1. **Military Security:** It encompasses the measures taken by a command to protect itself against espionage, enemy operation, sabotage, subversion or surprise
2. **Port boundary and Travel Security:** They has to do with the application of both military and civil security measures for counterintelligence control at point of entry and departure, international borders and boundaries
3. **Civil Security:** It encompasses active and passive counterintelligence measures affecting the non-military nationals permanently or temporarily residing in an area under military jurisdiction.
4. **Special Operations**: It focuses on counter subversion, sabotage and espionage

Brantly (2016) affirms that States are behaving rationally in cyberspace (. The rational behavior of states provides a substantial framework upon which to build future models for deterrence as well as within which to predict state actions in cyberspace. The book examines whether states rationally decide to engage in offensive cyber operations against other states. When a state decides to attack another state it is not concerned solely with its relative power to its adversary.but with the power of its adversary. It is concerned with its ability to conduct an attack against an adversary while maintaining anonymity.

The researcher builds a rationalist argument. By establishing a decision-making framework it is possible to examine why and when covert actions (such as OCOs) are employed. The lines between decision and action are drawn out.

Brantly points out that the U.S. government's approach to cyberspace has to this point relied on the military, with Admiral Mike Rogers currently the commander of both the National Security Agency and Cyber Command (CYBERCOM). The president has given **the military,** and **not the Central Intelligence Agency** (CIA), the lead as the main covert operator in the cyber domain.

The Department of Defense's "Joint Vision 2020" establishes the goal of information superiority on the battlefield. This information superiority enables decision superiority and favorably tilts the strategic and tactical balance.

Stuxnet 2010

The advent of Stuxnet in 2010 changed the overall tone and intensity of the debate on cyber warfare. Stuxnet represents the first strike in a new era of potential 'unchecked use of cyber-weapons in military-like aggression', although it is important to underline that the inherent inability of defending oneself against counterattacks in the cyberspace can offer a sufficient enough deterrence from undertaking actions in the field.

In order to provide such deterrence, actions of norm-building to restrict the availability of cyber-war are now under way. The experience of Stuxnet has proved useful in opening the debate on whether cyber- attacks fall under the definition of armed conflict under international law, as it is one of the few examples of such attacks that resulted in actual physical violence and damage against property. NATO does not categorizes cyber-attacks as clear military action, as it is not clear how much physical damage must be sustained by a state to qualify an attack as use of force and therefore demand an extension to the provisions of Article 5 of the Washington Treaty, even when just the demand of relief for collateral damage is concerned. Cyber-attacks have proven to be useful in warfare as they allow for sophisticated targeting, no recognition of the attacker, and less risk for military personnel and civilians involved.

The problem of cyber security has also arisen to be a particularly sensitive topic where the potential access to these weapons in the hands of terrorists is concerned, as cyber warfare creates an inherent advantage for the offensive party.

To understand the reasons behind the attack on the Iranian nuclear site of Natanz, it is necessary to reconstruct the international situation from the beginning. In 2002, it was announced to the world that Iran was building a secret nuclear enrichment plant in Natanz. This led to a crisis of the never good relations between the U.S. and the Iranian regime, but it also increased the fear that Iran could obtain the nuclear bomb, in particular in Israel and in the Western world, due to the radical extremism of the Iranian regime. The reaction was committed to the UN that enforced sanctions on Iran in 2006 and 2007, but with few results; Iran continued to enrich uranium and to implement the nuclear program with new sites.

In 2008, the Institute for Science and International Security (ISIS) examined the difficulties of a military strike on Iran's nuclear facilities. At that time, the discussions were focused on the possibility to attack Iran's nuclear plants militarily, in analogy with Israel's surgical strikes on Syria's clandestine nuclear reactor in September 2007, or Iraq's Osirak reactor in June 1981. In the case of Iran, the possible targets, mentioned in the discussions, could have been just two facilities, the Natanz enrichment plants and the Isfahan uranium conversion facility which would have significantly delayed Iran's ability to produce weapon-grade uranium for nuclear weapons.

U.S. and other intelligence agencies had poor or partial information about Iran's centrifuge manufacturing complex, making it difficult to support effective military strikes. Considering the modular, replicable nature of centrifuge plants, the ISIS report stated that an attack on Iran's nuclear program was unlikely to significantly degrade Iran's ability to reconstitute its gas centrifuge program. In addition, a possible military action would have discouraged Iran from allowing inspections, as more transparency would have given access to U.S. and Israel, to better target information. An increased pressure on Iran and its allies could have also affected the diplomatic solution to end Iran's growing nuclear weapons capabilities.

An alternative to military intervention was found. The Bush administration planned the so-called, but never officially confirmed, "Operation Olympic Games", a massive cyber-attack against the Iranian nuclear facilities.

The Israeli intelligence unit 8200 and the NSA / CIA collaborated in the creation of Stuxnet, showing that a cyber-weapon would have been a very valid strategy compared to a bombing: it would have generated confusion, the culprits could never have been found and they would have been capable of discovering important information about the Iranian nuclear program that otherwise would never have been recovered.

The program, in addition to slowing down the Iranian activities especially in Natanz, was probably also intended to prevent an eventual Israeli conventional attack to the Iranian sites like the ones to Osirak and Dayr-az-Zor: an action which would have surely lead to a retaliation or, in the worst case scenario, to a war.

REFERENCES

Brantly, A. (2016). *The decision to attack. Military and Intelligence Cyber Decision-making*. Studies in Security and International Affairs.

De Fazio, S. (2012). Nuove prospettive di ricerca in materia di atti persecutori: il fenomeno del cyberstalking. Rassegna Italiana di Criminologia, 3.

Jindals, S. (2016). *Electronic Warfare: An Indispensable Aspect Of Modern War.* Discussion in Indian Defence Forum.

Reno. (1999). *Cyberstalking: a new challenge for law enforcement and industry.* A report from the US Attorney General to the Vice President Al Gore.

Taylor, P. (2019). *From Information Warfare to Information Operation to the global war on terrorism.* Lecture 4, ICS, University of Leeds. Available in: https://slideplayer.com/slide/16461516/

Tonge, A., Kasture, S. S., & Chaudhari, S. (2013). Cyber Security: challenges for society – literature review. *IOSR Journal of Computer Engineering, 12*(2), 67-75. https://pdfs.semanticscholar.org/61fd/814aae913ed3f0ab6459625ffc6944952757.pdf?_ga=2.84089305.199330368.1560936122-811949187.1560936122

Wirtz, J. J. (2003). Review of Strategy: The Logic of War and Peace. *Journal of Cold War Studies, 5*(3), 115–116.

KEY TERMS AND DEFINITIONS

Cyber Terrorism: Janczewski and Colarik (2008) defines cyber terrorism as: "Cyber terrorism means pre-mediated, politically motivated attacks by sub national groups or clandestine agents or individuals against information and computer systems, computer programs, and data that results in violence against non-combatant targets."

Cyber Warfare: They are all those activities aimed at causing damage to computer systems of any kind. Unlike "normal" cyber attacks, these are actions carried out with specific political-military purposes by special military apparatus or by cyber criminal organizations financed, in any case, by government entities.

Information Warfare: It is a concept involving the battlespace use and management of information and communication technology (ICT) in pursuit of a competitive advantage over an opponent. It is an emerging asymmetric threat that forces us to innovate our security approach.

Section 3
Study Cases

Chapter 12

General George S. Patton and Our Climate Crisis:
The Stories People Need – Building New Myths for a Sustainable Earth

John Thomas Riley
The Big Moon Dig, USA

ABSTRACT

The story of General Patton at the Battle of the Bulge is an excellent example of a story with a message that can be applied to our climate crisis. Our climate crisis is the defining problem for human society in the 21st century. Although the current situation is chaotic, as in this story, several positive paths are now clear enough to allow useful plans for a worldwide effort. One alternative to fear is to build a vision of a viable future through stories. Stories have a long history of being a common tool for building unified societal efforts. The stories that society now needs require both a science-based background and believable characters in effective action on our climate crisis. The elements used to build stories, first the background and then the plot, are called beats. The background beats developed here include sea level rise, no-till farming, population peaking, and technology innovation for the period 2020 to 2100. These beats should enable fiction writers to place stories and characters in a world of action on our climate crisis.

DOI: 10.4018/978-1-7998-4339-9.ch012

Figure 1. General Patton and the Battle of the Bulge

Introductory Story: General Patton and the Battle of the Bulge

On D-Day during World War II, the Allies landed in Europe on June 6, 1944. By the time winter arrived six months later, and it was a harsh winter, the Allies had pushed Hitler mostly out of France. By that time, General Patton was leading the Third Army in eastern France, pushing toward the German border (Barron, 2014).

Then, on December 16, 1944, all hell broke loose. Hitler had committed all his remaining reserves on the western front into one last drive to the sea, attacking through the Ardennes forest again. It was an all-or-nothing play.

The result was chaos in the Allied lines as the area was heavily forested and poorly defended. The German army successfully pushed a salient deep into the Allied lines, which gave the battle its name, "The Battle of the Bulge."

When General Patton got word, he resisted the general panic and started to plan.

A few critical days later, the situation had crystalized; officers had some real idea of what was actually going on. General Eisenhower asked General Patton if he could relieve Allied forces desperately denying German access to a critical road hub, Bastogne. Patton did not answer with vague assertions; he answered with a detailed plan already worked out, right down to the orders for troop movements.

Over the next few days, Patton's Third Army disengaged from one major battle, pivoted 90 degrees, drove day and night in the dead of winter, and immediately took on the German army without sleep or hot food.

They broke through, relieving Bastogne and ending any chance of a German breakout to the coast (Note 1.).

~~~+++~~~

This is a great story from American history, which is mostly true, although it is a summary. It completely omits how much grief General Patton gave his supervisors or how hard he habitually drove his soldiers.

Still, it is a good story and a useful one today. Our current climate crisis has similarities to the Allied situation in the winter of 1944; our present situation is both confused and dangerous. This story can usefully be applied today with its moral about planning in the face of great confusion; planning that later turned out to make all the difference.

The question for this chapter then is thus: is planning for our climate crisis even possible right now? If so, are stories a good form to present that planning to the public, especially to our young people?

The State of Our Climate Crisis

In 1944, the security of the Allies was at stake and everybody knew it. The outcome of the war was still in doubt.

Numerous science-based reports (see reports at the end) document the scope of the current climate problem. Worrying incidents have already occurred, such as Category 5 hurricanes that stall for days, and droughts prolonging wild fire seasons.

For many, the chaos is being lived now. Yet other people are not moved to action. If the incidents become so severe that everyone is forced into action, will it then be too late?

Deep Climate History

The balance of oxygen and carbon dioxide in Earth's atmosphere is an artifact of life and geology. When life first arose, the atmosphere was heavy with carbon dioxide (CO_2) and almost no oxygen. Then life evolved photosynthesis, and sunlight powered the split of the CO_2 into its components. Much of the carbon slowly became stored, in the form of rock, coal, and oil. The oxygen was simply released into the atmosphere.

Earth's atmosphere now contains a number of gases, like CO_2, which allow visible light from the sun to pass through but block heat from getting back out. These are the greenhouse gases; they act like the glass panes in a greenhouse roof. Without them, the Earth would be a snowball. Over time, the average temperature of the Earth's surface tracks the amount of greenhouse gasses in the atmosphere very well.

Before the Industrial Revolution, the atmosphere contained about 280 parts per million (ppm) of CO_2. Today that level is about 412 ppm. Often in Earth's long history, the CO_2 has been as high as 1000 ppm. In those times, the surface temperature is four to ten degrees centigrade higher than what humans have grown to expect.

Over deep time, this CO_2 balance is affected naturally by the escape of stored carbon, volcanic gas release, and mountain-building adsorption.

Hothouse periods with average temperatures four to ten degrees centigrade above now were common. Most of the three ages of the dinosaurs were hothouse Earths, as was most of the time since. Then there was no ice anywhere to be found and, for a time, crocodiles lived in Greenland.

In contrast, there have only been two or three periods of Snowball Earth, where the glaciers extended nearly to the equator.

The recent ice age cycles, during which all human societies arose, were caused by the rise of the Himalayas, exposing an enormous amount of new rock that reacts with CO_2.

It is useful to note that all human civilizations have risen during the warmer interglacial periods. The human species prospers with some heat.

Chaos Theory

Earth's climate system is now formally in Chaos. This does not just describe a disrupted and uncertain state, but rather the formal state described in Chaos Theory (Gleick, 1987).

Chaotic systems typically contain non-linear parameters and powerful feedback loops. Moreover, while these systems appear to operate randomly or to show complex cycles, they do also show a few defining attributes.

For example, they are critically sensitive to initial conditions. Systems, like climate, may be usefully modeled on a computer. The internal parameters of the model are set to specific values, the system model is run for a while, and the results recorded. If the internal parameters are then changed ever so slightly, even in the fifth decimal place, when the model is run again, the results can vary wildly from the first run.

This property means that chaotic systems cannot be predicted very far in advance. For example, consider the predicted paths of hurricanes. Even a few days out, the possible path fans out into a wide cone.

This property does have at least one useful side effect. People's actions can affect the future of such systems dramatically. The small changes that people can accomplish may function as the initial conditions in future runs. Even if people's efforts can only affect the fifth decimal place, these efforts could powerfully affect the future output.

Accurately predicting the future of such systems is simply not possible. For this reason, it is not possible to predict what the climate of Earth will be decades out, but we might be able to affect it. All is not grim, however; if we could predict the climate, that would mean that the system was not Chaotic but linear. It would then be very unlikely that we could affect it, for good or for bad.

Tipping Point

Complex chaotic systems, like Earth's climate, often exhibit tipping points. Below the tipping point, slight perturbations tend to settle back to the original state. Beyond the tipping point, with even a small triggering event, the system moves quickly to a new state. After tipping, there is no clear path back to the initial state (Steffen, 2018).

There is one tipping point that Earth's climate seems to be near. It is in the Arctic, where the permafrost has been a storage place for the carbon in organic materials for thousands of years. There, much organic material is thawing, decomposing, and releasing methane (Wadhams, 2017; Shakhova, 2017). Methane is a potent greenhouse gas in its own right, and it oxidizes in Earth's atmosphere into CO_2 over about seven years.

If tripped for any reason, a warmer Arctic releases greenhouse gases that make the Arctic warmer in subsequent years, releasing even more gas. This may appear in long-term graphs as the CO_2 trailing the temperature.

If a tipping point is crossed, there is no going back. Society will have to plan a completely new future for itself.

Changing Climate

The Earth's climate has been remarkably stable for several thousand years. A number of perturbations, many manmade, are now driving the Earth's climate away from that stability.

Hot List

Here are some changes that are driving the Earth's climate to a hothouse Earth:

1. **Rising CO_2**

   The CO_2 in the atmosphere has risen from about 280 ppm to 412 ppm. (Carter, 2019) The average temperatures of both land and sea of Earth have historically tracked the CO_2 content of the atmosphere. Historically, by the time the CO_2 reaches 1000 ppm, the temperature is up four to ten degrees C and there is no ice left anywhere on Earth.

2. **Other human contributions**

   Humans are also leaking other greenhouse gases such as methane and industrial gases, like refrigerants, into the atmosphere. Much of this leakage could be avoided with sufficient effort. Now humans are even intentionally burning up the stored carbon in the Amazon rainforests.

3. **Stored CO_2 melting out**

   The Arctic is warming faster than the average. This rise results in organic material at the bottom of melt ponds and shallow seas rotting and releasing methane. In addition, Arctic peat is drying out and catching fire.

Cooling List

Some of the drivers of climate are changing in ways that cool the planet.

1. **Sun Cycles**

   The output of the Sun goes through cycle on top of cycle; the 11-year cycles are the best known. When the Sun becomes unusually quiet, the Earth cools. During the Little Ice Age, King Henry VIII rode in his heavy carriage to London over the foot-thick ice on the Thames. Today the Sun appears to be moving into a quiet period, but it is not known how deep or long this period will be.

2. **Volcanic Aerosols**

   Volcanic eruptions explode a large number of particles into the upper atmosphere that can result in cooling for a few years. The Russian Ebeko volcano has recently erupted, but its effects on atmospheric temperature are not yet clear.

3. **Human-Generated Aerosols**

   The exhaust of human machines, especially jet planes and large ships, also generates fine particles that, in turn, create clouds. The strength of this cooling effect, and whether it can be artificially increased, is not yet known.

4. **Next Ice Age**

Without interference from human beings, the Earth would now be slipping into a small ice age due to small changes in its orbit, the Milankovitch Cycles. However, since the invention of agriculture, human beings have been moving carbon out of long-term storage and into the atmosphere. Cutting down trees, depleting soils, and raising rice are the main culprits. This has produced enough greenhouse gases to stop our slip into a new ice age and, since the Industrial Revolution, to overwhelm these subtle cycles (It's Just Astronomical! 2019).

If human beings had not developed even farming, the Earth would now be cooling. However, we did, and the Earth is definitely warming. The extra CO2 in the atmosphere is now simply overriding all the cooling effects.

Playing Percentages

Even though the climate future cannot be accurately forecast, the chances for the possible outcomes can be estimated (Fischetti, 2019). In the lists above, the warming elements are simply overwhelming the cooling ones. Preparations are now needed against a hothouse Earth.

In a chaotic situation, those opposed to action can easily cherry-pick facts that run counter to the dominant argument and thus confuse the issue. This does not mean, however, that the overall direction can be ignored.

The amount of resources that should be put into addressing a possibility should be based both on the likelihood of that path and on the difficulties to society that it generates. Both the likelihood of a hothouse Earth and the great difficulties to society thus caused foreshadow enormous problems. Preparing society for the hot scenario is therefore warranted, even given that the effort and expense required is very large.

Society's Future

We need to first mitigate current problems and then plan for outcomes that are even more challenging.

There is still some small chance that an intense effort will successfully stop the temperature rise to below 1.5 degrees C. To do this, a substantial additional effort will be needed immediately.

Failing that, the Earth may cross tipping points and shift into a hothouse Earth. The challenge for humanity then will be to stop the rise after 2.0 C, if not then, after 2.5 C, if not then, after 3.0 C. The driving question for all humanity will be: can we stop the heat?

An enormous worldwide effort will be needed to put the brakes on climate change. Completely new technologies, new economic systems, and new ways of living will be needed.

This level of effort will require massive worldwide action. Fortunately, human beings are social animals (Wilson, 2012; Wilson, 2019; Christakis, 2019; Pinker, 2011). This level of activity is clearly possible given good leadership and an informed populous (Hawken, 2017).

The rest of this chapter is dedicated to using stories to build the mass action needed for such an effort.

~~~+++~~~

Stories

Current climate speakers may be distinguished and may have a good presentation, but their efforts are too often based on fear. Our leaders are still trying to scare people into action on our climate crisis.

Would our young people accept stories better?

Figure 2. Storytelling at the campfire

Long History of Stories

A few million years ago, the climate of Africa changed. Rainforests gave way to open savannas. Our human ancestors evolved to be bipedal to suit the new grasslands.

Grasslands have seasonal fires. These ancestors first learned to eat the animals killed by the fires and then they learned to control the fire themselves.

Cooked food provided a larger amount of nutrition. Evening campfires became a place for food and tales. These two innovations led to our large brains (Wilson, 2019).

People became more social, and their stories held together their tribal groups. In this way, they successfully managed their tribal assets, including the commons of their hunting grounds.

Purpose of New Stories

Faced with a challenging future, people need to see the new possibilities in their personal futures. These visions need to be in the form of stories; few people can accept direction from the complex technical documents that now often define our climate crisis.

Alternative to Fear

Too often fear has been used to get people into action on our climate crisis (Gore, 2006). Fear can get people into action quickly, but they often burn out and even resent the people who have frightened them.

The alternative to fear is to build a large social movement with both power and direction to take on our problem. Make action the thing society is doing right now. This requires strong leadership and persistence. New stories are needed to both build this movement and then to keep it in action.

Talk to the Young

Young people favor their information in the form of movies, TV, and videogames. Currently they are being taught to deal with zombie invasions and robots run amuck. This has nothing to do with the real problems they now face (Hawken, 2017) (Foundation for Climate Restoration, 2019) (Note 2. and Note 3.).

Cli-Fi Dystopias

Today there is an embryonic Climate Fiction (Cli-Fi) developing (Ellis, 2019; Tillman, 2018). Currently many stories in this field are dystopias (Example: *The Handmaid's Tale*).

Many such stories are very well written (El Akkad, 2018; Hunter, 2017). They provide the lesson that many human beings will survive a massive disruption of society. However, the story treatment of evolving technology and the likely order and timing of climate crisis events is weak.

These stories are not helpful. They play on people's fears. They do not teach what could be done to prevent problems for society. They lead people to inaction through resignation and away from useful action.

Society clearly needs new stories to address new problems. These stories must be far more than just comic book stories of heroes magically solving the problems. They must feature believable characters in affective action on the problems of our climate crisis. Sometimes the characters may win and sometimes they may lose. Always they will fight. The characters see the problems clearly and are in action.

Restoration Story

Historically the most common type of society-building story is the Restoration Story (Monbiot, 2019). This type of story has been successful over a great many years in building social unity.

As always in a Restoration Story, great forces have taken over the power and wealth of society. Our heroes, working against all odds, fight these forces and eventually prevail. He and she then go on to lead society to a new golden age.

In this case, the great forces are our own historic failures to sustain our Earth. The heroes are our young people who are seeking a life's work in addressing these great problems.

Humans are a social species who cooperate naturally and who have sustainably managed commons for thousands of years (Wilson, 2012; Wilson, 2019; Christakis, 2019; Pinker, 2011). Therefore, the society of the new golden age can be based upon altruism and the commons. Today's society vision must be enlarged to encompass the entire Earth as our commons.

Given a good Restoration Story, today's people could grow to be precisely the people who are needed to address our climate crisis. People love to identify with characters who fight the good fight.

Seeing the Future

Forecasting the future in chaotic times is difficult. Only a few people can do it well. Those who have the technical expertise needed are rarely the people who can actually produce professional-quality fiction.

People who can write professionally, in contrast, often take off on one idea while leaving everything else in society untouched (example: the film *Her*). This practice results in a vision of an unreal future not reflecting real problems and certainly not a believable whole.

The new stories must come from teams of technical people and writers.

Fictional worlds like the background here can be much loved by readers. Consider the success of *Star Trek: The Next Generation*, Hogwarts, *Dune*, and *Star Wars*. Is it possible to build a beloved fictional world for our climate crisis?

Aid to Writers

A good piece of fiction has a rhythm not unlike a piece of dance music (Trottier, 2014). The loose ideas that the author pulls together, his or her notes, are therefore called beats. It is the author's job to fit these beats into a unified whole that will invite the reader to mentally dance.

To aid this, the remainder of this chapter is a discussion of those major problems of our climate crisis that can be foreseen. Each problem has a description, proposed actions, and beats on how the problem might be handled in a story. These beats could then form the background of many great stories, and individual authors are welcome to add their front beats of characters and plot.

Rising Sea Levels

Problem: The sea level all over the Earth is on the rise. In the long view, the sea level has varied by several hundred meters up and down. It is lowest during ice ages and highest during hothouse Earths. That it has been stable for the entire history of human civilization is somewhat surprising.

The total amount of sea level rise since the start of the Industrial Revolution (Figure 6.) is about 165 mm (6.5 inches), or the width of a human hand. The rate of change, however, is not linear but is now increasing exponentially. Useful estimates for the future can be calculated by fitting an exponential curve to the satellite measurements from NASA. This curve shows a sea level rise of about 385 mm (12.8 inches) by 2050, which is about to mid-thigh. Looking out farther, the graph shows about 1532 mm (63.9 inches) by 2100, which is around eye height.

Figure 3. Sea Level Rise Extrapolated from current NASA readings

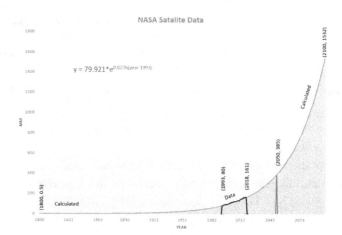

This rise could continue for many hundreds of years, eventually reaching the eye level of the Statue of Liberty.

Corrective Actions: There is no known human action that can now stop sea level rise. Reducing the CO_2 in the atmosphere should at least slow it down.

Human society must organize a retreat from the rising tides. Some shoreline facilities will have to be rebuilt due to recurrent high-tide flooding, but most of the retreat will be driven by great storms (Horton, 2017).

To be inhabitable, a house needs access, survivability from storms, potable water, power, and a functional waste system. If any of these are broken, whole communities may then become unlivable. This problem will be acute on barrier islands. In other places, floods at high tide will slowly make life unacceptable on more and more days in the month.

In the United States, residential housing near water is covered by special federally subsidized flood insurance. The cost of rebuilding houses time and time again is simply prohibitive. If a community is heavily damaged in a storm and flood, it will not be rebuilt in place but will be rebuilt on higher ground.

The vacation industry will also be hard hit. Investments in sea-view hotels and apartments will simply not be attractive if the viability of the area is not at least the life of the buildings.

Background Beats: The sea rising will not stop anytime soon.

- Flooded Out – The people will face the loss of their homes and family members, repeatedly. Many will have to abandon houses that their families built and lived in for decades. Many will have family members who were simply washed out to sea and never found.

- Picking the Bones – Workers will strip flooded-out hotels for recyclable materials. Copper and other metals will be the most valuable. The cores of the buildings are then simply abandoned to weather like giant standing snags. A few will be blasted down and left in place to serve as storm breaks.

- Moving Communities – Whole communities, after being destroyed by a storm, will then redesign themselves to be able to move and move again. Can a community be a community if it is forever on the move?

- Sea Level Refugees – The number of impoverished people driven from their homes by sea level rise will exceed 200 million people. This problem will cause major social disruptions.

- Military installations moved – Military people will be tied up in an unending fight to build new facilities as the sea level rises. They will be under great pressure to keep the lid on a distraught world while the readiness of unit after unit is compromised.

Figure 4. Dusty04 a cowboy AI

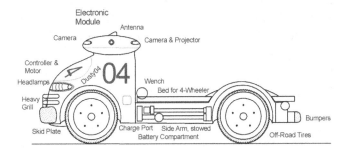

Farming, Soil, and Trees

Problem: Healthy soils can store an enormous amount of carbon that is taken by plants from the atmosphere. Current farming practices such as tilling and the heavy application of artificial chemicals do not support healthy soils and have caused reduction in the carbon content of soils. The needed soil-building effort will require major changes in farming practices worldwide, but it is a rare opportunity for carbon capture.

Corrective Actions: There is currently a major revolution in agriculture. The old practices of plowing the field, called tilling, planting a monocrop, using large amounts of fertilizers and pesticides are being replaced. Instead, the field is planted with a cover crop of many plants. The next crop is then drilled in rows through a crushed layer of organic material, disturbing the cover crops very little.

This no-till agriculture suppresses weeds and encourages beneficial insects. The major long-term advantage is that the process builds rich, deep soils. Such soils provide storage of large amounts of carbon taken from the atmosphere and readily adsorb rain.

The no-till approach to farming has been demonstrated successfully both in Africa and in the United States (Savory, 2016; Brown, 2018).

In the suburbs, the use of small gas motors used for lawn care is particularly polluting. Battery-powered devices redesigned for no-till work are needed.

Background Beats: This is a revolution in agriculture worldwide:

- Old ways, new ways – Many people will simply resist changing the ways of farming that have been practiced by their families for generations.
- No more feedlots – All the feedlots on Earth will simply be phased out. No-till practices provide enormous amounts of cover crops that need to be eaten. Meat will not be eliminated but its availability will be reduced; beef will be of better quality, if more expensive.
- AI Cowboy – The no-till system mimics the symbiotic relationship between ruminate animals and grasslands found in the wild. The livestock in this system need to be bunched in a tight herd and moved regularly. This is

Figure 5. No-Till Lawner

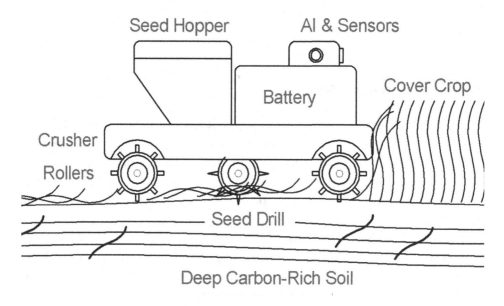

now accomplished by dividing the field into paddocks with electric fences. Specialty robots with AI could be designed to take over many of the new livestock responsibilities. (Figure 4.)

- New lawns – Neatly trimmed lawns are passé. They will be replaced by natural cover featuring many types of plants that are largely maintained by a robot that crushes the cover plants down to contact the carbon-rich soil. (Figure 5.) These new lawns will also feature many trees. Both the cover and the trees will largely be plants native to the region. The new "lawns" will require little or no water or chemicals and will build deep, rich soils.

Population Peaking

Problem: The human population of Earth will peak at about ten billion in about 2100. It will then drop to some number the Earth can sustain. The sustainable level cannot now be estimated.

Even if this problem were our only problem, it would result in major changes to society. No clear examples are currently available for a large sustainable human

Figure 6. Estimated Population of the Earth. 1800 to 2300

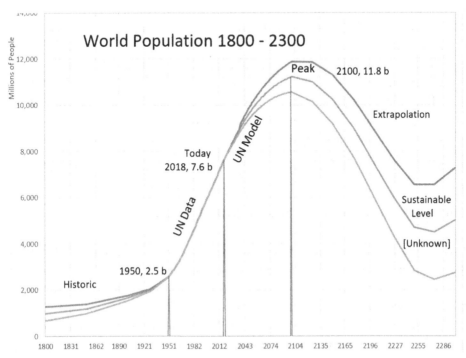

population. There are plenty of small island examples; some succeeded for a long time; many did not.

Corrective Actions: Somewhat surprisingly, the cessation of the population rise has already started naturally in the developed countries. There the number of children per productive woman is currently below the replacement value of 2.1. The developing countries are running a decade or two behind this figure but are on track too. It is important to understand that this is a natural occurrence and is not due to draconian laws but it is critical to avoiding tragic diebacks.

Other social changes such as the surprising success of the Gay Pride movement are strong indicators of the population approaching a peak. For example, a lesbian couple may give birth to one or two children but they almost never have the five it would take for them to increase the population. In addition, adoption is now very popular in the gay community.

Background Beats: Population peaking will strongly affect all plots set in the future:

- Every child valued – With fewer children, each child becomes more important; each child is valued. People who choose to delay having children will have opportunities to support those who are born.
- Aging Population – The average age of the population will rise considerably. Young people will not be the center of much attention.
- Virtual families – Each child will have a virtual family organized over the Internet. As the child grows, members of this family will come and go but powerful resources will always be available. One AI will be a member of this virtual family whose primary responsibility will be to provide security on the Internet.
- End of large family subsidies – Tax breaks and other laws that have historically supported large families will be phased out.
- Gay pride – Homosexuality will again be a normal part of society as it was in many ancient cultures.

Technical Innovation, Artificial Intelligence

It is very difficult to guess which new technologies will make a difference and which are pie-in-the-sky. A great effort will be needed on technical innovation even though no silver bullet can be expected. Technological innovation needs to be newly focused on the specific problems of our climate crisis.

Problem: The technology of Artificial Intelligence (AI) is developing rapidly and holds promise for addressing many aspects of our climate crisis. Electronic chip

Figure 7. JanetA, artificial intelligence

sets specifically designed for AI are expected on the market by 2020. These chips will increase the power of AIs while making them even more common.

With great promise comes real risk. A system to limit AI power to ethical action is needed. AI robots run amuck are a standard plot element of many dystopic movies (example: *The Terminator*).

Corrective Actions: The problem then is to harness the power of AIs while restricting them to ethical practices.

Background Beats: AIs will be part of the woodwork in all stories set in the future:

- **Symbionts, Not Slaves**: The relationship between humans and AI will be based on establishing a symbiosis. It will not be based on a master/slave relationship. It is simply not possible to guarantee that who is the master and who is the slave will not someday flip. A cooperative philosophy must therefore be established from the very beginning of the AI design process.
- **Many Avatars, Few Hominid Robots:** The vast majority of AI will either be beings that appear only on electronic screens or in machines with a purpose, like cars. AIs in human-like bodies will simply be an extravagant waste of resources. Major AIs will consist of both a chip set in a cell phone, car, etc., plus a larger system in a remote data center, sometimes called the cloud.
- **Human-AI Pairs:** Today intellectual workers cannot function without substantial computer skills. Soon most such workers will be a pair of a human and an AI. Anyone without this level of support will simply be passed over for hiring. Executives and technical people will be in a competition for who has the hottest AI.

Technical Innovation, Batteries

Problem: One technology area that is critical and where major advances are expected is rechargeable batteries.

The current technology, Lithium Ion, has limited energy storage, it fails after a few thousand charge-discharge cycles, and it can spontaneously catch fire.

Corrective Actions: An enormous amount of work is currently being done to improve the capacity and make a better battery. Different organizations keep promising new battery technologies, but mass production has proven elusive.

Background Beats: It is reasonable to assume that a battery technology four to ten times better than Lithium Ion will be developed very soon.

- **Cars:** Virtually all cars will be electric. Gas stations will be replaced by charging points. The cars will have AIs to make driving safer and to optimize the available power. Most cars will be small, streamlined, and have a one-charge range of at least 400 km. The windows will have a metallic sheen.
- **Trucks:** Even large trucks will be electric. They will have an AI capable of driving in convoys with only one human being for ten trucks, the supercargo.
- **Energy Storage:** Cars parked at night will serve as the energy storage system for the carbon-free power system. Their batteries will even out the power supplied by wind and photovoltaic systems.
- **Personal Appliances:** Personal devices, like cell phones, will need a charge only every few days and batteries will outlast the device. They will not catch fire in your pocket.

Technical Innovation, Drawdown

Problem: All the major plans require not only stopping more greenhouse gases from entering the atmosphere but also call for the removal of enormous amounts already there (see Major Climate Reports). This process is called drawdown (Hawken, 2017). This requires enormous amounts of energy that cannot come from fossil fuel sources.

Corrective Actions: A number of biological projects have been proposed, from planting trees, to no-till agriculture, to adding iron to the seas. All are worth small- and medium-sized trials (McAfee, 2019). None currently shows the level of drawdown needed without major unintended effects on the environment.

Basic technical approaches have been demonstrated in the laboratory but much work is needed to bring them to large scale (Voskina, 2019). The thermodynamics of these reactions will require massive amounts of power. Nuclear reactors of modern Gen IV design are needed to enlarge this effort (Illinois EnergyProf, 2019).

Background Beats

- **Massive Program –** To meet a 1.5 or even 2.0 C limit will require a massive drawdown industry. New technologies will need to be developed and large-scale ideas tested. A new generation of nuclear power stations will be needed. This will make the project very controversial.
- **Grassroots Drawdown:** There will be many small programs to use biology to pull CO_2 from the atmosphere. These include planting trees and no-till farming. The vacations of masses of people will go into these projects.
- **Iron Seas:** A program to sequester CO_2 from the seas by fertilizing plankton has been tried, but the effectiveness of the tests and their effects on adjacent environments proved problematic. A major effort in this area is warranted but a well-monitored effort will be needed to prove that the effort will do more good than harm.
- **Legality and Funds:** Significant political effort will be needed to empower people to take chances on new ideas and for funding agencies to support them.

Economic Growth

Problem: Granted, the one current worldwide neoliberal capitalist economic system has raised billions of people out of extreme poverty. Still, it has a problem that will get in the way of addressing our climate crisis.

The current economy is based on continuous economic growth. It does not place value on our commons, the Earth. There have been many efforts to address this deficiency (for example, the Clean Water Act). Major new efforts (for example, carbon cap and trade laws) have been put forward but have not been widely enacted.

This economic system has also generated an enormous wealth gap between the richest 1% and the poorest 50% of the population (Boghosian, 2019; Hanauer, 2019). Allowed to run to the extreme, such wealth gaps can result in violent revolutions (example, the French Revolution). Society does not have the time nor the resources for such a violent revolution. The current economic system will have to evolve to address our climate crisis.

Corrective Actions: If the temperature rise can be limited to only 1.5 degrees C, then many of the fundamental institutions of the current economy might be maintained with only reasonable adjustments (Bloom, 2017; Nordhaus, 2013; Menezes, 2019; Wagner, 2015). Even then, massive societal changes will be needed, including the move from carbon-based fuel, retreat from the rising seas, and population peaking.

If the temperature moves above the 1.5 C benchmark and the wealth gap persists, then poorly planned drastic changes or even violent revolutions become a major concern.

Background Beats: Our climate crisis will drive major economic changes:

- **No Violent Revolution:** Society simply does not have time for a violent revolution of any kind. If one starts, then all solutions for our climate crisis will be delayed and put in jeopardy. Plots that focus on a revolution are not helpful (El Akkad, 2018). They are dystopias and do not envision affective actions. Proposing an international authoritarian state to address this crisis is an invitation to violent revolution. Avoiding revolution can be a major plot point.

- **Carbon Cost:** There will be some system for carbon being included in product value. This will force major shifts in what products are available and at what cost.

- **Advertising:** Low carbon footprints will be a major selling point. Products with large carbon footprints, like distant vacations, will be seen as antisocial. A shift to recyclable packaging will be pervasive and visually boring.

- **Collapse of Fossil Fuels:** The current reserves of fossil fuels are valued at many trillions of dollars. Their value will collapse to perhaps one-tenth their present value in a short time when a phase-out becomes unavoidable. Can major financial institutions like stock markets and central banks survive this collapse? What new institutions could?

- **Under New Management:** Managers that understand how to protect the commons of the Earth will phase out wasters and spoilers. Women will hold between 40% and 60% of management positions. Old-style managers will be villains in many plots.

- **Metric:** All manufacturing worldwide will be metric. Americans will just have to get used to it.

- **The Quiet Super-Rich:** To avoid criticism for their excesses, the super-rich will keep a low profile. Investigative TV reporters will ferret them out and shame them.

~~~+++~~~

Fictional Environment

Pulling this all together, a useful story environment with dramatic potential might include:

Figure 8. Climate crisis story timeline

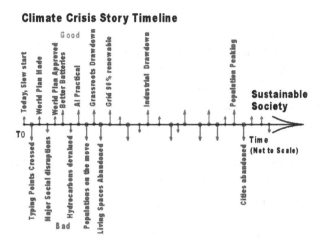

Story Timeline

It is important for the plots to reflect the major events in the order in which they are likely to occur:

- **Today, Slow Start**: The CO_2 in the air continues to climb. Most people only have vague misgivings and are not in action.

- **Tipping Points Crossed:** There is no going back from this point. The majority of people are now convinced and frightened. They demand action. The physical location of the major tipping points will be the Arctic.

- **World Plan Made:** The Paris Accord is expanded into a real plan. The next president of the United States will make an historic speech calling for unity and a focused international effort. The future of the human society of the Earth will turn on that speech. The massive worldwide effort will grow to be as large as all the efforts on both sides of World War II.

- **Major Social Disruptions:** The way people live their lives experiences major disruptions. Many of the beloved elements of society are vanishing or at risk.

- **World Plan Approved** – This time the governments pay attention and the plan has wide backing.

- **Better Batteries:** Mass production of a four-times-better battery is established. All cars, buses, and trucks manufactured are electric.

- **Hydrocarbon Reserves Devalued:** The economic value of all the coal, oil, and gas reserves is devalued to near zero. The government must step in to save the markets. Avoiding the collapse of the global economy is a close-fought battle.

- **AI Practical:** AIs are everywhere. They are designed based on symbiosis with humans, **not** master/slave. Most information workers are an IA/human pair. Many children have an AI virtual friend to protect them.
- **Populations on the Move:** Millions of climate refugees are on the move.
- **Living Spaces Abandoned:** Low-lying populated areas are not rebuilt after storms. Naval bases are hard hit.
- **Grassroots Drawdown:** Programs to plant trees, convert to no-till, and many other high-labor projects become the thing to do. This is how people now vacation.
- **Grid 90% Renewable:** Old power plants are shut down. Power now comes from renewables.
- **Industrial Drawdown:** Industrial plants to remove CO_2 from the air now have some effect. Some of these are powered with newly designed nuclear reactors.
- **Many Things Happen:** Many events, both good and bad, continue to occur, causing both hope and fear. Most of these cannot now be foreseen.
- **Population Peaking:** The human population of the Earth peaks at something under ten billion. This effect alone forces major changes to human societies.
- **Cities Abandoned:** Some coastal cities are cut back and then abandoned in a process spread over many years.

Through many disruptive events, a sustainable human society develops on Earth. It is a difficult and challenging time.

Background Beats: Here are many disruptions, good and bad, that the story characters must deal with:

- **The Natural World:** Many species, both plant and animal, will simply die off. Often a lost species will be a keystone species in a living environment (Carroll, 2016). There, diversity will fail and the few remaining species will be weeds, too often leaving a sad landscape of bleached coral, pigeons, rats, and kudzu.
- **Bad Weather:** The weather will simply not be what people expect and are counting on for their livelihoods. Often too hot, but sometimes too cold. Often too wet, but sometimes too dry. So many storms will come that people are not over one before the next one hits.
- **Heatwaves:** There will be major heatwaves that stall for weeks and that kill thousands of people, particularly if electric power is limited. These will support major wildfires and put stress on the ability of cities to provide even

drinking water. Many inland areas will become so hot, dry, and so short on water that most people will have to move away.

- **Retreat from the Seas:** The majesty of a great storm will be understood at a gut level. Whole cities on the seacoast will make plans to move after the next big storm. Many people will simply choose to risk death from storms one too many times. Perfectly good high-rise buildings will be stripped and then blasted down to make storm brakes. This process will drag on for hundreds of years.

- **Good Information from Science:** Scientists with the most reliable information will continue to restate that information for the public (Beckwith, 2019; Hansen, 2019).

- **Lots of People but Few Children:** There will be a large number of people around but few of them will be children. The population will be ageing and peaking. Rapid population growth will be gone, but millions of climate refugees will strain resources. The few children around will be highly valued.

- **Lots of Technology but No Trip to Mars:** New technologies will be applied specifically to the problems of our climate crisis. This will draw resources away from pie-in-the-sky ideas. Mars will have to wait. Robotic space missions with stronger and stronger AI will continue and be critical to keeping a positive vision of the future for all of society.

- **Lots of Ais**: Every person will regularly interact with AIs on ubiquitous screens, but there will be few humanoid robots. The first reaction of a person trying to use any machine will be to talk to it.

- **Transportation:** Most people will not actually own a car. Drivers will plug their small electric cars into the grid at night. The highways will be lined with convoys of trucks with perhaps one person per ten vehicles. Enormous container ships will exhaust great clouds of water vapor as they slowly cross the oceans.

- **Drawdown Grassroots:** Massive numbers of people will participate in grassroots programs to draw down CO_2 from the atmosphere. Every new idea will get at least a small trial. These efforts will be useful but not enough, not nearly enough.

- **New Settlers:** Only a few million people will move to northern areas in Russia, Alaska, and Canada. There only a few will live like 19th-century settlers. The summers will be long but it will take a lot of physical labor to convert old permafrost into farmland.

- **Food Limits:** Everybody will simplify their diets and reduce meat. Periodic food shortages will be a problem for many people. Everyone will work to reduce food waste.

- **Professional Deniers:** These are people who are paid by vested interests, like the fossil fuel industry, to confuse the public with half-truths and bad data (Mann, 2016). They are the natural villains for many stories.
- **The Way Most People Live:** People will pay attention to conservation and recycling about six times as much as Americans do now. There will be a new household appliance, the recycling center with an AI; some people will argue with them daily. Vacations will be for planting trees. Advertising will be about how to reduce your carbon footprint. Packaging will be easily recycled. Any product that is seen as out of line will be boycotted. More people will live in each housing unit. Not having a refugee family in residence will be seen as antisocial.

In short, the way people live will be very different from today, but people will live; society will go on. Surely, this time will be one of the most dramatic periods of human history.

CONCLUSION

Facing a chaotic future, people must have direction. Major societal changes are now unavoidable. For many people, it will be a series of slow changes; they buy a different kind of car; there are strict energy conservationist; their holidays are no such thing. For others the future will be dramatic, a storm destroys their house and it cannot be rebuilt; their family ends up in a refugee camp.

For many, the future of civilization now looks dire, but civilizations have survived disasters many, many times. Is this the end of society as we know it, yes; is it the end of all human society, **No**!

New stories are needed: new stories are critical to societies surviving; new stories are something that people can do. People can write stories about believable people in action on the real problems of our climate crisis. People can then turn them into TV series, feature movies, and videogames that talk to young people. Society has the capabilities in place to do this job, but time is short. Hopefully this chapter will facilitate this writing process.

~~~+++~~~

Figure 9. Air medal with four clusters, awarded to John A. Riley

Notes

1. The author's father, John A. Riley, flew gliders for the US Army Air Corps in Europe during the Second World War. He flew 18 missions total. Three of those missions were into Bastogne during this battle. He flew in ammunition and snatched out the severely wounded soldiers. He reported receiving German sniper fire from the edge of the landing zone.
2. The author's group, The Big Moon Dig, produced a book of science fiction short stories (Riley, 2019) about the near future. This effort has not generated strong results simply because science fiction short stories are not the current entertainment choice of young people.
3. The author's group, The Big Moon Dig, has written a screenplay, *Summer is Coming*, along the lines of this chapter and is now working to get it produced. It could be produced as either a TV or a web series.

Logline: Young people in a virtual family, who are faced with our climate crisis and unsure of themselves, get into action, and, with the help of an Artificial Intelligence, mold their life's work to be of real value in our challenging future.

REFERENCES

Barron, L. (2014). *Patton at the Battle of the Bulge: How the general's tanks turned the tide at Bastogne.* New York: Penguin Group.

Beckwith, P. (2019). *Paul Beckwith Climate Scientist.* Retrieved from web page https://paulbeckwith.net/

Bloom, M., & Pope, C. (2017). *Climate of Hope, How cities, businesses, and citizens can save the planet.* St. Martins.

Boghosian, B. M. (2019, November). The Inescapable Casino, A novel approach developed by physicists and mathematicians describes the distribution of wealth in modern economies with unprecedented accuracy. *Scientific American, 321*(5), 70–77.

Brown, G. (2018). *Dirt to Soil, One family's journey into regenerative agriculture.* Chelsea Green Publishing.

Carroll, S. B. (2016). *The Serengeti Rules, The quest to discover how life works and why it matters.* Princeton University Press.

Carter, P. (2019, June 25). *Spring 2019 Accelerating Global Warming & Atmospheric CO2.* Retrieved from TED Video at https://www.youtube.com/watch?v=RV3S4v5yTdA&t=658s

Christakis, N. A. (2019). *Blueprint, The evolutionary origins of a good society.* Little, Brown Spark.

El Akkad, O. (2018). American War. New York: Vintage Books.

Ellis, L., & Brady, A. (2019). *Can These Books Save the Planet? The Rise of Climate Fiction.* Retrieved from YouTube Video by HotMess/PBS at https://www.youtube.com/watch?v=zUnTcNzLIVg

Englander, J. (2013). *High Tide on Main Street, Rising sea level and the coming coastal crisis.* The Science Bookshelf.

Fischetti, M. (2019, November). Climate Clincher, The argument that global warming is part of a natural cycle is dead. *Scientific American, 321*(5), 86. doi:10.1038cien tificamerican1101-86

Foundation for Climate Restoration. (2019, September). *Climate Restoration: Solutions to the greatest threat facing humanity and nature today.* Retrieved from a white paper at https://foundationforclimaterestoration.org/wp-content/uploads/2019/09/20190916b_f4cr4_white-paper.pdf

Gleick, J. (1987). *Chaos, Making of a new science*. Viking.

Gore, A. (2006). *An Inconvenient Truth: The planetary emergency of global\warming and what we can do about it*. New York: Viking.

Hanauer, N. (2019). *The dirty secret of capitalism -- and a new way forward*. Retrieved from TED Video at https://www.youtube.com/watch?v=th3KE_H27bs

Hansen, J. (2011). *Storms of My Grandchildren, The truth about the coming climate catastrophe and our last chance to save humanity*. Bloomsbury Publishing.

Hawken, P. (2017). *Drawdown, The most comprehensive plan ever proposed to revers global warming*. Penguin Books.

Horton, T. (2017). *High Tide in Dorchester, A Bay Journal Documentary*. Retrieved from https://hightidedorchester.org/

Hunter, M. (2017). *The End We Start From*. Grove Press. A novel.

Illinois EnergyProf. (2019, May 14). *Reactors of the Future (Generation IV)*. University of Illinois at Urbana Champaign. Retrieved from a video lecture at https://www.youtube.com/watch?v=_mJ3S-VQuHY

It's Just Astronomical! (2019, October 13). *Where are we in the Milankovitch Cycles?* Retrieved from a TED Video at https://www.youtube.com/watch?v=eB3DJtQZVsw

Mann, M. E., & Roles, T. (2016). *The Madhouse Affect, How climate change denial is threatening our planet, destroying our politics, and driving us crazy*. Columbia University Press. doi:10.7312/mann17786

McAfee, A. (2019). *More from Less, The surprising story of how we learned to prosper using fewer resources – and what happens next*. Scribner.

Menezes, M. J. (2019). *Can we create an empathic alternative to the capitalist system?* Retrieved from World Economic Forum at https://www.weforum.org/agenda/2019/08/empathy-can-create-a-new-economic-system/

Nordhaus, W. (2013). *The Climate Casino, Risk, uncertainty, and economics of a warming world*. Yale University Press.

Pinker, S. (2011). *The Better Angels of Our Nature, Why Violence Has Declined*. Viking.

Riley, J. T., & dall'Acqua, L. (2019). *Narrative Thinking and Storytelling for Problem Solving in Science Education*. Hershey PA: IGI Global. Retrieved from https://www.igi-global.com/book/narrative-thinking-storytelling-problem-solving/217376

Riley, T. (2016). Big Moon Dig Stories" *The Big Moon Dig*. Retrieved from Web page at https://bigmoondig.com/Stories/BMDStories.html

Riley, T. (2018). Curse the Salt. *The Big Moon Dig/Stories*. Retrieved from short story at https://bigmoondig.com/Stories/BMDSalt.pdf

Russel, S. J., & Norvig, P. (2015). *Artificial Intelligence, A Modern Approach, Third Addition*. Person Education.

Savery, A. (2013, February). *How to green the world's deserts and reverse climate change*. Retrieved from TED video at https://www.ted.com/talks/allan_savory_how_to_green_the_world_s_deserts_and_reverse_climate_change?language=en

Savory, A., & Butterfield, J. (2016). *Holistic Management, A commonsense revolution to restore our environment*. Island Press.

Shakhova, N. (2017). *Current rates and mechanisms of subsea permafrost degradation in the East Siberian Arctic Shelf*. Retrieved from Nature Communications at https://www.nature.com/articles/ncomms15872

Steffen, W. (2018). Trajectories of the Earth System in the Anthropocene. *The Proceedings of the National Academy of Sciences*, *115*(33), 8252-8259. Retrieved from Web article at https://www.pnas.org/content/115/33/8252

Tillman, N. (2018). The Big Melt. South Branch Press.

Trottier, D. (2014). *The Screenwriter's Bible, A complete guide to writing, formatting and selling your script*. Silman-James Press.

Venkataraman, B. (2019). *The Optimist's Telescope, Thinking ahead in a reckless age*. Riverhead Books.

Voskina, S., & Alan Hatton, T. (2019, October 1). *Faradaic electro-swing reactive adsorption for CO_2 capture*. Retrieved from Energy & Environmental Science at https://pubs.rsc.org/en/content/articlelanding/2019/ee/c9ee02412c#!divAbstract

Wadhams, P. (2017). *A Farewell to Ice, A report from the Arctic*. Oxford Press.

Wagner, G., & Weitzman, M. L. (2015). *Climate Shock, The economic consequences of a hotter planet*. Princeton University Press. doi:10.1515/9781400865475

White, J. (2017). *Tides, The science and spirit of the ocean*. Trinity University Press.

Wilson, E. O. (2012). *The Social Conquest of Earth*. Liveright Publishing.

Wilson, E. O. (2019). *Genesis, the deep origin of societies*. Liveright Publishing.

APPENDIX

Major Climate Reports

The International Panel on Climate Change (IPCC) continues to issue authoritative reports of various aspects of our climate crisis. These reports can be retrieved from https://archive.ipcc.ch/publications_and_data/publications_and_data_reports.shtml

1. The Intergovernmental Panel on Climate Change (2018, October). Special Report 1.5" (IPCC SR1.5, UN). Retrieved from https://www.ipcc.ch/sr15/
2. United States Climate Research Program (2018, November). Fourth National Climate Assessment (NCA4) Retrieved fromhttps://www.globalchange.gov/nca4
3. Laurie Laybourn-Langton, Laurie & Lesley Rankin & Darren Baxter, (2019, February). This is a Crisis, Facing up to the age of environmental breakdown," Initial report, [Institute for Public Policy Research (IPPR), Great Britain. Retrieved from https://www.ippr.org/files/2019-02/this-is-a-crisis-february2019.pdf
4. Intergovernmental Science-Policy Platform on Biodiversity and Ecosystem Services (IPBES)
5. (2019, May). Intergovernmental Science-Policy Platform on Biodiversity and Ecosystem Services (#IPBES7). Retrieved from https://www.ipbes.net/
6. Ripple, William J, Christopher Wolf, Thomas M Newsome, Phoebe Barnard, William R Moomaw (BioScience, 05 November 2019). "World Scientists' Warning of a Climate Emergency." Retrieved from https://academic.oup.com/bioscience/advance-article/doi/10.1093/biosci/biz088/5610806

Figure Credits

1. *General Patton and the Battle of the Bulge* by Kenisha Eberhart.
2. *Storytelling at the campfire* by Kenisha Eberhart based on (Wilson, 2019) pp. 122.
3. *Sea Level Rise Extrapolated from current NASA readings* by Tom Riley of the Big Moon Dig. NASA data taken from ftp://podaac.jpl.nasa.gov/allData/merged_alt/L2/TP_J1_OSTM/global_mean_sea_level/GMSL_TPJAOS_4.2_199209_201803.txt
4. *Dusty04* by Tom Riley of the Big Moon Dig. Used in (Riley 2019).

5. *No-Till Lawner* by Tom Riley of The Big Moon Dig.
6. *Estimated Population of the Earth. 1800 to 2300* by Tom Riley of the Big Moon Dig. Data taken from United Nations Population, https://population.un.org/wpp/Download/Standard/Population/
7. *JanetA* by Kenisha Eberhart for The Big Moon Dig. Used in (Riley 2019).
8. *Climate Crisis Story Timeline* by Tom Riley.
9. *Air Medal with four clusters* photo by Tom Riley.

Chapter 13
Lobbying a Crucial Mechanism for NGOs to Obtain Funding for Poverty Alleviation Programs in Africa

Idahosa Igbinakhase
University of KwaZulu-Natal, South Africa

Vannie Naidoo
iD https://orcid.org/0000-0001-8435-4348
University of KwaZulu-Natal, South Africa

Thea van der Westhuizen
iD https://orcid.org/0000-0001-8795-4023
University of KwaZulu-Natal, South Africa

ABSTRACT

The need to unravel the organizational capabilities of youth-serving NGOs that may influence the replication of successful programmes designed to empower poor youths in order to make these programmes accessible to more youths and more geographical locations has motivated this study. This chapter will highlight the crucial role lobbying plays for NGOs in their efforts to obtain funding for poverty alleviation programs in Nigeria. Lobbying challenges experienced by youth-serving NGOs and factors that influence lobbying capabilities will be also be unpacked and discussed. A quantitative study was conducted on 196 youth-serving NGOs in Nigeria. Simple random sampling was used to collect data. This chapter will highlight the crucial role lobbying plays for NGOs in efforts to obtain funding for poverty alleviation programs. The results of the study indicated that lobbying is an important organizational capability for youth-serving NGOs in their bid to alleviate youth poverty in Nigeria.

DOI: 10.4018/978-1-7998-4339-9.ch013

INTRODUCTION AND BACKGROUND INTO THE STUDY

Youth-serving NGOs are among the key stakeholders fighting the scourge of youth poverty in Nigeria (Ohize & Adamu, 2009:48). NGO's are involved in many programmes that benefit the youth, such as the provision of shelter, food, medical services and education. Lobbying is very important in NGO management and plays a strategic role in the advocacy activities of NGOs. To establish the theoretical foundation for the investigation of the organisational capabilities of youth-serving NGOs to replicate successful programmes designed to empower poor youths in Nigeria, the deductive use of the SCALERS model is provided. The SCALERS model by Bloom and Chatterji (2009:115) proposes, "the extent to which an individual driver influence scaling success depends on various factors in the internal and external environment of the organisation that can enhance or suppress a driver's influence". In explaining the SCALERS model, Bloom and Chatterji (2009:116) and Bloom and Smith (2010:127 & 128) show that seven independent variables are considered, namely:

- Staffing
- Communication;
- Alliance building;
- Lobbying government agencies for support;
- Earnings generation;
- Replicating; and
- Stimulating market forces (organisational capabilities) in correlation with a dependent variable, which is the "scale of social impact" (see Bloom & Smith, 2010:128).

For this paper the focus is on lobbying government agencies for support that NGO's require and the important role lobbying plays to NGO management in the advocacy activities of NGOs.

H1: Lobbying is positively related to the replication of successful programmes designed to empower poor youths.

LITERATURE REVIEW

In the literature review various themes relating to lobbying challenges experienced by youth-serving NGOs and factors that influence lobbying capabilities will be unpacked and discussed.

Lobbying Challenges Experienced by Youth-Serving NGOs

Youth-serving NGOs encounter challenges in their attempt to lobby key stakeholders to assist in alleviating youth poverty in Nigeria. Momoh, Oluwasanu, Oduola, Delano & Ladipo (2015:1–2) considered the outcome of a reproductive health advocacy mentoring intervention by staff of selected NGOs in Nigeria and found that some of the NGOs lacked the capacity to negotiate with the state government. They also lacked a working system for influencing the policy formulation process and were unable to work together to act as an agent of change and to influence the political and social system to act for the benefit of their cause. Other major challenges were financial and time limitations (Momoh et al., 2015:6–7). Momoh et al. (2015:8) further state that the lobbying and advocacy challenges affected the effectiveness of NGOs to contribute positively to the reproductive health issues of adolescents and youths in Nigeria. Among the outcomes of the reproductive health advocacy mentoring for NGO staff were the provision of free airtime by a television station to educate the public on reproductive and maternal health issues and the donation of a landed property to build a youth-friendly centre (Momoh et al., 2015:1). Youth-serving NGOs encounter lobbying challenges in the form of financial challenges, time limitations, a lack of capacity to negotiate with state government, a lack of an effective operational system for influencing the policy formulation process among other challenges in their drive to alleviate the suffering of the youth with regard to reproductive health issues.

Factors that Influence the Lobbying Capability of NGOs

The following are some of the factors that affect the lobbying capability of NGOs.

NGO Leadership

NGO leadership is a significant determinant in an NGO lobbying capability. According to Luff (2015:3), "strengthening NGO influence on policy, strategy, or plans" is among NGO leadership roles in clusters. Leadership "is a process of social influence, which maximises the efforts of others, towards the achievement of a goal" (Kruse, 2013:3). According to Hailey (2006:2), four types of NGO leaders exist, namely paternalistic, activist, managerialist and catalytic leaders. It is the activist leaders who focus on advocacy and lobbying activities (Hailey, 2006:3). Hailey (2006:3) affirms that activist leaders are able to advocate their views to the relevant stakeholders to achieve the expected lobbying outcome. Ghere (2013:10) carried out a study on NGO leadership and human rights, and indicates that NGO leadership must show that the NGO's advocacy activities among other activities are credible and also necessary in the pursuit of the NGO's core mandate in society. NGO leadership manages the lobbying capability process of the NGO while ensuring that credibility is guaranteed in all the activities of the NGO.

The next section will present a discussion of networking with other NGOs as one of the factors that influence the lobbying capability of NGOs.

Networking with Other NGOs

Networking with other NGOs has a positive influence on NGO lobbying capability. According to Ivanov (1997:1), networking is "broadly defined as a structured communication for the achievement of similar goals in the conditions of interdependence". According to Holmén (2002:1), networking is a recommended strategy for NGOs to achieve performance and to create the desired social effect. Abelson (2003:9) affirms that networks play a strategic role in representing their members to advocate for policy change. Abelson (2003:9) further states that some networks mediate with their government for favourable legislation to enable their members to work effectively in achieving their goals. Moreover, Hennicke (2014:1) says there is evidence that NGOs benefit from indirect ties to networks and the positive side-effects come from indirect relationships with powerful NGOs that serve as advisers to expert groups of the European Commission. According to Hennicke (2014:4), the European Commission "created a system of advisory expert panels across its various policy areas to acquire technical information for their function in the EU institutions to develop political and legal initiatives". In addition and considering the networking effect on NGOs in the EU, Lee (2006:4) affirm that NGOs and national NGO networks have contributed considerably to the development of European policy. Lee (2006:4) further state that due to the structure of the EU, small NGOs are unable to be part of policy cycles that are influential as in terms of finance, only very large NGOs can maintain a major presence in the EU headquarters in Brussels. Using networks is one of the key strategies utilised by NGOs (Yasuda, 2015:17) and the sharing of resources is one of the major reasons for the creation of networks (Rhodes, 2007:1243–1250). This shows that NGOs in a network can have a bigger effect compared to NGOs who are lobbying independently for a cause with collaborative support. Networking offers many advantages for NGOs and increased lobbying capability is one of these.

The next section will present a discussion of financial resources as one of the factors that influence the lobbying capability of NGOs.

Financial Resources

Financial resources play a significant role in the running of an NGO and, more specifically, its lobbying activities. Financial resources represent funds available for immediate use.

The lack of financial resources has negative consequences as Lekorwe & Mpabanga (2007:2) affirm that inadequate financial resources could negatively affect the capability of an NGO to lobby among other NGO functions. One the other hand and focusing on NGOs with financial resources, Fitzgerald (2007:2) affirms that NGOs that are well funded and powerful wield considerable political influence in Australia. In addition, Carey (2009:p.iii) states that the NGO advocacy process needs both adequate staff and financial resources and proper preparation in the form of budgeting and fundraising. Schmid, Bar & Nirel (2008:597) suggest that in order to start the process of social and political change, NGOs must focus their resources on political activities using various sources of funds to increase their financial independence. Financial resources are essential for all NGO activities and the availability of a lobbying budget with adequate financial resources available enables an NGO to lobby effectively.

METHODOLOGY

The quantitative research approach was informed by the research problem that was investigated, the adapted SCALERS model that was applied and tested and also by the post positivist research philosophy which informed the quantitative approach for this study. According to Creswell (2013:48) and Nenty (2009:21), a quantitative approach allows the researcher to test a theory or apply a model with the intention of gaining insights into the relationships between defined variables in the theory and the model.

The population of a study is defined as the entire number of subjects or objects investigated by the researcher, such as "groups of people, events or things of interest" (Sekaran, 2009:265). The population for this study comprised youth-serving NGOs. According to NNNGO (a private organisation that has a database of NGOs in Nigeria and which is based in Lagos), there were about 400 active and registered youth-serving NGOs in Nigeria as at December 2015. Kumar (2005:347) defines simple random sampling as "a process of selecting the required sample size from the sample population, providing each element with an equal and independent chance of selection by any method designed to select a random sample". Simple random sampling is a widely used method of selecting a random sample (Kumar, 2005:348). In the present study, the simple random sampling design enabled the researcher to ensure that all youth-serving NGOs in the research population had an equal chance to be selected and to participate in the study. The study utilised Cohen, Manion & Morrison (2013:104) table on sample size for a defined population figure to determine the sample size for the research population of 400 youth-serving NGOs available for the study from the sampling frame provided by the NNNGO. The sample contained 196 youth-serving NGOs based on the 95% confidence level and the 5% margin of error. A total of 187 completed research questionnaires were returned after issues of improperly filled questionnaires had been addressed indicating a response rate of 95.4%, which was very good for the study (Baruch & Holtom, 2008:1141, 1155).

A survey was conducted in the study and a self-administered questionnaire was used to collect quantitative data from the respondents. Based on adopting the SCALERS research instrument and adapting it to this study, the research questionnaire was designed to have two sections, section A (Organisational Demographic Questions) with eight questions on a nominal scale (dichotomous and multi-choice questions) and section B (Main Research Questions – NGO Perceptions) with 28 questions on a 5-point Likert-type scale. A pilot study was carried out using a small sample of NGOs to pre-test and validate the research instrument. The outcome of the pilot study showed that the research instrument was reliable. According to Drost (2011:106), reliability is "the extent to which measurements are repeatable". A Chronbach alpha test was used to ascertain reliability in the study. According to Sullivan (2011:119), reliability may be calculated using different methods, and the preferred method will be influenced by the type of measurement instrument. A Cronbach coefficient alpha of .800 was found for the 28 items on the research instrument showing that the instrument was reliable. Since the Chronbach alpha score was 80% showed good reliability of the instrument.

DISCUSSION OF STUDY RESULTS

Both descriptive and inferential statistics emanating from the study will be put forward and discussed.

Descriptive Statistics

In the study the majority of youth-serving NGOs (80.2%) identified themselves as local NGOs. This was followed by respondents who indicated that they were international NGOs (19.3%). This shows that the majority of the sample group were local NGOs (80.2%).

The study also indicated that a high number of areas of expertise of youth-serving NGOs (29.4%) were related to education and training. This was followed by respondents who indicated that their area of expertise was in information technology (17.1%), agriculture (15.0%), health care services (12.8%), women development services (6.4%), legal representation services (4.8%), financial services (4.8), SME advisory services (4.8) and vocational training (4.3%).

The study further indicated that the majority of youth-serving NGOs (87.2%) targeted both male and female beneficiaries. This was followed by respondents who indicated that their NGO targeted only female beneficiaries (10.7%) and respondents who indicated that their NGOs targeted only male beneficiaries (2.1%). This shows that majority of the sample group were not gender exclusive and targeted both male and female beneficiaries (87.2%).

Inferential Statistics

Table 1. Lobbying will be positively related to the replication of successful programmes designed to empower poor youths

RSPDEPY	Lobbying
Pearson's correlation *Sig. (2-tailed)* *N*	*.426*** *.000* *187*

** Correlation is significant at the 0.001 level (2-tailed).
(Igbinakhase, 2018:229)

The hypothesized positive relationship between lobbying and the replication of successful programmes designed to empower poor youths in Nigeria (as proposed in the adapted SCALERS model) gained significant supporting evidence when it was tested in this study. The Pearson's correlation test carried out on the hypothesis indicated a significant correlation between lobbying and the replication of successful programmes designed to empower poor youths (r=.426, p < .0005). This finding shows that lobbying is an important organizational capability for youth-serving NGOs in their bid to alleviate youth poverty in Nigeria. The finding is consistent with the finding by Bloom and Smith (2010:128 & 134) who affirm the role lobbying plays in the scaling of social influence as reported in this study.

The implication of the results of the hypothesis test carried out on hypothesis 4 is that improved lobbying capabilities of youth-serving NGOs will be advantageous in the replication of successful programmes designed to empower poor youths. As a result of this implication, youth-serving NGOs should endeavor to resolve their lobbying challenges (Momoh et al., 2015:2) in time in order to achieve their youth poverty alleviation goals in the society.

IMPLICATIONS TO NGO MANAGEMENT

NGOs should ensure that efforts be made to convince local, state and federal government agencies and officials to provide supportive policies for their activities and efforts while they should also provide adequate financial support for the activities and efforts of the NGOs to enable the NGOs to be effective in their fight to eradicate youth poverty in Nigeria. In respect of earnings generation, NGOs should seek and identify long-term donors and sponsors who would provide the necessary funding for their activities and efforts to enable them to fight the scourge of youth poverty alleviation in Nigeria effectively. They should also ensure that alternative and sustainable sources of income be identified to boost their earnings generation and their financial capacity to remain relevant in the social sector.

CONCLUSION

This study is relevant in that it adds to the body of knowledge by providing evidence that showed earnings generation and lobbying as the two lagging organizational capabilities of youth-serving NGOs which needed serious improvement to be effective to enable youth-serving NGOs to achieve their social goals. NGO leadership is pivotal in maintaining contact with government organizations, business and society so that adequate lobbying takes place to raise awareness of youth unemployment and how to close this gap. NGO's must be more effective on social media and business and public forums to ensure adequate exposure to lobbying and the replication of successful programmes designed to empower poor youths in Nigeria.

REFERENCES

Abelson, A. (2003). *NGO networks: Strength in numbers? Office of Private and Voluntary Cooperation*. USAID. https://pdf.usaid.gov/pdf_docs/Pnacx190.pdf

Baruch, Y., & Holtom, B. C. (2008). Survey response rates and trends in organisational research. *Human Relations*, *61*(1), 1139–1160. doi:10.1177/0018726708094863

Bloom, P.N., & Chatterji, A.K. (2009). Scaling social entrepreneurship impact. *California Management Review*, *53*(1), 114–133.

Bloom, P.N., & Smith, B.R. (2010). Identifying the drivers of social entrepreneurial impact: Theoretical development and an exploratory empirical test of SCALERS. *Journal of Social Entrepreneurship*, (1), 126–145.

Carey, S. (2009). *Success at a price: How NGO advocacy led to changes in South Africa's People's Housing Process*. Planact, GGLN and Rooftops Canada. http://citeseerx.ist.psu.edu/viewdoc/download;jsessionid=5D7EC70FE94F0921DC8887 4FF43C0C6C?doi=10.1.1.484.9038&rep=rep1&type=pdf

Cohen, L., Manion, L., & Morrison, K. (2013). *Research methods in education*. Routledge. doi:10.4324/9780203720967

Creswell, J. W. (2013). *Research design-qualitative, quantitative and mixed method approaches* (4th ed.). Sage.

Drost, E.A. (2011). Validity and reliability in social science research. *Education Research and Perspectives*, *38*(1), 105–123.

Fitzgerald, J. (2007). *The need for transparency in lobbying. Democratic Audit of Australia*. Australian National University. https://www.parliament.sa.gov.au/Library/ ReferenceShare/Documents/lobbying.pdf

Ghere, R.K. (2013). *NGO leadership and human rights*. https://ecommons.udayton. edu/pol_fac_pub/47

Hailey, J. (2006). *NGO leadership development: A review of literature. Praxis paper no. 10*. International NGO Training and Research Centre. https://www.alnap.org/ pool/files/praxis-paper-10-ngo-leadership-development.pdf

Hennicke, M. (2014). Birds of a feather, stronger together? Network externalities in NGO cooperation. *Ecole de Sciences Economiques de Louvain*, 1-23. http://federation.ens.fr/ydepot/semin/texte1314/HEN2014BIR.pdf

Holme, N. H. (2002). *NGOs, networking, and problems of representation*. Linköpings University and ICER. https://www.icer.it/docs/wp2002/holmen33-02.pdf

Ivanov, A. (1997). Advanced networking: A conceptual approach to NGO-based early response strategies in conflict prevention. Occasional paper no. 11. Berlin: Berghof Research Center for Constructive Conflict Management.

Kruse, K. (2013). *What is leadership?* Forbes Magazine. http://www.forbes.com/ sites/kevinkruse/2013/04/09/what-is-leadership/#79016146713e

Kumar, R. (2005). *Research methodology: A step-by-step guide for beginners*. Pearson Longman.

Lee, J. (2006). *Comparing NGO influence in the EU and the U.S. Centre for Applied Studies in International Negotiations.* https://www.files.ethz.ch/isn/25102/ngoinfluenceinuandusa.pdf

Lekorwe, M., & Mpabanga, D. (2007). Managing non-governmental organisations in Botswana. *The Public Sector Innovation Journal, 12*(3), 1–18.

Luff, R. (2015). *Review of NGOs leadership roles in clusters.* International Council of Voluntary Agencies. www.alnap.org/pool/files/176-review-of-ngo-leadership-roles-in-clusters.pdf

Momoh, G. T., Oluwasanu, M. M., Oduola, O. L., Delano, G. E., & Ladipo, O. A. (2015). Outcome of a reproductive health advocacy mentoring intervention for staff of selected non-governmental organisations in Nigeria. *BMC Health Services Research, 15*(314), 1–9. doi:10.118612913-015-0975-0 PMID:26259953

Nenty, H. J. (2009). Writing a quantitative research thesis. *International Journal of Education Science, 1*(1), 19–32.

Ohize, E., & Adamu, M. J. (2009). Case study of youth empowerment scheme of Niger State, Nigeria in poverty alleviation. *AU Journal of Technology, 13*(1), 47–52.

Rhodes, R. A. (2007). Understanding governance: Ten years on. *Organization Studies, 28*(8), 1243–1264. doi:10.1177/0170840607076586

Schmid, H., Bar, M., & Nirel, R. (2008). Advocacy activities in nonprofit human service organisations: Implications for policy. *Nonprofit and Voluntary Sector Quarterly, 37*(4), 581–602. doi:10.1177/0899764007312666

Sullivan, G. M. (2011). A primer on the validity of assessment instruments. *Journal of Graduate Medical Education, 3*(2), 119–120. doi:10.4300/JGME-D-11-00075.1 PMID:22655129

Yasuda, Y. (2015). *Rules, norms and NGO advocacy strategies: Hydropower development on the Mekong River.* Routledge Taylor & Francis Group. doi:10.4324/9781315687179

Chapter 14
Dichotomy and Violent Student Protests:
Perceptions From Students

Thea van der Westhuizen
https://orcid.org/0000-0001-8795-4023
University of KwaZulu-Natal, South Africa

Yamkhela Nhleko
University of KwaZulu-Natal, South Africa

ABSTRACT

"How dare you!" was the opening line 16-year-old Greta Thunberg used in her address to world leaders at the United Nation Global Summit on Climate Change. This young woman demanded global political and business leaders to listen to her plea, as she firmly believes global systems are in crisis and politicians and business persons alike are not playing their part to resolve our people, planet, and profit crisis. Student protests in response to leadership in higher education institutions have become a generic form of expressing discontent. In a quantitative investigation, this study assessed student perceptions regarding higher education leadership in relation to three core leadership capabilities: a strategic approach, communication and collaboration, and institutional drivers and results. Data collection from students in their final year was done using a combination of simple and stratified sampling. SPSS version 25 was used for data analysis. Findings reiterated a current dichotomy and urge the need for social cohesion between student and university leadership.

DOI: 10.4018/978-1-7998-4339-9.ch014

INTRODUCTION

As major social institutions, universities both embody their times and produce the people who collectively act as catalysts for social change. (Webbstock & Fisher, 2016)

Violent student protests in South Africa is at an all-time high, with billions of Rands damages to Higher Education Institutions during the course of protest actions. Student protests centred on a multitude of unresolved problems they believe to experience. These problems are primarily centred on funding related issues for example fees must fall, free laptops and data, write-off from historical debt, and free accommodation and transportation. The aim of student protests are seemingly to convince all governance levels, from institutional to national governance, to resolve student demands. In 2019, violent protest actions rallied several deaths of students and security officers. It is debatable why students revert to violent protests and what prompts such deep-rooted anger, causes mostly perceived to have socio-economic development roots. Leaving lecturers fearful to come to work. Higher education is in large shaped by its leadership, and it is incumbent upon the leadership to project the values that students will hopefully wish to emulate. Rapidly changing global realities make academic leadership increasingly challenging, and especially so in developing countries such as South Africa (African Minds, 2016). In part, this is because South African institutions of higher education need leadership that can steer academic eco-systemic development to advance the country's socio-economic development. The task facing this leadership is two-fold: conserving and enhancing the quality of the tertiary education system while at the same time working to prepare its learners of the future world of work demands, especially in an era following Covid-19. Thompson (2016) emphasises the need for leaders to appreciate societal diversity, looking beyond individual behaviours to create understanding and appreciation of social and motivational differences and similarities.

The purpose of this research was to gain insight into perceptions of students in their final year, where the next step might be to potentially enter the world of work. A limitation of this study was that university leadership's perceptions were not investigated. The specific focus was on students' perceptions regarding three core leadership capabilities – strategic approach, communications and collaboration, and institutional drivers and results that potentially lead to student discontent expressed through protest actions.

Students are primary stakeholders in institutions of higher education, and including students to its strategic planning is therefore crucial to develop an academic environment conducive to learning. Violent student protest actions are not a new phenomenon in South Africa; they have always been a form in which students' express discontent with leadership, perceived managerial injustices, or promises made by politicians which remain perceivingly empty and unfulfilled (Tenza, 2015). Such violent expressions seem to have demographic and socio-economic development propensities, because not all South African universities experience violent student protests. In causal factors for student protest actions, Kiboiy (2013) distinguishes between external factors and internal factors. External factors are anything that arouses or provokes student unrest from outside the academic institution; internal factors are aspects that arise from within the academic institution and that the institution can to some extent deal with, such as mismanagement, lack of urgency in meeting student needs, lack of involvement in decision-making, or dissatisfaction with the learning environment (Alimba, 2008). A dichotomy arises in students' perceptions of cause-and-effect from internal and external factors, and university leadership's drive to implement its academic strategy. In this study, the focus was on internal factors that cause student protest actions. Within these perceived factors, a clear dichotomy is evident.

The Concept of Violent Student Protests

Violent student protest and student unrest, globally, are frequently regarded as synonymous (Omari & Mihyo, 1991; Uyanga, 2016; Darwin, 2016; Block, 2018). Brooks (2016), sees student protest as a global phenomenon that has been influenced by the continuous expansion of social media such as Twitter, Facebook, Instagram, and LinkedIn, exemplified in Twitter hashtags such as #RhodesMustFall in South Africa that prompted protests in Africa and beyond. One difference, however, is that Afrocentric student protests tend to be more violent, destructive and often leads to the death of activists in the movement. As Fomunyam (2017, p. 56) puts it, 'Students in Africa have inherited the culture of violence exhibited during the struggle against colonialism.' Badat (2016) notes that violent student protests took place at several major universities in South Africa: Walter Sisulu University, the University of KwaZulu Natal, where protests took place on all four campuses, the University of Witwatersrand, the University of Pretoria, and North-West University. At the University of Johannesburg alone, there was damage due to violent protest amounting to R100 million. Fomunyam (2017) notes that the phenomenon is not confined to Southern Africa: student protests have likewise been reported in many of the universities in West and Central Africa.

Leadership in Higher Education Institutions

Downton (as cited in Ofoegbu & Alonge, 2017, p. 112), describes leadership in higher education as requiring 'a dynamic amalgamation of spirit and heart, mind, will, character, savvy, wisdom and emotion to generate an increase in the level of congruity with the ethos, vision, conducts and values of the institution.' According to Ofoegbu and Alonge (2017), leadership in higher education requires continuous enhancement in pursuit of organisational goals, embracing the development of human minds, financial management and promotion of academic and developmental research. Doyle and Brady (2018) make the point that universities increasingly function as organisational actors expected to be committed to economic and social objectives as set by the policy framework within which they operate.

In a plea for the excellence in leadership and competence in management that South African universities and colleges need and deserve, Waghid and Davids (2016) call for reconsideration of the leadership role in response to the new complexities in these institutions, and in a Covid-19 era which changed the way of institutional architecture on both academic and operational fronts. Holistic and inclusive leadership decisions must be made in which there is openness to constructive criticism and an overall willingness to strive towards socio-economic development.

Leadership and Leadership Styles

Leadership signifies capacity (exercised by an individual or an organisation) to guide or lead other persons, teams or an organisation as a whole. With the end of apartheid, new leadership approaches emerged in South African higher education (Ngcamu & Teferra 2015). Pressure for transformation under the new government elicited differing responses from one institution to another, and often what this amounted to was market-oriented competition for students. Transformational leadership and managerial leadership were both seen in the various approaches to crisis management (Ngcamu & Teferra, 15).

In South Africa, Higher Education Institutes have three primary objectives: research, teaching, and community service. Violent student protests currently points toward a dichotomy on action deliverables in all three domains.

Leadership styles vary from leader to leader. Luthans (as cited in Khan et al., 2015, p. 87) defines leadership style as 'the way in which the leader influences the followers.' The leadership style adopted needs to be one that will lead to success in meeting the goals and objectives of the institution. In a university, the crucial factor in the leadership approach is its bearing on responses to national imperatives, as well as the United Nations Development Programme's sustainability goals, rather than the specific behaviour of an individual. The sense of embracing The Collective is therefore essential.

Institutional Leadership and Violent Protest Actions

The literature used in this research derives chiefly from work by African scholars, focused for the most part on student protest actions in African universities (Alimba, 2008; Badat, 2016; Bolden, 2008; Luescher-Mamashela, 2013; Mjema, 2013; Zuber-Skerrit, 2007). However, there has been relatively little investigation of the role of students' perceptions on institutional leadership as a possible factor in violent protest actions. Student protests are a regular occurrence in South African universities. Student grievances most often resulting in violent student protests, as listed by Alimba (2008), are accommodation, student funding and institutional or managerial styles. These same issues were listed by students in the recent 2019 student protest actions in universities in the province of KwaZulu-Natal, South Africa.

One of the reasons why students resort to violent protest actions is that they feel there is an unresponsive and remote institutional leadership, such as failure to enter into dialogue with student leaders (Langa, Ndelu, Edwin & Vilakazi, 2017). One many ask, are all students aware of discussions between student bodies and university leadership? Are students aware of multiple institutional and government proposed solutions to student grievances? And, are these dichotomic responses by students rooted in own initiative, or prompted by external political leaders? When protest actions ensue in breaking the law, the most common response by the leadership is a court interdict to prohibit student participation in the protest action (Langa et al., 2017), in an attempt to protect human lives and prevent destruction of university property. Other management strategies are calling for police intervention to disperse student demonstrators that threatens to result in a potential dangerous situation, suspending academic activities to protect safety of students and staff, and in some instances arresting student leaders who are breaking the law (Chinyere, 2008). There seems to be more dichotomy in what students perceive are acceptable ways to express discontent, students' interpretation of the country's law and university leadership principles. According to Watson (2000), everything hinges on the management strategy within which core activities of the institution are rooted, and since the students are the university's most important asset, its core commitment must be to develop and train them. But violent expressions by students and threats to public safety seem to prevent such important education to occur.

Conceptual framework

The focus of this research was on the perceptions of students regarding institutional leadership as related to protest actions. The conceptual framework for the study (see Figure 1) incorporates the leadership objectives that are involved in creating an academic environment that ensures the wellbeing of students. Strategic approach,

Figure 1. Conceptual framework used in the study. Adapted from McMaster University (n.d.)

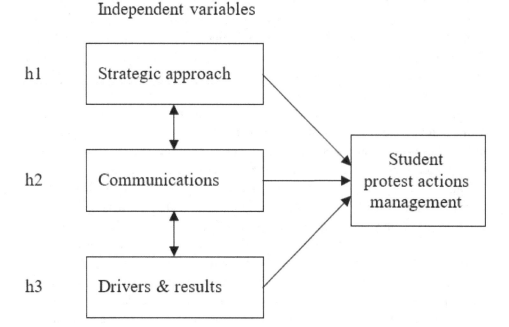

communication and collaboration, and drivers and results function as independent variables in the framework, and management of student protest actions is the dependent variable. The interrelatedness of the independent variables and the dependent variable explained in this study.

h1: There is a relationship between the strategic approach of the institution and its management of student protest actions

The first variable is the strategic approach that the institution chooses to take. According to Warner and Palfreyman (1996), the strategy that the institution chooses to adopt, and how it manages this strategy, is of utmost importance as it enables optimisation of the core activities of research, student development, and all broader economic and social services. A well-conceived and well-executed strategy captures the university's self-identity, attracts investors, and wins the attention of society (Warner & Palfreyman, 1996). The university leadership has a responsibility to execute the strategy as set out on paper and put it into effect. As several universities are millions of dollars in debt due to outstanding student fees. Incompliance from students to institutional financial strategy creates a dichotomic situation. In the spirit of all-inclusiveness, multiple conversations between students and many different stakeholders are taking place – but students remain increasingly insistent on waiving of fees. Which on the other side, might not be a financially viable decision to an organisation who are already in debt.

h2: There is a relationship between the communication and collaboration platforms used by institutional leadership and its management of student protest actions.

National and institutional governance have been communicating to student body governance, and all registered students to institutes on what are expected from them concerning fees. However, student bodies disagree. Institutional leadership follow an all-inclusive approach where students and the institute's eco-system are involved in remedial discussions. Students seemingly revert to the political sphere for assistance. Students as critical stakeholders, universities need to have both internal and community communication networks to encourage communication and collaboration among employees and students. Davis and Jones (2014,p. 368) make the point that 'as technological advances create yet more tools for collaboration, through social media connectivity, pressure remains to find more effective approaches to address likely disruptive change and increasing complexity that characterises the work of higher education leadership and management.' Information and communication technology platforms (email, mobile apps, and web services) are crucial element in these networks for speedy communication to large numbers of people (Boeren & Whittaker, 2018). But how conducive are these social media channels in cases where face news are distributed? Or when social media is misused to spur violent protests? The most popular communication channels adopted by universities in crisis management in South Africa are emails (76 per cent) and website (82 per cent); other channels such as Facebook, SMS, and WhatsApp all fell below 50 per cent (Grobler & Jansen van Rensburg, 2018; Sebola, 2017).

Collaboration between universities is vital as part of their research function, and Liew, Shahdan and Lim (2012) make a case for the involvement of project champions devoted to managing the collaboration and keeping the relationship going – the success of the collaboration being chiefly dependent on the strategic or tactical approach taken. The approach further underlines the importance of communication as a variable, closely linked to issues of leadership strategy in the conceptual framework and relating in particular to the ecosystem of the students (van der Westhuizen, 2017).

h3: There is a relationship between the institution's drivers and results and its management of student protest actions.

The framework also highlights the significance of drivers and results in university leadership. According to the University of Nottingham (2016), drivers and results define the enthusiasm and desire to meet and exceed the institution's objectives and advance its strategy. The university leadership plays an essential role in setting priorities for the institution and improving its performance; one aspect of this is getting all stakeholders to work together in pursuit of a common goal. The 2017–2021 Strategic Plan of this particular university states that adoption of the strategic plan provides an opportunity to review the achievements and failures of the university and focus on its core function as a knowledge agent, which is to achieve excellence and transformation. The strategy further outlines that the university strives to provide excellent teaching and learning; in this way, high potential students will be attracted and will be developed to their full potential so that they can become global leaders. Are students aware of the Bigger Picture socio-economic development plan of the university they attack with violent protests?

METHODOLOGY

The study adopted a quantitative approach to investigate ongoing protest actions and students' perceptions regarding the university leadership. The target population was students in their final year of study, more specifically honours students which are in a South African context post graduate students, in a subsequent final year (year four) of an undergraduate 3 year programme postgraduate students within the province of Kwa-Zulu Natal. In South Africa this signifies an honours year or year four of extended undergraduate qualification. Ethical clearance (Protocol no. HSS/0665/018H) was duly obtained to conduct this research. In accordance with ethical compliance, the sample sites are not disclosed. This specific student sample was considered because they were likely to have experienced three or more student protest actions at the university since their first year, regardless of whether they had chosen to participate in the protest action. A combination of simple convenience sampling and stratified sampling was employed to collect data for this study. Simple random sampling was used to administer 80 questionnaires to the study respondents within the province of KwaZulu-Natal, the largest geographical area with in the country. Convenience sampling was employed to select interdisciplinarity for the purpose of data collection (Sekaran & Bougie, 2016, Wilson, 2014). Stratified sampling strategy was used to segregate the students into strata based on four disciplines: Management, Entrepreneurship, Marketing, and Supply Chain. A total of 80 self-administered questionnaires were returned for analysis, which constituted a 100% response rate. SPSS version 25 was used to establish the relationships among the variables measured in the study.

Measurement

A five-point Likert scale ranging from 1 (strongly disagree) to 5 (strongly agree) was adopted as the measuring tool for this study. The Likert scale is 'designed to examine how strongly subjects agree or disagree with statements on a five-point scale' (Sekaran & Bougie, 2016, p. 215). The McMaster model was used to construct items to measure student perceptions on the core leadership capabilities (Miller, Ryan, Keitner, Bishop & Epstein, 2000). The items considered relevant to measure the constructs in this article are explained below.

Strategic Approach

Five constructs adapted from the McMaster University Core Leadership Capabilities model were listed as sub-items in assessing students' perceptions in the strategic approach category. The sub-items were aimed at measuring student perceptions on the promotion of culture and values in the university, on the university's understanding of global trends and impact, and on the university's anticipation of challenges, risks, and outcomes. Together, these items constituted a key construct in the strategic approach of the university that needed to be communicated to all the levels of management and reflected on the services offered. Universities face challenges that require them to adopt innovative and competent approaches that work as a model for providing support for decision making (Labib, Read, Gladstone-Millar, Tonge & Smith, 2013). The sub-items were as follows:

- **Sub-Item One:** 'The university promotes culture and values.'
- **Sub-Item Two:** 'The university understands global trends and impact.'
- **Sub-Item Three:** 'The university anticipates challenges, risks and outcomes.'
- **Sub-Item Four:** 'The university gathers key information and challenges.'
- **Sub-Item Five:** 'The university enables strategic plans through roles (e.g. management and administrative support).'

Cronbach Alpha reliability test for the five strategic approach sub-items was 0.80. This measurement implies that the tests were reliable, as it was above the statistically accepted threshold of 0.7.

Communications and Collaboration

Stressing the importance of communication and collaboration in higher education, Ezzeldin (2017, p. 6) notes that 'It is important for the success and effectiveness of academic institutions to become more aware of the communication system to keep improving its effectiveness and efficiency'.

Five constructs adapted from the McMaster University Core Leadership Capabilities model were listed as sub-items in assessment of students' perceptions in the communications and collaborations category:

- **Sub-Item One:** 'The university identifies opportunities to collaborate with students.'
- **Sub-Item Two:** 'The university generates trust and an inclusive environment for students.'
- **Sub-Item Three:** 'The university listens to students with insight and respect.'
- **Sub-Item Four:** 'The university maximises the use of internal and community networks to communicate with students.'
- **Sub-Item Five:** 'The university provides students with meaningful recognition.'

Cronbach alpha reliability test for the five communications and collaboration sub-items was 0.76.

Drivers and Results

In the drivers and results category four constructs for drivers or results were incorporated as sub-items in investigating perceptions of students:

- **Sub-Item One:** 'The university ensures the progression of the university strategy for students'
- **Sub-Item Two:** 'The university delivers student services with integrity.'
- **Sub-Item Three:** 'The university balances priorities to achieve success.'
- **Sub-Item Four:** 'The university takes well-judged risks that enable student innovation.'

Cronbach alpha reliability test for these four sub-items was 0.72.

RESULTS AND DISCUSSION

Outcomes of the statistical analysis shown in Table 1 suggest that the strategic approach has a significant positive association with communication and collaboration in the university ($r = 0.379$, N=80, $p < 0.01$). This result indicates that the strategic approach adopted by the university enhances communications and collaborations

Table 1. Correlation coefficient of the study main Constructs

Variables	1	2	3
1 Strategic approach	—		
2 Communications & Collaborations	0.379**	—	
3 Drivers & Results	0.376**	0.511**	—
4 Management of student protest actions	0.030	0.241*	430**

** Correlation is significant at the 0.01 level (2-tailed).
* Correlation is significant at the 0.05 level (2-tailed).

between the university leadership and the students. In other words, students perceive that a continuous improvement in the strategic approach adopted by the university will enhance communication and collaboration between the students and the university leadership.

Strategic Approach in Relation to Management of Student Protest Actions

The university's strategic approach (as in promotion of culture and values, awareness of global trends and impact, anticipation of challenges, risks and outcomes, gathering of key information and challenges, and enabling strategic plans through roles) is not correlated with management of student protest actions ($r = 0.030$, $N = 80$, $p > 0.05$).

The relationship between strategic approach and drivers and results showed significantly strong and positive association ($r = 0.376$, $N=80$, $p < 0.01$). This suggest that there might be a dichotomy between student perceptions and the vision of university strategy. Hypothesis one, which states that there is a relationship between the strategic approach of the institution and its management of student protest actions, is therefore not supported. This may be interpreted that students are not aware of national imperatives on socio-economic development goals, UNDP's goals for socio-economic development and university goals for socio-economic development. All systemic levels place youth development at its centre, however youth might not be able to fully understand complex system dynamics. Hypothesis one is therefore accepted.

Communications and Collaboration in Relation to Management of Student Protest Actions

The relationship between students' perceptions of communications and collaboration and management of student protest actions showed significant correlation ($r = 0.241$,

N = 80, p < 0.05). According to Coombs (2007), crises are considered as threat if they have adverse effects on the reputation of an organisation. Regular communication and engagement with students through collaboration could therefore help to douse tensions which may degenerate into protest actions. In addition, engagement with students by university leadership via the available communication platforms can be used as positive factor in the management of student protest actions. Based on this outcome, hypothesis two, which states that there is a relationship between the communication and collaboration platforms used by institutional leadership and its management of student protest actions, is accepted.

Drivers and Results in Relation to Management of Student Protest Actions

Similarly, drivers and results were positively associated with management of student protest actions in the university (r =0.430, N = 80, p < 0.01). From this it can be inferred that positive student perception of the university's drivers and results contributes to less protest actions, potentially not violent or dangerous to the university community. Hypothesis three, which states that there is a relationship between drivers and results and management of student protest actions, is accepted. Consistent with this finding, Armstrong (2016) lists the following as major drivers and results that contribute to management of student protest actions: career counselling, consultation, study training and workshops, individual assessments, campus health care and online education, balancing priorities to achieve success, and taking well-judged risks that enable student innovation. The outcome of the multiple regression analysis is presented in Table 2.

Table 2. Multiple regression analysis

Constructs	R	R square	Adjusted R square	F	Beta	T	P
Constant	.457[a]	.209	.178	6.697		5.157	.000[b]
Strategic approach					-.169	-1.494	.139
Communications & collaboration					.071	.584	.561
Drivers & results					.457	3.752	.000

a. Dependent variable: Management of student protest actions
b. Predictors (Constant): strategic approach; communications & collaboration; Drivers & results

The regression model in Table 2 shows R square of 0.209 and adjusted R square of 0.178. The result implies that that strategic approach, communications and collaboration, and drivers and results explain 20.9 per cent of variations in relation to management of student protest actions. The standardised coefficient Beta value and the P value for drivers and results were $\beta = 0.457$, $p < 0.001$. The result of the statistical analysis, as shown in Table 2, indicates that drivers and results are predictors of management of student protest actions. However, the standardised coefficient Beta values and the corresponding p values for strategic approach ($\beta = -0.169$, $p > 0.05$) and for communications and collaboration ($\beta = 0.584$, $p > 0.05$) show that communications and collaboration contribute more to the regression model than strategic approach; both constructs are statistically insignificant. This implies that strategic approach and communications and collaboration are not predictors of management of student protest actions. This finding is consistent with the outcome of the Pearson correlation coefficient, which showed that there was no relationship between strategic approach and management of student protest actions. Consistent with this finding, Langa et al. (2017) in their study on the #FeesMustFall movement at South Africa universities found that the lack of appropriate communication between all role-players involved, resulted in protest actions by students to attract the attention of the media on the perceived injustice prevalence in the university system – which yet indicates signs of dichotomy.

Suggestions for further study

The sample size was limited an we recommend to expand the research to include the other provinces in South Africa. This study investigated student perceptions on the perceived link between university leadership and the management of protest actions action in institutions of higher learning. A limitation of this study was that university leadership perceptions were not investigated. It is recommended to do more research on the dichotomy between student perceptions, university strategy and the eco-system of Higher Education Institutes.

Implications for Policy and Management

Implications for policy and management can be drawn from the analysed data on the ongoing student protest actions as reflecting perceptions on leadership in higher education. It is the responsibility of the entire ecosystem surrounding youth to provide good governance and raise them to become responsible and socio-economically contributive young citizens (van der Westhuizen, 2019). Judging from the viewpoint of student perceptions, the strategic approach employed by the university management to manage student protests actions was not effective. Again, the dichotomy can be debated on what the students demand and viable solutions to the problems. It is also questionable if students have sufficient and reliable information to ground decisions of violent protests.

The significant positive relationship between communication and collaboration and the management of student protest actions also has important implications for policy and practice in the university system. Enhanced communication and collaboration among all stakeholders in the university could help to forestall and manage the incessant protest actions among students in South African universities.

The drivers and results could be crucial in the handling of student protest actions by the university management. A continuous dialogue between students and university management could prove valuable in identifying and addressing the student needs that might result in protest actions if they are not properly managed.

CONCLUSION

The primary objective of this study was to investigate the perceptions of students on three core capabilities of university leadership: strategic approach, communications and collaboration, and drivers and results. The study sought to identify what role student perceptions of these leadership capabilities played in the on-going student protest actions in South African universities. The findings show that there is a dichotomy in the relationship between the strategic approach adopted by the university leadership and management of student protest actions. Further, cries from students in higher education institutes reflect "How dare you!" to leadership, especially from what students perceive as empty promises from political leadership, as they feel anxiously concerned about the demands higher education institutes bestow on them and in return, many students do not have financial means to support their studies. There is high uncertainty amongst students if they will become one of the unemployed statistics after completion of their degree. The article shows also that the platforms for communication and collaboration between students and university leadership and the drivers and results of the institution all have a significant relationship with the management of student protest actions. Lastly, it is acknowledged that there is a dichotomy between what students perceive they are entitled to demand, and what is realistic financial viable to universities. As not all South African universities have violent student protests, it might be concluded that this phenomenon is socio-economic demographic orientated

ACKNOWLEDGMENT

This article is based on research supported by the National Research Foundation of South Africa (Grant Number: 122002). The views expressed are those of the researcher and not the NRF.

REFERENCES

African Minds. (2016). *Reflections of South African HEI leaders:1981 to 2014*. Retrieved June 15, 2019 from http://www.che.ac.za/sites/default/files/publications/Reflections%20of%20South%20African%20HEI%20Leaders%201981-2014.pdf

Alimba, C. N. (2008). Lecturer–Students' perception of causes, effects and management patterns of students' unrest in tertiary institutions. *African Journal of Educational Management, 11*(1), 170–189.

Armstrong, L. (2016). Barriers to innovation and change in higher education. *TIAA-CREF Institute*. Retrieved from https://pdfs.semanticscholar.org/d513/141cb6af397d22a68d99fa9264875f888312.pdf

Badat, S. (2016). Deciphering the meanings and explaining the South African higher education student protests of 2015–16. *Pax Academica, 1*, 71–106.

Block, P. (2018). *Community: The structure of belonging*. San Francisco, CA: Berrett-Koehler. Retrieved June 15, 2019 from https://books.google.co.za/books?hl=en&lr=&id=9guXL4Yl8ekC&oi=fnd&pg=PR1&ots=mPJJF8eCDs&sig=P-ihsPZUjQCGYFU2hgZlna8qKqw&redir_esc=y#v=onepage&q&f=false

Boeren, E., & Whittaker, S. (2018). A typology of education and training provisions for low educated adults: Categories and definitions. *Studies in the Education of Adults, 50*(1), 4–18. doi:10.1080/02660830.2018.1520017

Bolden, R. (20078). Distributed leadership. university of Leadership. In A. Marturano & J. Gosling (Eds.), *Leadership: The Key Concepts* (1st ed., p. 1). Routledge., doi:10.4324/9780203099643

Brooks, R. (2019). Politics and protest – Students rise up worldwide. *University World News*. Retrieved June 15, 2019 from https://www.HEIworldnews.com/post.php?story=20160510173152311

Brooks-Tatum, S. R. (2016). Delaware State University Guides Patrons into more Effective Research with Standardized Lib Guides. *Against the Grain (Charleston, S.C.), 24*(1), 7.

Chinyere, N. A. (2008). Lecturer-students. *African Journal of Education Management, 11*(1), 170–189.

Coombs, W. T. (2007). Protecting organization reputations during a crisis: The development and application of situational crisis communication theory. *Corporate Reputation Review, 10*(3), 163-176. doi:10.1057/palgrave.crr.1550049

Davies, K. U., Ekwere, G. E., & Uyanga, U. U. (2016). Factors influencing students unrest in institutions of higher learning and its implications on the academic performance of students in University of Uyo, Akwa Ibom State, Nigeria. *Istraživanja u pedagogiji, 6*(1), 27-42. doi:10.17810/2015.21

Davis, H., & Jones, S. (2014). The work of leadership in higher education management. *Journal of Higher Education Policy and Management, 36*(4), 367–370. doi:10.10 80/1360080X.2014.916463

Doyle, T., & Brady, M. (2018). Reframing the university as an emergent organisation: Implications for strategic management and leadership in higher education. *Journal of Higher Education Policy and Management, 40*(4), 305–320. doi:10.1080/1360 080X.2018.1478608

Ezzeldin, A. M. G. (2017). Faculty perceptions of the importance of communication in Saudi Arabia Higher Education Najran Community College: Case study. *Cogent Business & Management, 4*(1). doi: 10.1080/23311975.2017.1319007

Fomunyam, K. G. (2017). Student protest and the culture of violence at African universities: An inherited ideological trait. *Yesterday and Today*, (17), 38-63. doi:10.17159/2223-0386/2017/n17a3

Grobler, A., & Jansen van Rensburg, M. (2018). Organisational climate, person–organisation fit and turn over intention: A generational perspective within a South African Higher Education Institution. *Studies in Higher Education*, 1–13. doi:10.1 080/03075079.2018.1492533

Habib, A. (2016). Transcending the past and reimagining the future of the South African university. *Journal of Southern African Studies, 42*(1), 35–48. doi:10.108 0/03057070.2016.1121716

Khan, M. S., Khan, I., Qureshi, Q. A., Ismail, H. M., Rauf, H., Latif, A., & Tahir, M. (2015). The styles of leadership: A critical review. *Public Policy and Administration Research*, *5*(3), 87–92.

Kiboiy, K. L. (2013). *The dynamics of student unrests in Kenya's higher education: the case of Moi University* (Doctoral dissertation, University of Pretoria). Retrieved April 5, 2019 from https://repository.up.ac.za/bitstream/handle/2263/32399/kiboiy_dynamics_2013.pdf?sequence=4

Labib, A., Read, M., Gladstone-Millar, C., Tonge, R., & Smith, D. (2013). Formulation of higher education institutional strategy using operational research approaches. *Studies in Higher Education*, *39*(5), 885–904. doi:10.1080/03075079.2012.754868

Langa, M., Ndelu, S., Edwin, Y., & Vilakazi, M. (2017). *Hashtag: An Analysis of the #FeesMustFall Movement at South African Universities* (1st ed.). Africa Portal. Retrieved from https://www.africaportal.org/publications/hashtag-an-analysis-of-the-feesmustfall-movement-at-south-african-universities/

Liew, M. S., Shahdan, T. T., & Lim, E. S. (2012). Strategic and tactical approaches on university-industry collaboration. *Procedia: Social and Behavioral Sciences*, *56*, 405–409. doi:10.1016/j.sbspro.2012.09.669

Luescher-Mamashela, T. M. (2013). Student representation in university decision making: Good reasons, a new lens? *Studies in Higher Education*, *38*(10), 1442–1456. doi:10.1080/03075079.2011.625496

McMaster University. (n.d.). *McMaster's Core Leadership Capabilities*. Retrieved from https://cauce-aepuc.ca/documents/conference/2018/Mac-Core-Leadership-Capabilities-Card.pdf

Miller, I. W., Ryan, C. E., Keitner, G. I., Bishop, D. S., & Epstein, N. B. (2000). The McMaster approach to families: Theory, assessment, treatment and research. *Journal of Family Therapy*, *22*(2), 168–189. doi:10.1111/1467-6427.00145

Mjema, M. M. (2013). *The Causes and Management of Students' Unrest at the University of Arusha in Tanzania* (Doctoral dissertation). The Open University of Tanzania.

Ngcamu, B. S., & Teferra, D. (2015). How well do university staff understand transformation? A case of a merged South African University. *International Journal of Educational Sciences, 8*(2), 305-312. doi:10.1080/09751122.2015.11890252

Ofoegbu, F. O., & Alonge, H. O. (2017). Effective university leadership as predictor of academic excellence in Southern Nigerian universities. *Journal of Education and Practice*, *8*(8), 111–116.

Omari, I. M., & Mihyo, P. B. (1991). *Roots of student unrest in African universities*. Retrieved from https://idl-bnc-idrc.dspacedirect.org/bitstream/handle/10625/9855/92427.pdf?sequence=1

Sebola, M. P. (2017). Communication in the South African public participation process-the effectiveness of communication tools. *African Journal of Public Affairs*, *9*(6), 25–35. https://hdl.handle.net/10520/EJC-754d2f95f

Sekaran, U., & Bougie, R. (2016). *Research methods for business*. John Wiley & Sons.

Shaw, C. (2013). How should universities respond to student protests? 10 views. *The Guardian*. Retrieved June 15, 2019 from https://www.theguardian.com/higher-education-network/blog/2013/dec/11/student-protest-how-should-management-respond

Tenza, M. (2015). An investigation into the causes of violent protest actions in South Africa: Some lessons from foreign law and possible solutions. *Law. Democracy & Development*, *19*(1), 211–231. doi:10.4314/ldd.v19i1.11

Thompson, N. (2016). *Anti-discriminatory practice: Equality, diversity and social justice*. Macmillan International Higher Education. doi:10.1007/978-1-137-58666-7

University of Nottingham. (2016). *Drive for results*. Retrieved from https://www.nottingham.ac.uk/hr/guidesandsupport/performanceatwork/pdpr/pdpr-behavioural-competency-guide/achieving-and-delivery/drive-for-results.aspx

Waghid, Y., & Davids, N. (2016). Educational leadership as action: Towards an opening of rhythm. *South African Journal of Higher Education*, *30*(1), 1753–5913. doi:10.20853/30-1-554

Warner, D., & Palfreyman, D. (1996). *Higher education management: The key elements*. Retrieved from https://books.google.co.za/books/about/Higher_education_management.html?id=6JklAQAAIAAJ&redir_esc=y

Watson, D. (2000). *Managing universities and colleges: Guides to good practice Managing strategy*. Open University.

Webbstock, D., & Fisher, G. (2016). *South African higher education reviewed: Two decades of democracy.* Retrieved June 15, 2019 from https://www.che.ac.za/sites/default/files/publications/CHE_South%20African%20higher%20education%20reviewed%20-%20electronic.pdf

Wilson, J. (2014). *Essentials of business research: A guide to doing your research project.* Sage.

Zuber-Skerritt, O. (2007). Leadership development in South African higher education: The heart of the matter. *South African Journal of Higher Education, 21*(7), 984–1005.

Compilation of References

A Guide to the Project Management Body of Knowledge. (2017). (6th ed.). PMBOK® Guide. Project Management Institute.

Abelson, A. (2003). *NGO networks: Strength in numbers? Office of Private and Voluntary Cooperation.* USAID. https://pdf.usaid.gov/pdf_docs/Pnacx190.pdf

Achakulvisut, T., Acuna, D. E., Ruangrong, T., & Kording, K. (2016). Science concierge: A fast content-based recommendation system for scientific publications. *PLoS One, 11*(7), e0158423. doi:10.1371/journal.pone.0158423 PMID:27383424

African Minds. (2016). *Reflections of South African HEI leaders: 1981 to 2014.* Retrieved June 15, 2019 from http://www.che.ac.za/sites/default/files/publications/Reflections%20of%20South%20African%20HEI%20Leaders%201981-2014.pdf

Akhil, P. V., & Joseph, S. (2017). A survey of recommender system types and its classification. *International Journal of Advanced Research in Computer Science, 8*(9), 486–491. doi:10.26483/ijarcs.v8i9.5017

Alač, M. (2009). Moving android: On social robots and body-in-interaction. *Social Studies of Science, 39*(4), 491–528. doi:10.1177/0306312709103476 PMID:19848108

Alač, M., Movellan, J., & Tanaka, F. (2011). When a robot is social: Spatial arrangements and multimodal semiotic engagement in the practice of social robotics. *Social Studies of Science, 41*(6), 893–926. doi:10.1177/0306312711420565 PMID:22400423

Alimba, C. N. (2008). Lecturer–Students' perception of causes, effects and management patterns of students' unrest in tertiary institutions. *African Journal of Educational Management, 11*(1), 170–189.

Amatriain, X., & Basilico, J. (2015). Recommender Systems in Industry: A Netflix Case Study. In Recommender Systems Handbook. doi:10.1007/978-1-4899-7637-6_11

Anantatmula, V. S., & Anantatmula, M. (2008). *Use of Agile Methodology for IT Consulting Projects.* Paper presented at PMI® Research Conference: Defining the Future of Project Management, Warsaw, Poland.

Ankiewicz, P. (2015). *The implications of the philosophy of technology for the academic majors of technology student teachers. In PATT 29 conference proceedings.* Presses Universitaires de Provence.

Archer, M. (2000). *Being human: The problem of agency.* Cambridge University Press. doi:10.1017/CBO9780511488733

Armstrong, L. (2016). Barriers to innovation and change in higher education. *TIAA-CREF Institute.* Retrieved from https://pdfs.semanticscholar.org/d513/141cb6af397d22a68d99fa926 4875f888312.pdf

Arnuphaptrairong, T. (2011). Top Ten Lists of Software Project Risks: Evidence from the Literature Survey. *Proceedings of the International Multi Conference of Engineering and Computer Scientists.*

Aslett, M. & Curtis, J. (2019). *Accelerating AI with Data Management; Accelerating Data Management with AI.* Pathfinder Report. 451 Research.

Asnicar, F., & Tasso, C. (1997). ifWeb: a Prototype of User Model-based Intelligent Agent for Documentation Filtering and Navigation in the Word Wide Web. *Proceedings of the First International Workshop on Adaptive Systems and User Modeling on the World Wide Web, Sixth International Conference on User Modeling,* 3–12.

Avoiding Groupthink. Avoiding Fatal Flaws in Group Decision Making. (2019). *Mindtools.* Available in https://www.mindtools.com/pages/article/newLDR_82.htm

Badat, S. (2016). Deciphering the meanings and explaining the South African higher education student protests of 2015–16. *Pax Academica, 1,* 71–106.

Balabanovic, M., & Shoham, Y. (1997). Fab: Content-based, collaborative recommendation. *Commun Assoc Comput Mach, 40*(3), 66–72.

Bandler, R., Robert, A., & Fitzpatrick, O. (2013). *An Introduction To Nlp.* Harper Collins Publishers.

Bandura, A. (2002). Social cognitive theory in cultural context. *Applied Psychology, 51*(2), 269–290. doi:10.1111/1464-0597.00092

Barron, L. (2014). *Patton at the Battle of the Bulge: How the general's tanks turned the tide at Bastogne.* New York: Penguin Group.

Baruch, Y., & Holtom, B. C. (2008). Survey response rates and trends in organisational research. *Human Relations, 61*(1), 1139–1160. doi:10.1177/0018726708094863

Basu, C., Hirsh, H., & Cohen, W. (1998). Recommendation as classification: using social and content-based information in recommendation. *Proceedings of the fifteenth national conference on artificial intelligence (AAAI-98),* 714–720.

Baudet, M. B. (2019, March 26). Perché il Belgio è il focolaio del jihadismo europeo. *Internazionale.* Retrieved November 25, 2019 from https://www.internazionale.it/notizie/2016/03/23/belgio-jihadismo-europeo

BBC News. (2015, November 16). *Why is this Belgian suburb linked to so many terrorist attacks?* Retrieved November 27, 2019 from https://www.bbc.co.uk/programmes/p0385tzj

BBC News. (2016, April 9). *Brussels explosions: What we know about airport and metro attacks.* Retrieved November 30, 2019 from https://www.bbc.com/news/world-europe-35869985

BBC. (2018). Home – A VR Spacewalk. Retrieved from https://www.bbc.co.uk/taster/pilots/home-a-vr-spacewalk

Beckwith, P. (2019). *Paul Beckwith Climate Scientist.* Retrieved from web page https://paulbeckwith.net/

Behzadan, V., Munir, A., & Yampolskiy, R. V. (2018). A Psychopathological Approach to Safety Engineering in AI and AGI. *Proceedings of International Conference on Computer Safety, Reliability, and Security.* 10.1007/978-3-319-99229-7_46

Belhassein, K., Cochet, H., Clodic, A., Guidetti, M., & Alami, R. (2019). *From Children to Robots: How the parallel with developmental psychology can improve human-robot joint activities.* Academic Press.

Best VR headsets for 2020. (n.d.). Retrieved from https://www.gamespot.com/articles/best-vr-headsets-for-2020-half-life-alyx-compatibi/1100-6473057

Best VR headsets Review. (n.d.). Retrieved from https://www.tomsguide.com/us/best-vr-headsets,review-3550.html

Betts, R. (2007). *Enemies of Intelligence: Knowledge and Power in American National Security.* Columbia University Press.

Billinghurst, M., & Dünser, A. (2012). Augmented Reality in the Classroom. *Comput. (Long Beach Calif.), 45,* 56–63.

Blackburn, S. (2005). *The Oxford dictionary of philosophy.* OUP Oxford.

Bloch, M., Blumberg, S., & Laartz, J. (2012). *Delivering Large-Scale IT Projects on Time, on Budget, and on Value.* Retrieved from https://www.mckinsey.com/business-functions/mckinsey-digital/our-insights/delivering-large-scale-it-projects-on-time-on-budget-and-on-value#

Block, P. (2018). *Community: The structure of belonging.* San Francisco, CA: Berrett-Koehler. Retrieved June 15, 2019 from https://books.google.co.za/books?hl=en&lr=&id=9guXL4Yl8ekC&oi=fnd&pg=PR1&ots=mPJJF8eCDs&sig=P-ihsPZUjQCGYFU2hgZlna8qKqw&redir_esc=y#v=onepage&q&f=false

Bloom, P.N., & Chatterji, A.K. (2009). Scaling social entrepreneurship impact. *California Management Review, 53*(1), 114–133.

Bloom, P.N., & Smith, B.R. (2010). Identifying the drivers of social entrepreneurial impact: Theoretical development and an exploratory empirical test of SCALERS. *Journal of Social Entrepreneurship,* (1), 126–145.

Bloom, M., & Pope, C. (2017). *Climate of Hope, How cities, businesses, and citizens can save the planet.* St. Martins.

Bobadilla, J., Ortega, F., Hernando, A., & Gutiérrez, A. (2013). Recommender systems survey. *Knowledge-Based Systems, 46*, 109–132. doi:10.1016/j.knosys.2013.03.012

Boeren, E., & Whittaker, S. (2018). A typology of education and training provisions for low educated adults: Categories and definitions. *Studies in the Education of Adults, 50*(1), 4–18. do i:10.1080/02660830.2018.1520017

Boghosian, B. M. (2019, November). The Inescapable Casino, A novel approach developed by physicists and mathematicians describes the distribution of wealth in modern economies with unprecedented accuracy. *Scientific American, 321*(5), 70–77.

Bolden, R. (20078). Distributed leadership. university of Leadership. In A. Marturano & J. Gosling (Eds.), *Leadership: The Key Concepts* (1st ed., p. 1). Routledge., doi:10.4324/9780203099643

Bonabeau, E. (2002). Agent-Based Modeling: Methods and Techniques for Simulating Human Systems. *Proceedings of the National Academy of Sciences.*

Booker, C. (2018). *GLOBALWARMING. A case study in groupthink. How science can shed new light on the most important 'non-debate' of our time.* The Global Warming Policy Foundation GWPF Report 28.

Borum, R. (2003). Understanding the terrorist mindset. *FBI Law Enforcement Bulletin, 72*(7), 7-10. Retrieved November 30, 2019 from https://www.ncjrs.gov/pdffiles1/nij/grants/201462.pdf

Bosnić, I., Čavrak, I. & Žagar, M. (2019) Assessing the Impact of the Distributed Software Development Course on the Careers of Young Software Engineers. *ACM Transactions on Computing Education (TOCE), 19*(2).

Bouneffouf, D., Bouzeghoub, A., & Ganarski, A. L. (2013). Risk-aware recommender systems. In *Neural Information Processing* (pp. 57–65). Springer. doi:10.1007/978-3-642-42054-2_8

Brantly, A. (2016). *The decision to attack. Military and Intelligence Cyber Decision-making.* Studies in Security and International Affairs.

Britovšek, J., Tičar, B., & Sotlar, A. (2018). Private intelligence in the Republic of Slovenia: Theoretical, legal, and practical aspects. *Security Journal, 31*(2), 410–427. doi:10.105741284-017-0107-0

Brooks, R. (2019). Politics and protest – Students rise up worldwide. *University World News.* Retrieved June 15, 2019 from https://www.HEIworldnews.com/post.php?story=20160510173152311

Brooks, J. (2018). Promises of the virtual museum. *XRDS, 25*(2), 46–50. doi:10.1145/3301483

Brooks-Tatum, S. R. (2016). Delaware State University Guides Patrons into more Effective Research with Standardized Lib Guides. *Against the Grain (Charleston, S.C.), 24*(1), 7.

Brown, G. (2018). *Dirt to Soil, One family's journey into regenerative agriculture*. Chelsea Green Publishing.

Bruner, J. S. (1990). *Acts of meaning* (Vol. 3). Harvard University Press.

Burke, R. (2002). *User Modeling and User-Adapted Interaction*. doi:10.1023/A:1021240730564

Butti, G. (2016). *La tutela del capitale intellettuale*. http://www.sicurezzanazionale.gov.it

Caillou, P., Gaudou, B., Grignard, A., Truong, C. Q., & Taillandier, P. (2015). A Simple-to-Use BDI Architecture for Agent-based Modelling and Simulation. *Proceedings of the Eleventh Conference of the European Social Simulation Association (ESSA 2015)*.

Carey, S. (2009). *Success at a price: How NGO advocacy led to changes in South Africa's People's Housing Process*. Planact, GGLN and Rooftops Canada. http://citeseerx.ist.psu.edu/viewdoc/download;jsessionid=5D7EC70FE94F0921DC88874FF43C0C6C?doi=10.1.1.484.9038&rep=rep1&type=pdf

Carroll, S. B. (2016). *The Serengeti Rules, The quest to discover how life works and why it matters*. Princeton University Press.

Carter, N., Levin, S., Barlow, A. & Grimm, V. (2015). *Modelling Tiger Population and Territory Dynamics Using an Agent-Based Approach*. Ecol. Model.

Carter, P. (2019, June 25). *Spring 2019 Accelerating Global Warming & Atmospheric CO2*. Retrieved from TED Video at https://www.youtube.com/watch?v=RV3S4v5yTdA&t=658s

Carter, D. (2009). *Law Enforcement Intelligence: A Guide for State, Local, and Tribal Law Enforcement Agencies*. Office of Community Oriented Policing Services.

Charsky, D. (2010). From edutainment to serious games: A change in the use of game characteristics. *Games and Culture, 5*(2), 177–198. doi:10.1177/1555412009354727

Chen, L. S., Hsu, F. H., Chen, M. C., & Hsu, Y. C. (2008). Developing recommender systems with the consideration of product profitability for sellers. *Inf. Sci., 178*(4), 1032–1048. doi:10.1016/j.ins.2007.09.027

Chen, L., & Sycara, K. (1998). WebMate: A Personal Agent for Browsing and Searching. In *Proceedings of the 2nd International Conference on Autonomous Agents*, (pp. 9–13). ACM Press. 10.1145/280765.280789

Cheong, R.K.F., & Tsui, E. (2011). From Skills and Competencies to Outcome-based Collaborative Work: Tracking a Decade's Development of Personal Knowledge Management (PKM) Models, Knowledge and Process Management. *The Journal of Corporate Transformation, 18*(3), 175-193.

Cheong, R. K. F., & Tsui, E. (2010). The Roles and Values of Personal Knowledge Management: An exploratory study. *VINE Journal of Information and Knowledge Management Systems, 40*(2), 204–227.

Cheville, J. (2006). The bias of materiality in sociocultural research: Reconceiving embodiment. *Mind, Culture, and Activity, 13*(1), 25–37. doi:10.120715327884mca1301_3

Chin, K. O., Gan, K. S., Alfred, R., Anthony, P. & Lukose, D. (2014). Agent Architecture: An Overview. *Transactions on Science and Technology, 1*(1).

Chinyere, N. A. (2008). Lecturer-students. *African Journal of Education Management, 11*(1), 170–189.

Chois, K. (2012). A hybrid online-product recommendation system: Combining implicit rating-based collaborative filtering and sequential pattern analysis. *Electronic Commerce Research and Applications, 11*(4), 309–317. doi:10.1016/j.elerap.2012.02.004

Chomsky, N. (2017). *"10 Strategies of Manipulation" by the Media.* Retrieved in: https://politics1660.wordpress.com/2017/01/05/noam-chomsky-10-strategies-of-manipulation-by-the-media/

Christakis, N. A. (2019). *Blueprint, The evolutionary origins of a good society.* Little, Brown Spark.

Chui, M., Henke, N., & Miremadi, M. (2018, July). Most of AI's Business Uses Will Be in Two Areas. *Harvard Business Review,* 20.

Chu, W. T., & Tsai, Y. L. (2017). A hybrid recommendation system considering visual information for predicting favorite restaurants. *World Wide Web (Bussum), 20*(6), 1313–1331. doi:10.100711280-017-0437-1

Clancy, T. (1994). *The Chaos Report.* The Standish Group.

Clark, A. (2008). *Supersizing the mind: Embodiment, action, and cognitive extension.* OUP USA. doi:10.1093/acprof:oso/9780195333213.001.0001

Clarke, S. N., Howley, I., Resnick, L., & Penstein Rosé, C. (2016). Student agency to participate in dialogic science discussions. *Learning, Culture and Social Interaction, 10,* 27–39. Advance online publication. doi:10.1016/j.lcsi.2016.01.002

Claypool, M., Gokhale, A., & Miranda, T. (1999). Combining content-based and collaborative filters in an online newspaper. *Proceedings of the SIGIR-99 workshop on recommender systems: algorithms and evaluation.*

Clayton, M. (2019). *7 Uncomfortable Truths for Project Managers. Project Management Update.* Retrieved from https://www.projectmanagementupdate.com/ estimate/monitoring/?open-article-id= 9629696&article-title=7-uncomfortable-truths-for-project-managers &blog-domain=projectmanager.com&blog-title=projectmanager-com

Cohen, L., Manion, L., & Morrison, K. (2013). *Research methods in education.* Routledge. doi:10.4324/9780203720967

Cole, M. (1996). *Cultural psychology: A once and future discipline.* Harvard University Press.

Coombs, W. T. (2007). Protecting organization reputations during a crisis: The development and application of situational crisis communication theory. *Corporate Reputation Review*, *10*(3), 163-176. doi:10.1057/palgrave.crr.1550049

Coronado, S., & Jaén, J. A. (2002). *A Software Project Management Method: A3.* Paper presented at PMI® Research Conference 2002: Frontiers of Project Management Research and Applications, Seattle, WA.

Costanzo, B. (2014). *La protezione del segreto industriale.* http://www.sicurezzanazionale.gov.it

Cotter, P., & Smyth, B. (2000). PTV: intelligent personalized TV guides. *Twelfth conference on innovative applications of artificial intelligence*, 957–964.

Creswell, J. W. (2013). *Research design-qualitative, quantitative and mixed method approaches* (4th ed.). Sage.

Cristoferri, G. (2016). *Elan: "Le figure più richieste e meno reperibili".* Retrieved in: https://www.repubblica.it/economia/affari-e-finanza/2016/02/01/news/elan_le_figure_pi_richieste_e_meno_reperibili-132532463/

Cruickshank, P. (2017, October 30). The inside story of the Paris and Brussels attacks. *CNN.* Retrieved November 25, 2019 from https://edition.cnn.com/2016/03/30/europe/inside-paris-brussels-terror-attacks/index.html

Dalgaard-Nielsen, A. (2010). Violent radicalization in Europe: What we know and what we do not know. *Studies in Conflict and Terrorism*, *33*(9), 797–814. Retrieved November 27, 2019, from. doi:10.1080/1057610X.2010.501423

dall'Acqua, L. (2011). Didactical suggestion for a Dynamic Hybrid Intelligent e-Learning Environment (DHILE) applying the PENTHA ID Model. In *AIP, Conference Proceedings, Special Edition of the WCECS2010* (Vol. 1373, pp. 159-173). Academic Press.

dall'Acqua, L. (2014). Needs and strategies of KM in a multi-user environment: PENTHA Model view and analysis. *Jekpot KM19.*

dall'Acqua, L. (2019). Scientific Intelligence, Decision-Making and Cyber-Security. In *Forecasting and Managing Risk in the Health and Safety Sectors.* IGI Global.

dall'Acqua, L., & Santo, M. (2014). Orientism, the basic pedagogical approach of PENTHA ID Model vs. 2, to manage decisions in unpredictability conditions. *Proceedings of World Congress on Engineering and Computer Science WCECS2014*, *1*, 316-21.

Dall'Acqua, L. (2018). Risk Taxnomoy and Strategic Rationality in Enterprise Decision-Making Process. A Metacognitive Analysis. In *Improving Business Performance.* IGI Global.

Daugherty, P. R., & Wilson, H. J. (2019, Apr.). Using AI to Make Knowledge Workers More Effective. *Harvard Business Review*, 19.

Davidson, J., Liebald, B., Liu, J., Nandy, P., Van Vleet, T., Gargi, U., Gupta, S., He, Y., Lambert, M., Livingston, B., & Sampath, D. (2010). The YouTube video recommendation system. In *RecSys'10, Proceeding of the fourth ACM Conference Recommender Systems* (pp. 293-296). Academic Press.

Davies, K. U., Ekwere, G. E., & Uyanga, U. U. (2016). Factors influencing students unrest in institutions of higher learning and its implications on the academic performance of students in University of Uyo, Akwa Ibom State, Nigeria. *Istraživanja u pedagogiji, 6*(1), 27-42. doi:10.17810/2015.21

Davis, H., & Jones, S. (2014). The work of leadership in higher education management. *Journal of Higher Education Policy and Management, 36*(4), 367–370. doi:10.1080/1360080X.2014.916463

De Fazio, S. (2012). Nuove prospettive di ricerca in materia di atti persecutori: il fenomeno del cyberstalking. Rassegna Italiana di Criminologia, 3.

DeAngelis, D. L. & Diaz, S. G. (2019). Decision-Making in Agent-Based Modelling: A Current Review and Future Prospectus. *Journal of Frontiers in Ecology and Evolution, 6.*

DiGironimo, N. (2011). What is technology? Investigating student conceptions about the nature of technology. *International Journal of Science Education, 33*(10), 1337–1352. doi:10.1080/09500693.2010.495400

Discenza, R., & Forman, J. B. (2007). *Seven Causes of Project Failure: How to Recognize Them and How to Initiate Project Recovery.* Paper presented at PMI® Global Congress 2007.

Dourish, P. (2004). *Where the action is: The foundations of embodied interaction.* MIT Press.

Doyle, T., & Brady, M. (2018). Reframing the university as an emergent organisation: Implications for strategic management and leadership in higher education. *Journal of Higher Education Policy and Management, 40*(4), 305–320. doi:10.1080/1360080X.2018.1478608

Drost, E.A. (2011). Validity and reliability in social science research. *Education Research and Perspectives, 38*(1), 105–123.

Dusek, V. (2007). *Philosophy of technology: An introduction.* Blackwell Publishing.

Duus, R., Cooray, M., & Page, N. C. (2018). Exploring human-tech hybridity at the intersection of extended cognition and distributed agency: A focus on self-tracking devices. *Frontiers in Psychology, 9,* 9. doi:10.3389/fpsyg.2018.01432 PMID:30150957

Ealing, M. (2018). *PEST analysis identifying "big picture" opportunities and threats.* London: University of Westminster. Retrieved November 30, 2019 from https://www.academia.edu/37754145/PEST_Analysis

Eaton, J. (2001). Management communication: The threat of groupthink. *Corporate Communications, 6*(4), 183–192. doi:10.1108/13563280110409791

Edwards, A. (2005). Relational agency: Learning to be a resourceful practitioner. *International Journal of Educational Research, 43*(3), 168–182. doi:10.1016/j.ijer.2006.06.010

Edwards, J. (2010). A Process View of Knowledge Management: It ain't What You Do, It's the Way That You Do It. *Proceedings of the 11th European Conference on Knowledge Management.*

El Akkad, O. (2018). American War. New York: Vintage Books.

Ellis, L., & Brady, A. (2019). *Can These Books Save the Planet? The Rise of Climate Fiction.* Retrieved from YouTube Video by HotMess/PBS at https://www.youtube.com/watch?v=zUnTcNzLIVg

Elnakhala, D. (n.d.). *Ct overview: Belgium, 4TU Center for Ethics and Technology.* Retrieved November 20, 2019 from http://counterterrorismethics.com/the-belgian-counter-terrorism-landscape/

Enfei, L. (2015). *Risk Factors of Software Development Projects in Chinese IT Small and Medium Sized Enterprises.* KTH Royal Institute of Technology.

Engeström, Y. (2015). *Learning by expanding: An activity-theoretical approach to developmental research* (2nd ed.). Cambridge University Press.

Englander, J. (2013). *High Tide on Main Street, Rising sea level and the coming coastal crisis.* The Science Bookshelf.

European Council, Council of the European Union. (n.d.). *EU counter-terrorism strategy.* Retrieved November 21, 2019 from https://www.consilium.europa.eu/en/policies/fight-against-terrorism/eu-strategy/

European Council, Council of the European Union. (n.d.). *Response to the terrorist threat and recent terrorist attacks in Europe.* Retrieved November 21, 2019 from https://www.consilium.europa.eu/en/policies/fight-against-terrorism/foreign-fighters/

Europol. (2018). *European Union terrorism situation and trend.* Report. Retrieved November 20, 2019 from https://www.europol.europa.eu/activities-services/main-reports/european-union-terrorism-situation-and-trend-report-2018-tesat-2018

Ezzeldin, A. M. G. (2017). Faculty perceptions of the importance of communication in Saudi Arabia Higher Education Najran Community College: Case study. *Cogent Business & Management, 4*(1). doi: 10.1080/23311975.2017.1319007

Feinstein, N. (2010). Salvaging science literacy. *Science Education, 95*(1), 168–185. doi:10.1002ce.20414

Ferrando, F. (2019). *Philosophical Posthumanism.* Bloomsbury Publishing. doi:10.5040/9781350059511

Fiore, S. (2019). *Becoming Transhuman: A roadmap for Augmentation Cognition in the 21tst Century.* University of Central Florida.

Fischetti, M. (2019, November). Climate Clincher, The argument that global warming is part of a natural cycle is dead. *Scientific American, 321*(5), 86. doi:10.1038cientificamerican1101-86

Fisher, R. (2018). *Introduction to Security*. Butterworth-Heinemann.

Fitzgerald, J. (2007). *The need for transparency in lobbying. Democratic Audit of Australia.* Australian National University. https://www.parliament.sa.gov.au/Library/ReferenceShare/Documents/lobbying.pdf

Fomunyam, K. G. (2017). Student protest and the culture of violence at African universities: An inherited ideological trait. *Yesterday and Today*, (17), 38-63. doi:10.17159/2223-0386/2017/n17a3

Foundation for Climate Restoration. (2019, September). *Climate Restoration: Solutions to the greatest threat facing humanity and nature today.* Retrieved from a white paper at https://foundationforclimaterestoration.org/wp-content/uploads/2019/09/20190916b_f4cr4_white-paper.pdf

Gagné, R. M. (1985). *The Condition of Learning and Theory of Instruction.* CBS College Publishing.

Ghere, R.K. (2013). *NGO leadership and human rights.* https://ecommons.udayton.edu/pol_fac_pub/47

Gillespie, A. (2010). Position exchange: The social development of agency. *New Ideas in Psychology, 30*(1), 32–46. doi:10.1016/j.newideapsych.2010.03.004

Girardi, R., & Leite, A. (2013). A Survey on Software Agent Architectures. *IEEE Intelligent Informatics Bulletin, 14*(1).

Gironacci, I. (2012). *Virtual Environment modelling and development with Unity3D game engine.* Academic Press.

Gironacci, I. (2015). *Interactive Augmented Reality Mobile Applications.* Academic Press.

Gleick, J. (1987). *Chaos, Making of a new science.* Viking.

Gleick, J. (2000). *Faster: The acceleration of just about everything.* Little, Brown.

Goldsmith, M., Morgan, H., & Ogg, A. (2004). *Effectively Influencing Up:Ensuring That Your Knowledge, Makes a Difference. In Leading Organizational Learning.* Jossey-Bass.

Goller, M., & Harteis, C. (2017). Human Agency at Work: Towards a Clarification and Operationalisation of the Concept. In M. Goller & S. Paloniemi (Eds.), *Agency at Work. Professional and Practice-based Learning, 20.* Springer. doi:10.1007/978-3-319-60943-0_5

Good, N. (1999). Combining collaborative filtering with personal agents for better recommendations. *Proceedings of the sixteenth national conference on artificial intelligence (AAAI-99)*, 439–446.

Gore, A. (2006). *An Inconvenient Truth: The planetary emergency of global \warming and what we can do about it.* New York: Viking.

Greisman, H. C. (1979). Terrorism and the closure of society: A social-impact projection. *Technological Forecasting and Social Change, 14*(2), 135–146. doi:10.1016/0040-1625(79)90100-8

Grieger, T. (2006). Psychiatric and societal impacts of terrorism. *The Psychiatric Times, 23*(7), 1–2. Retrieved December 10, 2019, from https://www.psychiatrictimes.com/disaster-psychiatry/psychiatric-and-societal-impacts-terrorism

Griffin, R. (1991). Introduction. *Journal of Management, 17*(4), 787-787.

Grobler, A., & Jansen van Rensburg, M. (2018). Organisational climate, person–organisation fit and turn over intention: A generational perspective within a South African Higher Education Institution. *Studies in Higher Education*, 1–13. doi:10.1080/03075079.2018.1492533

Guattari, F. (1987). As creches e a iniciação. In F. Guattari (Ed.), *Revolução molecular: pulsações políticas do desejo* (pp. 50–55). Brasiliense.

Guo, Y., Wang, M., & Li, X. (2017). Application of an improved Apriori algorithm in a mobile e-commerce recommendation system. *Industrial Management & Data Systems, 117*(2), 287–303. doi:10.1108/IMDS-03-2016-0094

Ha, H., & Coghill, K. (2008). E-Government in Singapore a SWOT and PEST Analysis. *Asia-Pacific Social Science Review, 6*(2), 103-130. Retrieved April 13, 2020 from https://www.researchgate.net/publication/242314776_E-Government_in_Singapore_a_SWOT_and_PEST_Analysis

Haapasaari, A., & Kerosuo, H. (2015). Transformative agency: The challenges of sustainability in a long chain of double stimulation. *Learning, Culture and Social Interaction, 4*, 37–47. doi:10.1016/j.lcsi.2014.07.006

Habib, A. (2016). Transcending the past and reimagining the future of the South African university. *Journal of Southern African Studies, 42*(1), 35–48. doi:10.1080/03057070.2016.1121716

Hailey, J. (2006). *NGO leadership development: A review of literature. Praxis paper no. 10.* International NGO Training and Research Centre. https://www.alnap.org/pool/files/praxis-paper-10-ngo-leadership-development.pdf

Hall, H. (n.d.). *What Project Managers Should Know About Monitoring Project Risks.* Project Risk Coach. Retrieved from https://projectriskcoach.com/monitoring-project-risks/

Hanauer, N. (2019). *The dirty secret of capitalism -- and a new way forward.* Retrieved from TED Video at https://www.youtube.com/watch?v=th3KE_H27bs

Hansen, J. (2011). *Storms of My Grandchildren, The truth about the coming climate catastrophe and our last chance to save humanity.* Bloomsbury Publishing.

Hasted, G. P. (1987). The New Context of Intelligence Estimating: Politicization or Publicizing? Intelligence and Intelligence Policy in a Democratic Society. Transnational Publishers, Inc.

Hawken, P. (2017). *Drawdown, The most comprehensive plan ever proposed to revers global warming*. Penguin Books.

Hayles, N. K. (2010). How we became posthuman: Ten years on an interview with N. katherine hayles. *Paragraph, 33*(3), 318–330. doi:10.3366/para.2010.0202

Hays, J. (2009). *Ninjas in Japan and their history*. Retrieved in: http://factsanddetails.com/japan/cat16/sub107/item498.html

Hennicke, M. (2014). Birds of a feather, stronger together? Network externalities in NGO cooperation. *Ecole de Sciences Economiques de Louvain*, 1-23. http://federation.ens.fr/ydepot/semin/texte1314/HEN2014BIR.pdf

Hofmann, T. (1999). Probabilistic latent semantic analysis. In *Proceedings of the fifteenth conference on uncertainty in artificial intelligence*. Morgan Kaufmann.

Holme, N. H. (2002). *NGOs, networking, and problems of representation*. Linköpings University and ICER. https://www.icer.it/docs/wp2002/holmen33-02.pdf

Horton, T. (2017). *High Tide in Dorchester, A Bay Journal Documentary*. Retrieved from https://hightidedorchester.org/

Hunter, M. (2017). *The End We Start From*. Grove Press. A novel.

Illinois EnergyProf. (2019, May 14). *Reactors of the Future (Generation IV)*. University of Illinois at Urbana Champaign. Retrieved from a video lecture at https://www.youtube.com/watch?v=_mJ3S-VQuHY

Ineke, F., Sonneveld, W., & de Vries, M. (2010). Teaching and learning the nature of technical artifacts. *International Journal of Technology and Design Education, 21*, 277–290.

INFOSEC. (2018, February 3). *The role of technology in modern terrorism*. Retrieved November 22, 2019 from https://resources.infosecinstitute.com/the-role-of-technology-in-modern-terrorism/

It's Just Astronomical! (2019, October 13). *Where are we in the Milankovitch Cycles?* Retrieved from a TED Video at https://www.youtube.com/watch?v=eB3DJtQZVsw

Ivanov, A. (1997). Advanced networking: A conceptual approach to NGO-based early response strategies in conflict prevention. Occasional paper no. 11. Berlin: Berghof Research Center for Constructive Conflict Management.

Janis, I.L. (1972). Victims of Groupthink. *Political Psychology, 12*(2), 247-278.

Janis, I. L. (1982). *Groupthink: Psychological studies of policy decisions and fiascoes*. Houghton Mifflin.

Jannach, D., & Hegelich, K. (2009). A case study on the effectiveness of recommendations in the mobile internet. *Proceedings of the 3rd ACM Conference on Recommender Systems*, 205–208. 10.1145/1639714.1639749

Jiménez, M., Piattini, M. & Vizcaíno, A. (2009). Challenges and Improvements in Distributed Software Development: A Systematic Review. *Advance in Software Engineering*.

Jindals, S. (2016). *Electronic Warfare: An Indispensable Aspect Of Modern War*. Discussion in Indian Defence Forum.

Jing, Y., Liu, D., Kislyuk, D., Zhai, A., Xu, J., Donahue, J., & Tavel, S. (2015). Visual Search at Pinterest. *KDD'15, Proceedings of the 21th ACM SIGKDD International Conference Knowledge Discovery and Data Mining*, 1889-1898. 10.1145/2783258.2788621

Kajamaa, A., & Kumpulainen, K. (2019). Agency in the making: Analyzing students' transformative agency in a school-based makerspace. *Mind, Culture, and Activity, 26*(3), 266–281. doi:10.108 0/10749039.2019.1647547

Keefe, P. (2010). *Privatized spying: the emerging intelligence industry*. Loch Johnson.

Khan, M. S., Khan, I., Qureshi, Q. A., Ismail, H. M., Rauf, H., Latif, A., & Tahir, M. (2015). The styles of leadership: A critical review. *Public Policy and Administration Research, 5*(3), 87–92.

Kiboiy, K. L. (2013). *The dynamics of student unrests in Kenya's higher education: the case of Moi University* (Doctoral dissertation, University of Pretoria). Retrieved April 5, 2019 from https://repository.up.ac.za/bitstream/handle/2263/32399/kiboiy_dynamics_2013.pdf?sequence=4

Kilhefner, J. (2019). *Groupthink Examples in Business*. Available in: https://work.chron.com/groupthink-examples-business-21692.html

Kirer Silva Lecuna, H. (2016). A Survey of Agent-Based Approach of Complex Networks. *Ekonomik Yaklasim., 27*(98), 1. doi:10.5455/ey.35900

Kirshenbaum, E., Forman, G., & Dugan, M. (2012). A live comparison of methods for personalized article recommendation at Forbes.com. In *Machine Learning and Knowledge Discovery in Databases* (pp. 51–66). Springer. doi:10.1007/978-3-642-33486-3_4

Knorr Cetina, K. D. (2001). Objectual practice. In The practice turn in contemporary theory. Routledge.

Knorr Cetina, K. D. (2009). *Epistemic cultures: How the sciences make knowledge*. Harvard University Press. doi:10.2307/j.ctvxw3q7f

Kroet, C. (2016, January 1). Belgium has most foreign fighters per head: Anti-terror report says most radicalized fighters come from Just 4 EU countries. *Politico*. Retrieved November 25, 2019 from https://www.politico.eu/article/a-third-of-isil-foreign-fighters-return-to-europe-report/

Kruse, K. (2013). *What is leadership?* Forbes Magazine. http://www.forbes.com/sites/kevinkruse/2013/04/09/what-is-leadership/#79016146713e

Krystal. (2019). *Top 8 Causes of Project Failure in 2020*. Retrieved from https://www.softwaresuggest.com/blog/top-causes-project-failure/

Kumar, R. (2005). *Research methodology: A step-by-step guide for beginners*. Pearson Longman.

Kumpulainen, K., Rajala, A., & Kajamaa, A. (2019). Researching the materiality of communication in an educational makerspace The meaning of social objects. In N. Mercer, R. Wegerif, & L. Major (Eds.), *The Routledge International Handbook of Research on Dialogic Education. Routledge.* doi:10.4324/9780429441677-36

Labib, A., Read, M., Gladstone-Millar, C., Tonge, R., & Smith, D. (2013). Formulation of higher education institutional strategy using operational research approaches. *Studies in Higher Education, 39*(5), 885–904. doi:10.1080/03075079.2012.754868

Langa, M., Ndelu, S., Edwin, Y., & Vilakazi, M. (2017). *Hashtag: An Analysis of the #FeesMustFall Movement at South African Universities* (1st ed.). Africa Portal. Retrieved from https://www.africaportal.org/publications/hashtag-an-analysis-of-the-feesmustfall-movement-at-south-african-universities/

Lasoen, K. L. (2017). For Belgian eyes only: Intelligence cooperation in Belgium. *International Journal of Intelligence and CounterIntelligence, 30*(3), 464–490. doi:10.1080/08850607.2017.1297110

Lasoen, K. L. (2018). Plan B(ruxellles): Belgian intelligence and the terrorist attacks of 2015-16. *Terrorism and Political Violence,* 1–19. doi:10.1080/09546553.2018.1464445

Latour, B. (1991). Technology is society made durable. In J. Law (Ed.), *A sociology of monster: Essays 132.* Routledge.

Latour, B. (1996). On actor-network theory: A few clarifications plus more than a few complications. *Soziale Welt, 47,* 369–381.

Latour, B. (2012). *We have never been modern.* Harvard University Press.

Lawrence, N. D., & Urtasun, R. (2009). Non-linear matrix factorization with gaussian processes. *Proceedings of the 26th Annual International Conference on Machine Learning.* doi:10.1145/1390156.1390267

Lee, J. (2006). *Comparing NGO influence in the EU and the U.S. Centre for Applied Studies in International Negotiations.* https://www.files.ethz.ch/isn/25102/ngoinfluenceinuandusa.pdf

Lee, J. K., & Rao, H. R. (2005). *Risk of Terrorism, Trust in Government, and e-Government Services: An Exploratory Study of Citizens' Intention to use e-Government Services in a Turbulent Environment.* YCISS Working Paper Number 30, pp.1-27. Retrieved April 13, 2020 from https://yorkspace.library.yorku.ca/xmlui/bitstream/handle/10315/1348/YCI0020.pdf?

Lee, J., Sun, M., & Lebanon, G. (2012). *A Comparative Study of Collaborative Filtering Algorithms.* ArXiv, abs/1205.3193

Lee, L. N., Kim, M. J., & Hwang, W. J. (2019). Potential of Augmented Reality and Virtual Reality Technologies to Promote Wellbeing in Older Adults. Applied Sciences (Basel, Switzerland), 2019(9), 3556. doi:10.3390/app9173556

Lee, D., & Seung, H. (1999). Learning the parts of objects by non-negative matrix factorization. *Nature*, *401*(6755), 788–791. doi:10.1038/44565 PMID:10548103

Lee, S. K., Cho, Y. H., & Kim, S. H. (2010). Collaborative filtering with ordinal scale-based implicit ratings for mobile music recommendations. *Information Sciences*, *180*(11), 2142–2155. doi:10.1016/j.ins.2010.02.004

Lekorwe, M., & Mpabanga, D. (2007). Managing non-governmental organisations in Botswana. *The Public Sector Innovation Journal*, *12*(3), 1–18.

Lenovo Mirage Solo Specs. (n.d.). Retrieved from https://www.lenovo.com/ca/en/virtual-reality-and-smart-devices/virtual-and-augmented-reality/lenovo-mirage-solo/Mirage-Solo/p/ZZIRZRHVR01

Lenovo Mirage Solo with Daydream Review. (n.d.). Retrieved from https://www.theverge.com/2018/5/4/17318648/lenovo-mirage-solo-google-daydream-standalone-vr-headset-review

Lenz Taguchi, H., & Palmer, A. (2014). Reading a Deleuzio-Guattarian cartography of young girls'"school-related" ill-/well-being. *Qualitative Inquiry*, *20*(6), 764–771. doi:10.1177/1077800414530259

Lieberman, H. (1995). Letizia: an Agent that Assists Web Browsing. *Proceedings of the International Joint Conference on Artificial Intelligence*, 924–929.

Liew, M. S., Shahdan, T. T., & Lim, E. S. (2012). Strategic and tactical approaches on university-industry collaboration. *Procedia: Social and Behavioral Sciences*, *56*, 405–409. doi:10.1016/j.sbspro.2012.09.669

Linden, G., Smith, B., & York, J. (2003). Amazon.com recommendations: Item-to-item collaborative filtering. *IEEE Internet Computing*, *7*(1), 76–80. doi:10.1109/MIC.2003.1167344

Liu, J., Dolan, P., & Pedersen, E. R. (2010). Personalized news recommendation based on click behavior. *Proceedings of the 15th International Conference on Intelligent User Interfaces, IUI '10*, 31–40. 10.1145/1719970.1719976

Luescher-Mamashela, T. M. (2013). Student representation in university decision making: Good reasons, a new lens? *Studies in Higher Education*, *38*(10), 1442–1456. doi:10.1080/03075079.2011.625496

Luff, R. (2015). *Review of NGOs leadership roles in clusters*. International Council of Voluntary Agencies. www.alnap.org/pool/files/176-review-of-ngo-leadership-roles-in-clusters.pdf

Mandin, J. (2014). *An overview of integration policies in Belgium.* INTERACT RR 2014/20, Robert Schuman Centre for Advanced Studies, San Domenico di Fiesole (FI): European University Institute. Retrieved November 21, 2019 from http://diana-n.iue.it:8080/bitstream/handle/1814/33133/INTERACT-RR-2014%20-%2020.pdf?sequence=1&isAllowed=y

Mann, M. E., & Roles, T. (2016). *The Madhouse Affect, How climate change denial is threatening our planet, destroying our politics, and driving us crazy.* Columbia University Press. doi:10.7312/mann17786

Marr, B. (2019). *Why Every Company Needs An Artificial Intelligence (AI) Strategy For 2019.* Forbes. Retrieved from https://www.forbes.com/sites/bernardmarr/2019/03/21/why-every-company-needs-an-artificial-intelligence-ai-strategy-for-2019/#18da0fd468ea

Marrin, S. (2013). Revisiting Intelligence and Policy: Problems with Politicization and Receptivity. In Intelligence and National Security. Routledge.

Marschark, M., Lang, H. G., & Albertini, J. A. (2002). *Educating Deaf Students: From Research to Practice.* University Press.

Martiniello, M. (2003). Belgium's immigration policy. *The International Migration Review*, *37*(1), 225–232. doi:10.1111/j.1747-7379.2003.tb00135.x

Matheson, R. (2019a, Nov. 2). *Better Autonomous "Reasoning" At Tricky Intersections: Model Alerts Driverless Cars When It's Safest to Merge into Traffic at Intersections with Obstructed Views.* MIT News.

Matheson, R. (2019b, May 22). *Bringing Human-Like Reasoning to Driverless Car Navigation: Autonomous Control System 'Learns' to Use Simple Maps and Image Data to Navigate New, Complex Routes.* MIT News.

McAfee, A. (2019). *More from Less, The surprising story of how we learned to prosper using fewer resources – and what happens next.* Scribner.

McMaster University. (n.d.). *McMaster's Core Leadership Capabilities.* Retrieved from https://cauce-aepuc.ca/documents/conference/2018/Mac-Core-Leadership-Capabilities-Card.pdf

Mele, S. (2014). *Le best practice in materia di cyber-security per le PMI.* http://www.sicurezzanazionale.gov.it

Melville, P., Mooney, R. J., & Nagarajan, R. (2002). Content-boosted collaborative filtering for improved recommendations. *Proceedings of the eighteenth national conference on artificial intelligence (AAAI-02)*, 187–192.

Menezes, M. J. (2019). *Can we create an empathic alternative to the capitalist system?* Retrieved from World Economic Forum at https://www.weforum.org/agenda/2019/08/empathy-can-create-a-new-economic-system/

Mercer, N., Wegerif, R., & Major, L. (2019). The Routledge International Handbook of Research on Dialogic Education. Taylor & Francis Ltd. doi:10.4324/9780429441677

Miller, I. W., Ryan, C. E., Keitner, G. I., Bishop, D. S., & Epstein, N. B. (2000). The McMaster approach to families: Theory, assessment, treatment and research. *Journal of Family Therapy*, *22*(2), 168–189. doi:10.1111/1467-6427.00145

Mills, K. (2019, June). How AI Could Help Small Businesses. *Harvard Business Review*, 3.

Mintz A., Wayne C. (2016). *The Polythink Syndrome: U.S. Foreign Policy Decisions on 9/11, Afghanistan, Iraq, Iran, Syria, and ISIS*. Stanford University Press.

Mintz, A., & Schneiderman, I. (2018). From groupthink to polythink in the yom kippur war decisions of 1973. *European Review of International Studies.*, 5(1), 48–66. doi:10.3224/eris.v5i1.03

Mintz, A., & Wayne, C. (2014). Group decision making in conflict: From groupthink to polythink in the war in Iraq. In P. T. Coleman, M. Deutsch, & E. C. Marcus (Eds.), *The handbook of conflict resolution: Theory and practice* (pp. 331–352). Jossey-Bass.

Mirza, N. M., Grossen, M., de Diesbach-Dolder, S., & Nicollin, L. (2014). Transforming personal experience and emotions through secondarisation in education for cultural diversity: An interplay between unicity and genericity. *Learning, Culture and Social Interaction*, 3(4), 263–273. doi:10.1016/j.lcsi.2014.02.004

Mitcham, C. (1994). *Thinking through technology*. The University of Chicago Press.

Mixed Reality Specs. (n.d.). Retrieved from https://www.tomshardware.com/reviews/hp-windows-mixed-reality-headset,5665.html

Miyahara, K., & Pazzani, M. J. (2002). *Improvement of collaborative filtering with the simple bayesian classifier*. Academic Press.

Miyahara, K., & Pazzani, M. J. (2000). Collaborative filtering with the simple bayesian classifier. *Proceedings of the 6th Pacific Rim International Conference on Artificial Intelligence*, 679–689. 10.1007/3-540-44533-1_68

Mjema, M. M. (2013). *The Causes and Management of Students' Unrest at the University of Arusha in Tanzania* (Doctoral dissertation). The Open University of Tanzania.

Mladenic, D. (1999). Text-learning and Related Intelligent Agents: A Survey. *IEEE Intelligent Systems*, 14(4), 44–54. doi:10.1109/5254.784084

Moghaddam, F. M. (2005). The staircase to terrorism: A psychological exploration. *American Psychological Association, 60*(2), 161–169. Retrieved December 2, 2019 from https://www.academia.edu/3450594/The_staircase_to_terrorism_a_psychological_on

Momoh, G. T., Oluwasanu, M. M., Oduola, O. L., Delano, G. E., & Ladipo, O. A. (2015). Outcome of a reproductive health advocacy mentoring intervention for staff of selected non-governmental organisations in Nigeria. *BMC Health Services Research*, 15(314), 1–9. doi:10.118612913-015-0975-0 PMID:26259953

Moore, J. W. (2016). What is the sense of agency and why does it matter? *Frontiers in Psychology*, 7, 1272. doi:10.3389/fpsyg.2016.01272 PMID:27621713

Morano, C. P. (2015). *Cyber security, intrusion detection systems e intelligenza artificiale*. http://www.sicurezzanazionale.gov.it

Moscovici, S., & Zavalloni, M. (1969). The group as a polarizer of attitudes. *Journal of Personality and Social Psychology, 12*(2), 125–135. doi:10.1037/h0027568

Moukas, A. (1997). Amalthaea Information Discovery and Filtering Using a Multiagent Evolving Ecosystem. *Applied Artificial Intelligence, 11*(5), 437–457. doi:10.1080/088395197118127

Muslims in Belgium. (2008). *Insights, 1*(2), 119-144. Retrieved November 19, 2019 from http://www.euro-islam.info/spip/article.php3?id_article=2168

Nadeem, M. A. & Lee, S. U-J. (2019). Dynamic Agile Distributed Development Method. *Mathematics, 7*(10).

Name, J. (2019). Deep Learning for Audio-Based Music Classification and Tagging. IEEE Signal Processing Magazine, 36(1).

Nelson, R., & Sanderson, T. M. (2011). *A threat transformed: Al Qaeda and associated movements in 2011*. Center for Strategic and International Studies. Retrieved December 10, 2019 from https://csis-prod.s3.amazonaws.com/s3fs-public/legacy_files/files/publication/110203_Nelson_AThreatTransformed_web.pdf

Nenty, H. J. (2009). Writing a quantitative research thesis. *International Journal of Education Science, 1*(1), 19–32.

Ngcamu, B. S., & Teferra, D. (2015). How well do university staff understand transformation? A case of a merged South African University. *International Journal of Educational Sciences, 8*(2), 305-312. doi:10.1080/09751122.2015.11890252

Niantic, I. (n.d.). Pokémon GO Plus System Requirements and Compatibility–Pokémon Support. Available online: https://support.pokemon.com/hc/en-us/articles/360000938393-Pokémon-GO-Plus-system-requirements-and-compatibility

Ninja Museum of Igaryu Igaueno. (2019). Retrieved in: https://www.iganinja.jp/en/museum/index.html

NIS Cooperation Group. (2019). *EU coordinated risk assessment of the cybersecurity of 5G networks*.

Nordhaus, W. (2013). *The Climate Casino, Risk, uncertainty, and economics of a warming world*. Yale University Press.

Oculus Go Specs. (n.d.). Retrieved from https://www.theverge.com/2018/5/1/17306458/oculus-go-standalone-vr-headset-review

Oculus Quest Pro and Cons. (n.d.). Retrieved from https://www.engadget.com/2019/04/30/oculus-quest-review-wireless-vr

Oculus Quest. (n.d.). Retrieved from https://www.forbes.com/sites/solrogers/2019/05/03/oculus-quest-the-best-standalone-vr-headset/#64d6e4e08ed8

Oculus Rift S Specs by RoadVR. (n.d.). Retrieved from https://www.roadtovr.com/palmer-luckey-oculus-founder-rift-s-optimal-70-population-ipd/

Oculus Rift S vs HTC Vive. (n.d.). Retrieved from https://versus.com/en/htc-vive-vs-oculus-rift-s

Oculus Rift S vs Oculus Quest. (n.d.). Retrieved from https://www.windowscentral.com/oculus-rift-s-vs-oculus-quest

Oculus Rift. (n.d.). Specifications. Retrieved from https://www.tomshardware.com/reviews/oculus-rift-s-vr-headset,6148.html

OECD. (2002). Economic consequences of terrorism. *Economic Outlook*, *71*, 117–140. Retrieved November 23, 2019, from https://www.oecd.org/economy/outlook/1935314.pdf

Ofoegbu, F. O., & Alonge, H. O. (2017). Effective university leadership as predictor of academic excellence in Southern Nigerian universities. *Journal of Education and Practice*, *8*(8), 111–116.

OHCHR. (2018, May 23). *France: UN expert says new terrorism laws may undermine fundamental rights and freedoms.* Retrieved November 22, 2019 from https://www.ohchr.org/EN/NewsEvents/Pages/DisplayNews.aspx?NewsID=23130&LangID=E

Ohize, E., & Adamu, M. J. (2009). Case study of youth empowerment scheme of Niger State, Nigeria in poverty alleviation. *AU Journal of Technology*, *13*(1), 47–52.

Omari, I. M., & Mihyo, P. B. (1991). *Roots of student unrest in African universities.* Retrieved from https://idl-bnc-idrc.dspacedirect.org/bitstream/handle/10625/9855/92427.pdf?sequence=1

Pasquale, L., De Gemmis, M., & Semeraro, G. (2010). *Recommender Systems Handbook. Springer Science Business Media, LLC.* doi:10.1007/978-0-387-85820-3_3

Pawlak, M., & Poniszewska-Marańda, A. (2018). Software Test Management Approach for Agile Environments. *Information Systems Management*, *7*(1).

Pazzani, M. J. (1999). A framework for collaborative, content-based and demographic filtering. *Artificial Intelligence Review*, *13*(5–6), 393–408. doi:10.1023/A:1006544522159

Pazzani, M. J., & Billsus, D. (2007). Content-Based Recommendation Systems. In P. Brusilovsky, A. Kobsa, & W. Nejdl (Eds.), Lecture Notes in Computer Science: Vol. 4321. *The Adaptive Web.* Springer. doi:10.1007/978-3-540-72079-9_10

Pazzani, M. J., Muramatsu, J., & Billsus, D. (1996). Syskill and Webert: Identifying Interesting Web Sites. In *Proceedings of the Thirteenth National Conference on Artificial Intelligence and the Eighth Innovative Applications of Artificial Intelligence Conference*, (pp. 54–61). AAAI Press / MIT Press.

Pea, R., & Cole, M. (2019). The Living Hand of the Past: The Role of Technology in Development. *Human Development*, *62*(1-2), 14–39. doi:10.1159/000496073

Perez, A. (2019, Jan.). Leveraging the Beliefs-Desires-Intentions Agent Architecture. *MSDN Magazine*.

Pesheva, E. & Menting, A. M. (2020, Winter). One Giant Step: Researchers are Building an Artificial Intelligence System that can Mimic Human Clinical Decision Making. *Harvard Medicine*.

Pinker, S. (2011). *The Better Angels of Our Nature, Why Violence Has Declined*. Viking.

Pitt, J. (2000). *Thinking about technology - Foundations of the philosophy of technology*. Seven Bridges Press.

Popescul, A., Ungar, L., Pennock, D. M., & Lawrence, S. (2001). Probabilistic models for unified collaborative and content-based recommendation in sparse-data environments. In *Proceedings of the seventeenth conference on uncertainity in artificial intelligence*. University of Washington.

Procházka, A., Dostálová, T., Kašparová, M., Vyšata, O., Charvátová, H., Sanei, S., & Mařík, V. (2019). Augmented Reality Implementations in Stomatology. Applied Sciences (Basel, Switzerland), 9(14), 2929. doi:10.3390/app9142929

Prunckun, H. (2013). *Intelligence and Private Investigation: Developing Sophisticated Methods for Conducting Inquiries*. Charles Thomas.

Puyvelde, V. (2019). *Outsourcing US Intelligence*. Edinburgh University Press. doi:10.3366/edinburgh/9781474450225.001.0001

Rao, A., Likens, S., Baccala, M., & Shehab, M. (2019). *AI Predictions Six AI priorities you can't afford to ignore*. PWC. Retrieved from https://www.pwc.com/us/en/services/consulting/library/artificial-intelligence-predictions-2019.html

Reno. (1999). *Cyberstalking: a new challenge for law enforcement and industry*. A report from the US Attorney General to the Vice President Al Gore.

Rhodes, R. A. (2007). Understanding governance: Ten years on. *Organization Studies*, *28*(8), 1243–1264. doi:10.1177/0170840607076586

Riley, J. T., & dall'Acqua, L. (2019). *Narrative Thinking and Storytelling for Problem Solving in Science Education*. Hershey PA: IGI Global. Retrieved from https://www.igi-global.com/book/narrative-thinking-storytelling-problem-solving/217376

Riley, T. (2016). Big Moon Dig Stories" *The Big Moon Dig*. Retrieved from Web page at https://bigmoondig.com/Stories/BMDStories.html

Riley, T. (2018). Curse the Salt. *The Big Moon Dig/Stories*. Retrieved from short story at https://bigmoondig.com/Stories/BMDSalt.pdf

Ring, M., & Orseau, L. (2011). Delusion, Survival, and Intelligent Agents. *Proceedings of the 4th International Conference, AGI 2011*.

Ronald, N., Sterling, L., & Kirley, M. (2007). An agent-based approach to modelling pedestrian behaviour. *Simulation*, *8*(1), 1473–8031.

Ross, S. (2019, May 20). *Top 5 ways terrorism impacts the economy.* Investopedia. Retrieved December 10, 2019 from https://www.investopedia.com/articles/markets/080216/top-5-ways-terrorism-impacts-economy.asp

Rozenes, S., Vitner, G., & Spraggett, S. (2006). Project Control: Literature Review. *Project Management Journal, 37*(4), 5–14. doi:10.1177/875697280603700402

Russel, S. J., & Norvig, P. (2015). *Artificial Intelligence, A Modern Approach, Third Addition.* Person Education.

Saccone, U. (2014). *Lo sviluppo di un sistema antifrode: considerazioni programmatiche e ruolo della Security.* http://www.sicurezzanazionale.gov.it

Saccone, U. (2015). *Security aziendale e protezione dei lavoratori all'estero.* http://www.sicurezzanazionale.gov.it

Sageman, M. (2008). A strategy for fighting international islamist terrorists. *The Annals of the American Academy of Political and Social Science, 618*(1), 223–231. doi:10.1177/0002716208317051

Salakhutdinov, R., & Mnih, A. (2008). Bayesian probabilistic matrix factorization using markov chain monte carlo. *Proceedings of the International Conference on Machine Learning.*

Salakhutdinov, R., & Mnih, A. (2008). Probabilistic matrix factorization. *Advances in Neural Information Processing Systems.*

Samata, S. (2016). Language, exclusion and violent jihad: Are they related? *International Journal of Bilingual Education and Bilingualism,* 1–10. Retrieved November 23, 2019, from. doi:10.10 80/13670050.2016.1208143

Sarwar, B. M., Karypis, G., Konstan, J., & Riedl, J. (2002). Recommender systems for largescale e-commerce: Scalable neighborhood formation using clustering. *Proceedings of the 5th International Conference on Computer and Information Technology.*

Savery, A. (2013, February). *How to green the world's deserts and reverse climate change.* Retrieved from TED video at https://www.ted.com/talks/allan_savory_how_to_green_the_world_s_deserts_and_reverse_climate_change?language=en

Savory, A., & Butterfield, J. (2016). *Holistic Management, A commonsense revolution to restore our environment.* Island Press.

Schein, A. I., Popescul, A., Ungar, L. H., & Pennock, D. M. (2002). Methods and metrics for cold-start recommendations. In *SIGIR '02: proceedings of the 25th annual international ACM SIGIR conference on research and development in information retrieval.* ACM. 10.1145/564376.564421

Schlesinger, M. & Parisi, D. (2001). The Agent-Based Approach: A New Direction for Computational Models of Development. Developmental Review. *Science Direct, 21*(1).

Schmid, H., Bar, M., & Nirel, R. (2008). Advocacy activities in nonprofit human service organisations: Implications for policy. *Nonprofit and Voluntary Sector Quarterly*, *37*(4), 581–602. doi:10.1177/0899764007312666

Schreuer, M. (2019, January 5). Belgium bans religious slaughtering practices, drawing praise and protest. *The New York Times*. Retrieved November 27, 2019 from https://www.nytimes.com/2019/01/05/world/europe/belgium-ban-jewish-muslim-animal-slaughter.html

Sebola, M. P. (2017). Communication in the South African public participation process-the effectiveness of communication tools. *African Journal of Public Affairs*, *9*(6), 25–35. https://hdl.handle.net/10520/EJC-754d2f95f

Sekaran, U., & Bougie, R. (2016). *Research methods for business*. John Wiley & Sons.

Shakhova, N. (2017). *Current rates and mechanisms of subsea permafrost degradation in the East Siberian Arctic Shelf*. Retrieved from Nature Communications at https://www.nature.com/articles/ncomms15872

Shaw, C. (2013). How should universities respond to student protests? 10 views. *The Guardian*. Retrieved June 15, 2019 from https://www.theguardian.com/higher-education-network/blog/2013/dec/11/student-protest-how-should-management-respond

Shorrock, T. (2008). *Spies for hire: the secret world of intelligence outsourcing*. Simon & Schuster.

Silber, M. D., & Bhatt, A. (2007). *Radicalization in the West: The homegrown threat*. The New York City Police Department.

Smith, C. H. (2019). Reality Hacking as Intelligence Augmentation. Creative Innovation 2019, Melbourne, Australia.

Soboroff, I., & Nicholas, C. (2000). Collaborative filtering and the generalized vector space model (poster session). *Proceedings of the 23rd annual international conference on Research and development in information retrieval*, 351–353. 10.1145/345508.345646

Spalek, S. (2005). *Critical Success Factors in Project Management: To Fail or Not to Fail, That is the Question!* Paper presented at PMI® Global Congress 2005—EMEA, Edinburgh, UK.

Srebro, N., Rennie, J. D. M., & Jaakola, T. S. (2005). *Maximum-margin matrix factorization* (Vol. 17). MIT Press.

Srivastava, R., Palshikar, G. K., Chaurasia, S., & Dixit, A. (2018). What's Next? A Recommendation System for Industrial Training. *Data Sci. Eng.*, *3*(3), 232–247. doi:10.100741019-018-0076-2

Steffen, W. (2018). Trajectories of the Earth System in the Anthropocene. *The Proceedings of the National Academy of Sciences*, *115*(33), 8252-8259. Retrieved from Web article at https://www.pnas.org/content/115/33/8252

Stetsenko, A. (2017). *The transformative mind: Expanding Vygotsky's approach to development and education*. Cambridge University Press. doi:10.1017/9780511843044

Stoner, J. (1968, October). Risky and cautious shifts in group decisions: The influence of widely held values. *Journal of Experimental Social Psychology*, *4*(4), 442–459. doi:10.1016/0022-1031(68)90069-3

Su, X., Greiner, R., Khoshgoftaar, T. M., & Zhu, X. (2007). Hybrid collaborative filtering algorithms using a mixture of experts. Web Intelligence, 645–649. doi:10.1109/WI.2007.10

Sullivan, G. M. (2011). A primer on the validity of assessment instruments. *Journal of Graduate Medical Education*, *3*(2), 119–120. doi:10.4300/JGME-D-11-00075.1 PMID:22655129

Taylor, P. (2019). *From Information Warfare to Information Operation to the global war on terrorism*. Lecture 4, ICS, University of Leeds. Available in: https://slideplayer.com/slide/16461516/

Team, F. M. E. (2013). *PESTLE analysis: Strategy skills. Electronic Publication: Free Management Ebooks*. Retrieved December 10, 2019 from https://docplayer.net/9768722-Pestle-analysis-strategy-skills team-fme-www-free-management ebooks-com-isbn-978-1-62620-998-5.html

Techcrunch. (2014). *Netflix's Neil Hunt Says Personalized Recommendations Will Replace The Navigation Grid*. Retrieved from https://techcrunch.com/2014/05/19/netflix-neil-hunt-internet-week/

Tenza, M. (2015). An investigation into the causes of violent protest actions in South Africa: Some lessons from foreign law and possible solutions. *Law. Democracy & Development*, *19*(1), 211–231. doi:10.4314/ldd.v19i1.11

Terzi, M. (2019). E-Government and Cyber Terrorism: Conceptual Framework, Theoretical Discussion and Possible Solutions. *TESAM Akademi Dergisi - Turkish Journal of TESAM Academy*, *6*(1), 213-247. Retrieved April 13, 2020 from https://dergipark.org.tr/en/pub/tesamakademi/article/528011

Test Institute. (n.d.). *What is Software Risk and Software Risk Management?* Retrieved from https://www.test-institute.org/What_Is_Software_Risk_And_Software_Risk_Management.php

The National Interest. (2019, February 22). *Technology is making terrorists more effective and harder to thwart*. Retrieved November 22, 2019 from https://nationalinterest.org/feature/technology-making-terrorists-more-effective—and-harder-thwart-45452

The Verge. (2017). Sephora's latest app updated lets you try virtual makeup on at home with AR. Retrieved from https://www.theverge.com/2017/3/16/14946086/sephora-virtual-assistant-ios-app-update-ar-makeup

Thompson, N. (2016). *Anti-discriminatory practice: Equality, diversity and social justice*. Macmillan International Higher Education. doi:10.1007/978-1-137-58666-7

Tillman, N. (2018). The Big Melt. South Branch Press.

Timmerman, C., Vanderwaeren, E., & Crul, M. (2003). The second generation in Belgium. *The International Migration Review*, *37*(4), 1065–1090. doi:10.1111/j.1747-7379.2003.tb00170.x

Tonge, A., Kasture, S. S., & Chaudhari, S. (2013). Cyber Security: challenges for society – literature review. *IOSR Journal of Computer Engineering, 12*(2), 67-75. https://pdfs.semanticscholar.org/6 1fd/814aae913ed3f0ab6459625ffc6944952757.pdf?_ga=2.84089305.199330368.1560936122-811949187.1560936122

Towards Data Science. (2019). *Product Recommender using Amazon Review dataset.* Retrieved from https://towardsdatascience.com/product-recommender-using-amazon-review-dataset-e69d479d81dd

Traynor, I. (2015, November 15). Molenbeek: The Brussels borough becoming known as Europe's jihadi central. *The Guardian.* Retrieved November 26, 2019 from https://www.theguardian.com/world/2015/nov/15/molenbeek-the-brussels-borough-in-the spotlight-after-paris-attacks

Trottier, D. (2014). *The Screenwriter's Bible, A complete guide to writing, formatting and selling your script.* Silman-James Press.

Trump, D. J. (2018). *National strategy for counterterrorism of the United States of America.* Washington, DC: The White House. Retrieved 28 November 2019 from https://www.whitehouse.gov/wp-content/uploads/2018/10/NSCT.pdf

Ungar, L. H., & Foster, D. P. (1998). Clustering methods for collaborative filtering. *AAAI Workshop on Recommendation Systems.*

University of Nottingham. (2016). *Drive for results.* Retrieved from https://www.nottingham.ac.uk/hr/guidesandsupport/performanceatwork/pdpr/pdpr-behavioural-competency-guide/achieving-and-delivery/drive-for-results.aspx

Valdéz, E. R. (2012). Implicit feedback techniques on recommender systems applied to electronic books. *Computers in Human Behavior, 28*(4), 1186–1193. doi:10.1016/j.chb.2012.02.001

Valsiner, J. (2000). Culture and human development. *Sage (Atlanta, Ga.).*

Valsiner, J. (2014). *An invitation to cultural psychology.* Sage. doi:10.4135/9781473905986

Valve Index Official Website. (n.d.). Retrieved from https://www.valvesoftware.com/en/index

Valve Index Review. (n.d.). Retrieved from https://www.tomshardware.com/reviews/valve-index-vr-headset-controllers,6205.html

Van Ostaeyen, P. (2016). Belgian radical networks and the road to the Brussels attacks. *CTC Sentinel, 9*(613), 7-12. Retrieved December 2, 2019 from https://ctc.usma.edu/belgian-radical-networks-and-the-road-to-the-brussels-attacks/

Venkataraman, B. (2019). *The Optimist's Telescope, Thinking ahead in a reckless age.* Riverhead Books.

Venture Scanner. (2017). *Artificial Intelligence Startup Highlights.* Author.

Vetoshkina, L. (2019). *ANCHORING: CRAFT. The object as an intercultural and intertemporal unifying factor* (PhD Thesis). Helsinki Studies in Education.

Vive Pro Features. (n.d.). Retrieved from https://www.vive.com/us/product/vive-pro/

Vive Std Features. (n.d.). Retrieved from https://www.vive.com/

Voskina, S., & Alan Hatton, T. (2019, October 1). *Faradaic electro-swing reactive adsorption for CO_2 capture*. Retrieved from Energy & Environmental Science at https://pubs.rsc.org/en/content/articlelanding/2019/ee/c9ee02412c#!divAbstract

Vucetic, S., & Obradovic, Z. (2005). Collaborative filtering using a regression-based approach. *Knowledge and Information Systems*, *7*(1), 1–22. doi:10.100710115-003-0123-8

Vygotsky, L. S. (1978). *Mind in society* (M. Cole, V. John-Steiner, S. Scribner, & E. Souberman, Eds.). Harvard University Press.

Wadhams, P. (2017). *A Farewell to Ice, A report from the Arctic*. Oxford Press.

Waghid, Y., & Davids, N. (2016). Educational leadership as action: Towards an opening of rhythm. *South African Journal of Higher Education*, *30*(1), 1753–5913. doi:10.20853/30-1-554

Wagner, G., & Weitzman, M. L. (2015). *Climate Shock, The economic consequences of a hotter planet*. Princeton University Press. doi:10.1515/9781400865475

Wang, Y., Chan, C. F., & Ngai, G. (2012). *Applicability of demographic recommender system to tourist attractions: A case study on trip advisor*. Paper Presented at *IEEE/WIC/ACM International Conference on Web Intelligence and Intelligent Agent Technology*. 10.1109/WI-IAT.2012.133

Warner, D., & Palfreyman, D. (1996). *Higher education management: The key elements*. Retrieved from https://books.google.co.za/books/about/Higher_education_management.html?id=6JklAQAAIAAJ&redir_esc=y

Waterfield, B. (2011, December 6). Belgium to have new government after world record 541 days. *The Telegraph*. Retrieved November 27, 2019 from https://www.telegraph.co.uk/news/worldnews/europe/belgium/8936857/Belgium-to-have-new government-after-world-record-541-days.html

Watson, D. (2000). *Managing universities and colleges: Guides to good practice Managing strategy*. Open University.

Webbstock, D., & Fisher, G. (2016). *South African higher education reviewed: Two decades of democracy*. Retrieved June 15, 2019 from https://www.che.ac.za/sites/default/files/publications/CHE_South%20African%20higher%20education%20reviewed%20-%20electronic.pdf

Weimann, G. (2004). Cyberterrorism. How Real Is the Threat? *United State Institute of Peace*. Retrieved April 13, 2020 from https://www.usip.org/sites/default/files/sr119.pdf

Which VR headsets can you actually buy? (n.d.). Retrieved from https://www.theverge.com/2019/5/16/18625238/vr-virtual-reality-headsets-oculus-quest-valve-index-htc-vive-nintendo-labo-vr-2019

White, J. (2017). *Tides, The science and spirit of the ocean*. Trinity University Press.

Wiktorowicz, Q. (2004). *Joining the cause: Al-Muhajiroun and radical Islam.* Paper: Department of International Studies, Rhodes College. Retrieved November 26, 2019 from https://securitypolicylaw.syr.edu/wp-content/uploads/2013/03/Wiktorowicz.Joining-the-Cause.pdf

Williams, L. K., Koch, T. M., & Smith, J. M. (2013). The political consequences of terrorism: Terror events, casualties, and government duration. *International Studies Perspectives, 14*(3), 343–361. doi:10.1111/j.1528-3585.2012.00498.x

Wilner, A. S., & Dubouloz, C. J. (2010). Homegrown terrorism and transformative learning: An interdisciplinary approach to understanding radicalization. *Global Change, Peace & Security, 22*(1), 33–51. doi:10.1080/14781150903487956

Wilson, E. O. (2012). *The Social Conquest of Earth.* Liveright Publishing.

Wilson, E. O. (2019). *Genesis, the deep origin of societies.* Liveright Publishing.

Wilson, J. (2014). *Essentials of business research: A guide to doing your research project.* Sage.

Wired. (2017). Ikea's new app flaunts what you'll love more about AR. Retrieved from: https://www.wired.com/story/ikea-place-ar-kit-augmented-reality/

Wirtz, J. J. (2003). Review of Strategy: The Logic of War and Peace. *Journal of Cold War Studies, 5*(3), 115–116.

Wonderful Wanderings. (2015, May 19). *Belgium explained: Language and political structure.* YouTube Video. Retrieved December 2, 2019 from https://www.youtube.com/watch?v=2ehWO-f_6uk

Wu, H.-K., Lee, S. W.-Y., Chang, H.-Y., & Liang, J.-C. (2013). Current status, opportunities and challenges of augmented reality in education. *Computers & Education, 62*, 41–49. doi:10.1016/j.compedu.2012.10.024

Wu, L. (2014). The browsemaps: Collaborative filtering at LinkedIn. *CEUR Workshop Proceedings,* •••, 1271.

Xue, G. R. (2005). Scalable collaborative filtering using cluster-based smoothing. In *Proceedings of the 28th annual international ACM SIGIR conference on Research and development in information retrieval,* (pp. 114–121). ACM.

Yasuda, Y. (2015). *Rules, norms and NGO advocacy strategies: Hydropower development on the Mekong River.* Routledge Taylor & Francis Group. doi:10.4324/9781315687179

Yen, J.-C., Tsai, C.-H., & Wu, M. (2013). Augmented reality in the higher education: Students' science concept learning and academic achievement in astronomy. *Procedia: Social and Behavioral Sciences, 103*, 165–173. doi:10.1016/j.sbspro.2013.10.322

Yu, K., Zhu, S., Lafferty, J., & Gong, Y. (2009). Fast nonparametric matrix factorization for large-scale collaborative filtering. *Proc. of the international ACM SIGIR conference on Research and development in information retrieval.* 10.1145/1571941.1571979

Zaltman, G., & Zaltman, L. (2008). *Marketing Metaphoria: What Deep Metaphors Reveal about the Minds of Consumers*. Harvard Business School Press.

Zhao, W. X., Li, S., He, Y., Wang, L., Wen, J.-R., & Li, X. (2016). Exploring demographic information in social media for product recommendation. *Knowledge and Information Systems, 49*(1), 61–89. doi:10.100710115-015-0897-5

Zuber-Skerritt, O. (2007). Leadership development in South African higher education: The heart of the matter. *South African Journal of Higher Education, 21*(7), 984–1005.

Related References

To continue our tradition of advancing information science and technology research, we have compiled a list of recommended IGI Global readings. These references will provide additional information and guidance to further enrich your knowledge and assist you with your own research and future publications.

Aasi, P., Rusu, L., & Vieru, D. (2017). The Role of Culture in IT Governance Five Focus Areas: A Literature Review. *International Journal of IT/Business Alignment and Governance, 8*(2), 42-61. doi:10.4018/IJITBAG.2017070103

Abdrabo, A. A. (2018). Egypt's Knowledge-Based Development: Opportunities, Challenges, and Future Possibilities. In A. Alraouf (Ed.), *Knowledge-Based Urban Development in the Middle East* (pp. 80–101). Hershey, PA: IGI Global. doi:10.4018/978-1-5225-3734-2.ch005

Abu Doush, I., & Alhami, I. (2018). Evaluating the Accessibility of Computer Laboratories, Libraries, and Websites in Jordanian Universities and Colleges. *International Journal of Information Systems and Social Change*, *9*(2), 44–60. doi:10.4018/IJISSC.2018040104

Adeboye, A. (2016). Perceived Use and Acceptance of Cloud Enterprise Resource Planning (ERP) Implementation in the Manufacturing Industries. *International Journal of Strategic Information Technology and Applications*, *7*(3), 24–40. doi:10.4018/IJSITA.2016070102

Adegbore, A. M., Quadri, M. O., & Oyewo, O. R. (2018). A Theoretical Approach to the Adoption of Electronic Resource Management Systems (ERMS) in Nigerian University Libraries. In A. Tella & T. Kwanya (Eds.), *Handbook of Research on Managing Intellectual Property in Digital Libraries* (pp. 292–311). Hershey, PA: IGI Global. doi:10.4018/978-1-5225-3093-0.ch015

Adhikari, M., & Roy, D. (2016). Green Computing. In G. Deka, G. Siddesh, K. Srinivasa, & L. Patnaik (Eds.), *Emerging Research Surrounding Power Consumption and Performance Issues in Utility Computing* (pp. 84–108). Hershey, PA: IGI Global. doi:10.4018/978-1-4666-8853-7.ch005

Afolabi, O. A. (2018). Myths and Challenges of Building an Effective Digital Library in Developing Nations: An African Perspective. In A. Tella & T. Kwanya (Eds.), *Handbook of Research on Managing Intellectual Property in Digital Libraries* (pp. 51–79). Hershey, PA: IGI Global. doi:10.4018/978-1-5225-3093-0.ch004

Agarwal, R., Singh, A., & Sen, S. (2016). Role of Molecular Docking in Computer-Aided Drug Design and Development. In S. Dastmalchi, M. Hamzeh-Mivehroud, & B. Sokouti (Eds.), *Applied Case Studies and Solutions in Molecular Docking-Based Drug Design* (pp. 1–28). Hershey, PA: IGI Global. doi:10.4018/978-1-5225-0362-0.ch001

Ali, O., & Soar, J. (2016). Technology Innovation Adoption Theories. In L. Al-Hakim, X. Wu, A. Koronios, & Y. Shou (Eds.), *Handbook of Research on Driving Competitive Advantage through Sustainable, Lean, and Disruptive Innovation* (pp. 1–38). Hershey, PA: IGI Global. doi:10.4018/978-1-5225-0135-0.ch001

Alsharo, M. (2017). Attitudes Towards Cloud Computing Adoption in Emerging Economies. *International Journal of Cloud Applications and Computing*, 7(3), 44–58. doi:10.4018/IJCAC.2017070102

Amer, T. S., & Johnson, T. L. (2016). Information Technology Progress Indicators: Temporal Expectancy, User Preference, and the Perception of Process Duration. *International Journal of Technology and Human Interaction*, 12(4), 1–14. doi:10.4018/IJTHI.2016100101

Amer, T. S., & Johnson, T. L. (2017). Information Technology Progress Indicators: Research Employing Psychological Frameworks. In A. Mesquita (Ed.), *Research Paradigms and Contemporary Perspectives on Human-Technology Interaction* (pp. 168–186). Hershey, PA: IGI Global. doi:10.4018/978-1-5225-1868-6.ch008

Anchugam, C. V., & Thangadurai, K. (2016). Introduction to Network Security. In D. G., M. Singh, & M. Jayanthi (Eds.), Network Security Attacks and Countermeasures (pp. 1-48). Hershey, PA: IGI Global. doi:10.4018/978-1-4666-8761-5.ch001

Anchugam, C. V., & Thangadurai, K. (2016). Classification of Network Attacks and Countermeasures of Different Attacks. In D. G., M. Singh, & M. Jayanthi (Eds.), Network Security Attacks and Countermeasures (pp. 115-156). Hershey, PA: IGI Global. doi:10.4018/978-1-4666-8761-5.ch004

Anohah, E. (2016). Pedagogy and Design of Online Learning Environment in Computer Science Education for High Schools. *International Journal of Online Pedagogy and Course Design*, 6(3), 39–51. doi:10.4018/IJOPCD.2016070104

Anohah, E. (2017). Paradigm and Architecture of Computing Augmented Learning Management System for Computer Science Education. *International Journal of Online Pedagogy and Course Design*, 7(2), 60–70. doi:10.4018/IJOPCD.2017040105

Anohah, E., & Suhonen, J. (2017). Trends of Mobile Learning in Computing Education from 2006 to 2014: A Systematic Review of Research Publications. *International Journal of Mobile and Blended Learning*, 9(1), 16–33. doi:10.4018/IJMBL.2017010102

Assis-Hassid, S., Heart, T., Reychav, I., & Pliskin, J. S. (2016). Modelling Factors Affecting Patient-Doctor-Computer Communication in Primary Care. *International Journal of Reliable and Quality E-Healthcare*, 5(1), 1–17. doi:10.4018/IJRQEH.2016010101

Bailey, E. K. (2017). Applying Learning Theories to Computer Technology Supported Instruction. In M. Grassetti & S. Brookby (Eds.), *Advancing Next-Generation Teacher Education through Digital Tools and Applications* (pp. 61–81). Hershey, PA: IGI Global. doi:10.4018/978-1-5225-0965-3.ch004

Balasubramanian, K. (2016). Attacks on Online Banking and Commerce. In K. Balasubramanian, K. Mala, & M. Rajakani (Eds.), *Cryptographic Solutions for Secure Online Banking and Commerce* (pp. 1–19). Hershey, PA: IGI Global. doi:10.4018/978-1-5225-0273-9.ch001

Baldwin, S., Opoku-Agyemang, K., & Roy, D. (2016). Games People Play: A Trilateral Collaboration Researching Computer Gaming across Cultures. In K. Valentine & L. Jensen (Eds.), *Examining the Evolution of Gaming and Its Impact on Social, Cultural, and Political Perspectives* (pp. 364–376). Hershey, PA: IGI Global. doi:10.4018/978-1-5225-0261-6.ch017

Banerjee, S., Sing, T. Y., Chowdhury, A. R., & Anwar, H. (2018). Let's Go Green: Towards a Taxonomy of Green Computing Enablers for Business Sustainability. In M. Khosrow-Pour (Ed.), *Green Computing Strategies for Competitive Advantage and Business Sustainability* (pp. 89–109). Hershey, PA: IGI Global. doi:10.4018/978-1-5225-5017-4.ch005

Basham, R. (2018). Information Science and Technology in Crisis Response and Management. In M. Khosrow-Pour, D.B.A. (Ed.), Encyclopedia of Information Science and Technology, Fourth Edition (pp. 1407-1418). Hershey, PA: IGI Global. doi:10.4018/978-1-5225-2255-3.ch121

Batyashe, T., & Iyamu, T. (2018). Architectural Framework for the Implementation of Information Technology Governance in Organisations. In M. Khosrow-Pour, D.B.A. (Ed.), Encyclopedia of Information Science and Technology, Fourth Edition (pp. 810-819). Hershey, PA: IGI Global. doi:10.4018/978-1-5225-2255-3.ch070

Bekleyen, N., & Çelik, S. (2017). Attitudes of Adult EFL Learners towards Preparing for a Language Test via CALL. In D. Tafazoli & M. Romero (Eds.), *Multiculturalism and Technology-Enhanced Language Learning* (pp. 214–229). Hershey, PA: IGI Global. doi:10.4018/978-1-5225-1882-2.ch013

Bennett, A., Eglash, R., Lachney, M., & Babbitt, W. (2016). Design Agency: Diversifying Computer Science at the Intersections of Creativity and Culture. In M. Raisinghani (Ed.), *Revolutionizing Education through Web-Based Instruction* (pp. 35–56). Hershey, PA: IGI Global. doi:10.4018/978-1-4666-9932-8.ch003

Bergeron, F., Croteau, A., Uwizeyemungu, S., & Raymond, L. (2017). A Framework for Research on Information Technology Governance in SMEs. In S. De Haes & W. Van Grembergen (Eds.), *Strategic IT Governance and Alignment in Business Settings* (pp. 53–81). Hershey, PA: IGI Global. doi:10.4018/978-1-5225-0861-8.ch003

Bhatt, G. D., Wang, Z., & Rodger, J. A. (2017). Information Systems Capabilities and Their Effects on Competitive Advantages: A Study of Chinese Companies. *Information Resources Management Journal*, 30(3), 41–57. doi:10.4018/IRMJ.2017070103

Bogdanoski, M., Stoilkovski, M., & Risteski, A. (2016). Novel First Responder Digital Forensics Tool as a Support to Law Enforcement. In M. Hadji-Janev & M. Bogdanoski (Eds.), *Handbook of Research on Civil Society and National Security in the Era of Cyber Warfare* (pp. 352–376). Hershey, PA: IGI Global. doi:10.4018/978-1-4666-8793-6.ch016

Boontarig, W., Papasratorn, B., & Chutimaskul, W. (2016). The Unified Model for Acceptance and Use of Health Information on Online Social Networks: Evidence from Thailand. *International Journal of E-Health and Medical Communications*, 7(1), 31–47. doi:10.4018/IJEHMC.2016010102

Brown, S., & Yuan, X. (2016). Techniques for Retaining Computer Science Students at Historical Black Colleges and Universities. In C. Prince & R. Ford (Eds.), *Setting a New Agenda for Student Engagement and Retention in Historically Black Colleges and Universities* (pp. 251–268). Hershey, PA: IGI Global. doi:10.4018/978-1-5225-0308-8.ch014

Burcoff, A., & Shamir, L. (2017). Computer Analysis of Pablo Picasso's Artistic Style. *International Journal of Art, Culture and Design Technologies*, 6(1), 1–18. doi:10.4018/IJACDT.2017010101

Byker, E. J. (2017). I Play I Learn: Introducing Technological Play Theory. In C. Martin & D. Polly (Eds.), *Handbook of Research on Teacher Education and Professional Development* (pp. 297–306). Hershey, PA: IGI Global. doi:10.4018/978-1-5225-1067-3.ch016

Calongne, C. M., Stricker, A. G., Truman, B., & Arenas, F. J. (2017). Cognitive Apprenticeship and Computer Science Education in Cyberspace: Reimagining the Past. In A. Stricker, C. Calongne, B. Truman, & F. Arenas (Eds.), *Integrating an Awareness of Selfhood and Society into Virtual Learning* (pp. 180–197). Hershey, PA: IGI Global. doi:10.4018/978-1-5225-2182-2.ch013

Carlton, E. L., Holsinger, J. W. Jr, & Anunobi, N. (2016). Physician Engagement with Health Information Technology: Implications for Practice and Professionalism. *International Journal of Computers in Clinical Practice, 1*(2), 51–73. doi:10.4018/IJCCP.2016070103

Carneiro, A. D. (2017). Defending Information Networks in Cyberspace: Some Notes on Security Needs. In M. Dawson, D. Kisku, P. Gupta, J. Sing, & W. Li (Eds.), Developing Next-Generation Countermeasures for Homeland Security Threat Prevention (pp. 354-375). Hershey, PA: IGI Global. doi:10.4018/978-1-5225-0703-1.ch016

Cavalcanti, J. C. (2016). The New "ABC" of ICTs (Analytics + Big Data + Cloud Computing): A Complex Trade-Off between IT and CT Costs. In J. Martins & A. Molnar (Eds.), *Handbook of Research on Innovations in Information Retrieval, Analysis, and Management* (pp. 152–186). Hershey, PA: IGI Global. doi:10.4018/978-1-4666-8833-9.ch006

Chase, J. P., & Yan, Z. (2017). Affect in Statistics Cognition. In *Assessing and Measuring Statistics Cognition in Higher Education Online Environments: Emerging Research and Opportunities* (pp. 144–187). Hershey, PA: IGI Global. doi:10.4018/978-1-5225-2420-5.ch005

Chen, C. (2016). Effective Learning Strategies for the 21st Century: Implications for the E-Learning. In M. Anderson & C. Gavan (Eds.), *Developing Effective Educational Experiences through Learning Analytics* (pp. 143–169). Hershey, PA: IGI Global. doi:10.4018/978-1-4666-9983-0.ch006

Chen, E. T. (2016). Examining the Influence of Information Technology on Modern Health Care. In P. Manolitzas, E. Grigoroudis, N. Matsatsinis, & D. Yannacopoulos (Eds.), *Effective Methods for Modern Healthcare Service Quality and Evaluation* (pp. 110–136). Hershey, PA: IGI Global. doi:10.4018/978-1-4666-9961-8.ch006

Cimermanova, I. (2017). Computer-Assisted Learning in Slovakia. In D. Tafazoli & M. Romero (Eds.), *Multiculturalism and Technology-Enhanced Language Learning* (pp. 252–270). Hershey, PA: IGI Global. doi:10.4018/978-1-5225-1882-2.ch015

Cipolla-Ficarra, F. V., & Cipolla-Ficarra, M. (2018). Computer Animation for Ingenious Revival. In F. Cipolla-Ficarra, M. Ficarra, M. Cipolla-Ficarra, A. Quiroga, J. Alma, & J. Carré (Eds.), *Technology-Enhanced Human Interaction in Modern Society* (pp. 159–181). Hershey, PA: IGI Global. doi:10.4018/978-1-5225-3437-2. ch008

Cockrell, S., Damron, T. S., Melton, A. M., & Smith, A. D. (2018). Offshoring IT. In M. Khosrow-Pour, D.B.A. (Ed.), Encyclopedia of Information Science and Technology, Fourth Edition (pp. 5476-5489). Hershey, PA: IGI Global. doi:10.4018/978-1-5225-2255-3.ch476

Coffey, J. W. (2018). Logic and Proof in Computer Science: Categories and Limits of Proof Techniques. In J. Horne (Ed.), *Philosophical Perceptions on Logic and Order* (pp. 218–240). Hershey, PA: IGI Global. doi:10.4018/978-1-5225-2443-4.ch007

Dale, M. (2017). Re-Thinking the Challenges of Enterprise Architecture Implementation. In M. Tavana (Ed.), *Enterprise Information Systems and the Digitalization of Business Functions* (pp. 205–221). Hershey, PA: IGI Global. doi:10.4018/978-1-5225-2382-6.ch009

Das, A., Dasgupta, R., & Bagchi, A. (2016). Overview of Cellular Computing-Basic Principles and Applications. In J. Mandal, S. Mukhopadhyay, & T. Pal (Eds.), *Handbook of Research on Natural Computing for Optimization Problems* (pp. 637–662). Hershey, PA: IGI Global. doi:10.4018/978-1-5225-0058-2.ch026

De Maere, K., De Haes, S., & von Kutzschenbach, M. (2017). CIO Perspectives on Organizational Learning within the Context of IT Governance. *International Journal of IT/Business Alignment and Governance, 8*(1), 32-47. doi:10.4018/ IJITBAG.2017010103

Demir, K., Çaka, C., Yaman, N. D., İslamoğlu, H., & Kuzu, A. (2018). Examining the Current Definitions of Computational Thinking. In H. Ozcinar, G. Wong, & H. Ozturk (Eds.), *Teaching Computational Thinking in Primary Education* (pp. 36–64). Hershey, PA: IGI Global. doi:10.4018/978-1-5225-3200-2.ch003

Deng, X., Hung, Y., & Lin, C. D. (2017). Design and Analysis of Computer Experiments. In S. Saha, A. Mandal, A. Narasimhamurthy, S. V, & S. Sangam (Eds.), Handbook of Research on Applied Cybernetics and Systems Science (pp. 264-279). Hershey, PA: IGI Global. doi:10.4018/978-1-5225-2498-4.ch013

Denner, J., Martinez, J., & Thiry, H. (2017). Strategies for Engaging Hispanic/ Latino Youth in the US in Computer Science. In Y. Rankin & J. Thomas (Eds.), *Moving Students of Color from Consumers to Producers of Technology* (pp. 24–48). Hershey, PA: IGI Global. doi:10.4018/978-1-5225-2005-4.ch002

Devi, A. (2017). Cyber Crime and Cyber Security: A Quick Glance. In R. Kumar, P. Pattnaik, & P. Pandey (Eds.), *Detecting and Mitigating Robotic Cyber Security Risks* (pp. 160–171). Hershey, PA: IGI Global. doi:10.4018/978-1-5225-2154-9.ch011

Dores, A. R., Barbosa, F., Guerreiro, S., Almeida, I., & Carvalho, I. P. (2016). Computer-Based Neuropsychological Rehabilitation: Virtual Reality and Serious Games. In M. Cruz-Cunha, I. Miranda, R. Martinho, & R. Rijo (Eds.), *Encyclopedia of E-Health and Telemedicine* (pp. 473–485). Hershey, PA: IGI Global. doi:10.4018/978-1-4666-9978-6.ch037

Doshi, N., & Schaefer, G. (2016). Computer-Aided Analysis of Nailfold Capillaroscopy Images. In D. Fotiadis (Ed.), *Handbook of Research on Trends in the Diagnosis and Treatment of Chronic Conditions* (pp. 146–158). Hershey, PA: IGI Global. doi:10.4018/978-1-4666-8828-5.ch007

Doyle, D. J., & Fahy, P. J. (2018). Interactivity in Distance Education and Computer-Aided Learning, With Medical Education Examples. In M. Khosrow-Pour, D.B.A. (Ed.), Encyclopedia of Information Science and Technology, Fourth Edition (pp. 5829-5840). Hershey, PA: IGI Global. doi:10.4018/978-1-5225-2255-3.ch507

Elias, N. I., & Walker, T. W. (2017). Factors that Contribute to Continued Use of E-Training among Healthcare Professionals. In F. Topor (Ed.), *Handbook of Research on Individualism and Identity in the Globalized Digital Age* (pp. 403–429). Hershey, PA: IGI Global. doi:10.4018/978-1-5225-0522-8.ch018

Eloy, S., Dias, M. S., Lopes, P. F., & Vilar, E. (2016). Digital Technologies in Architecture and Engineering: Exploring an Engaged Interaction within Curricula. In D. Fonseca & E. Redondo (Eds.), *Handbook of Research on Applied E-Learning in Engineering and Architecture Education* (pp. 368–402). Hershey, PA: IGI Global. doi:10.4018/978-1-4666-8803-2.ch017

Estrela, V. V., Magalhães, H. A., & Saotome, O. (2016). Total Variation Applications in Computer Vision. In N. Kamila (Ed.), *Handbook of Research on Emerging Perspectives in Intelligent Pattern Recognition, Analysis, and Image Processing* (pp. 41–64). Hershey, PA: IGI Global. doi:10.4018/978-1-4666-8654-0.ch002

Filipovic, N., Radovic, M., Nikolic, D. D., Saveljic, I., Milosevic, Z., Exarchos, T. P., ... Parodi, O. (2016). Computer Predictive Model for Plaque Formation and Progression in the Artery. In D. Fotiadis (Ed.), *Handbook of Research on Trends in the Diagnosis and Treatment of Chronic Conditions* (pp. 279–300). Hershey, PA: IGI Global. doi:10.4018/978-1-4666-8828-5.ch013

Fisher, R. L. (2018). Computer-Assisted Indian Matrimonial Services. In M. Khosrow-Pour, D.B.A. (Ed.), Encyclopedia of Information Science and Technology, Fourth Edition (pp. 4136-4145). Hershey, PA: IGI Global. doi:10.4018/978-1-5225-2255-3.ch358

Fleenor, H. G., & Hodhod, R. (2016). Assessment of Learning and Technology: Computer Science Education. In V. Wang (Ed.), *Handbook of Research on Learning Outcomes and Opportunities in the Digital Age* (pp. 51–78). Hershey, PA: IGI Global. doi:10.4018/978-1-4666-9577-1.ch003

García-Valcárcel, A., & Mena, J. (2016). Information Technology as a Way To Support Collaborative Learning: What In-Service Teachers Think, Know and Do. *Journal of Information Technology Research*, *9*(1), 1–17. doi:10.4018/JITR.2016010101

Gardner-McCune, C., & Jimenez, Y. (2017). Historical App Developers: Integrating CS into K-12 through Cross-Disciplinary Projects. In Y. Rankin & J. Thomas (Eds.), *Moving Students of Color from Consumers to Producers of Technology* (pp. 85–112). Hershey, PA: IGI Global. doi:10.4018/978-1-5225-2005-4.ch005

Garvey, G. P. (2016). Exploring Perception, Cognition, and Neural Pathways of Stereo Vision and the Split–Brain Human Computer Interface. In A. Ursyn (Ed.), *Knowledge Visualization and Visual Literacy in Science Education* (pp. 28–76). Hershey, PA: IGI Global. doi:10.4018/978-1-5225-0480-1.ch002

Ghafele, R., & Gibert, B. (2018). Open Growth: The Economic Impact of Open Source Software in the USA. In M. Khosrow-Pour (Ed.), *Optimizing Contemporary Application and Processes in Open Source Software* (pp. 164–197). Hershey, PA: IGI Global. doi:10.4018/978-1-5225-5314-4.ch007

Ghobakhloo, M., & Azar, A. (2018). Information Technology Resources, the Organizational Capability of Lean-Agile Manufacturing, and Business Performance. *Information Resources Management Journal*, *31*(2), 47–74. doi:10.4018/IRMJ.2018040103

Gianni, M., & Gotzamani, K. (2016). Integrated Management Systems and Information Management Systems: Common Threads. In P. Papajorgji, F. Pinet, A. Guimarães, & J. Papathanasiou (Eds.), *Automated Enterprise Systems for Maximizing Business Performance* (pp. 195–214). Hershey, PA: IGI Global. doi:10.4018/978-1-4666-8841-4.ch011

Gikandi, J. W. (2017). Computer-Supported Collaborative Learning and Assessment: A Strategy for Developing Online Learning Communities in Continuing Education. In J. Keengwe & G. Onchwari (Eds.), *Handbook of Research on Learner-Centered Pedagogy in Teacher Education and Professional Development* (pp. 309–333). Hershey, PA: IGI Global. doi:10.4018/978-1-5225-0892-2.ch017

Gokhale, A. A., & Machina, K. F. (2017). Development of a Scale to Measure Attitudes toward Information Technology. In L. Tomei (Ed.), *Exploring the New Era of Technology-Infused Education* (pp. 49–64). Hershey, PA: IGI Global. doi:10.4018/978-1-5225-1709-2.ch004

Grace, A., O'Donoghue, J., Mahony, C., Heffernan, T., Molony, D., & Carroll, T. (2016). Computerized Decision Support Systems for Multimorbidity Care: An Urgent Call for Research and Development. In M. Cruz-Cunha, I. Miranda, R. Martinho, & R. Rijo (Eds.), *Encyclopedia of E-Health and Telemedicine* (pp. 486–494). Hershey, PA: IGI Global. doi:10.4018/978-1-4666-9978-6.ch038

Gupta, A., & Singh, O. (2016). Computer Aided Modeling and Finite Element Analysis of Human Elbow. *International Journal of Biomedical and Clinical Engineering*, *5*(1), 31–38. doi:10.4018/IJBCE.2016010104

H., S. K. (2016). Classification of Cybercrimes and Punishments under the Information Technology Act, 2000. In S. Geetha, & A. Phamila (Eds.), *Combating Security Breaches and Criminal Activity in the Digital Sphere* (pp. 57-66). Hershey, PA: IGI Global. doi:10.4018/978-1-5225-0193-0.ch004

Hafeez-Baig, A., Gururajan, R., & Wickramasinghe, N. (2017). Readiness as a Novel Construct of Readiness Acceptance Model (RAM) for the Wireless Handheld Technology. In N. Wickramasinghe (Ed.), *Handbook of Research on Healthcare Administration and Management* (pp. 578–595). Hershey, PA: IGI Global. doi:10.4018/978-1-5225-0920-2.ch035

Hanafizadeh, P., Ghandchi, S., & Asgarimehr, M. (2017). Impact of Information Technology on Lifestyle: A Literature Review and Classification. *International Journal of Virtual Communities and Social Networking*, *9*(2), 1–23. doi:10.4018/IJVCSN.2017040101

Harlow, D. B., Dwyer, H., Hansen, A. K., Hill, C., Iveland, A., Leak, A. E., & Franklin, D. M. (2016). Computer Programming in Elementary and Middle School: Connections across Content. In M. Urban & D. Falvo (Eds.), *Improving K-12 STEM Education Outcomes through Technological Integration* (pp. 337–361). Hershey, PA: IGI Global. doi:10.4018/978-1-4666-9616-7.ch015

Haseski, H. İ., Ilic, U., & Tuğtekin, U. (2018). Computational Thinking in Educational Digital Games: An Assessment Tool Proposal. In H. Ozcinar, G. Wong, & H. Ozturk (Eds.), *Teaching Computational Thinking in Primary Education* (pp. 256–287). Hershey, PA: IGI Global. doi:10.4018/978-1-5225-3200-2.ch013

Hee, W. J., Jalleh, G., Lai, H., & Lin, C. (2017). E-Commerce and IT Projects: Evaluation and Management Issues in Australian and Taiwanese Hospitals. *International Journal of Public Health Management and Ethics*, 2(1), 69–90. doi:10.4018/IJPHME.2017010104

Hernandez, A. A. (2017). Green Information Technology Usage: Awareness and Practices of Philippine IT Professionals. *International Journal of Enterprise Information Systems*, 13(4), 90–103. doi:10.4018/IJEIS.2017100106

Hernandez, A. A., & Ona, S. E. (2016). Green IT Adoption: Lessons from the Philippines Business Process Outsourcing Industry. *International Journal of Social Ecology and Sustainable Development*, 7(1), 1–34. doi:10.4018/IJSESD.2016010101

Hernandez, M. A., Marin, E. C., Garcia-Rodriguez, J., Azorin-Lopez, J., & Cazorla, M. (2017). Automatic Learning Improves Human-Robot Interaction in Productive Environments: A Review. *International Journal of Computer Vision and Image Processing*, 7(3), 65–75. doi:10.4018/IJCVIP.2017070106

Horne-Popp, L. M., Tessone, E. B., & Welker, J. (2018). If You Build It, They Will Come: Creating a Library Statistics Dashboard for Decision-Making. In L. Costello & M. Powers (Eds.), *Developing In-House Digital Tools in Library Spaces* (pp. 177–203). Hershey, PA: IGI Global. doi:10.4018/978-1-5225-2676-6.ch009

Hossan, C. G., & Ryan, J. C. (2016). Factors Affecting e-Government Technology Adoption Behaviour in a Voluntary Environment. *International Journal of Electronic Government Research*, 12(1), 24–49. doi:10.4018/IJEGR.2016010102

Hu, H., Hu, P. J., & Al-Gahtani, S. S. (2017). User Acceptance of Computer Technology at Work in Arabian Culture: A Model Comparison Approach. In M. Khosrow-Pour (Ed.), *Handbook of Research on Technology Adoption, Social Policy, and Global Integration* (pp. 205–228). Hershey, PA: IGI Global. doi:10.4018/978-1-5225-2668-1.ch011

Huie, C. P. (2016). Perceptions of Business Intelligence Professionals about Factors Related to Business Intelligence input in Decision Making. *International Journal of Business Analytics*, *3*(3), 1–24. doi:10.4018/IJBAN.2016070101

Hung, S., Huang, W., Yen, D. C., Chang, S., & Lu, C. (2016). Effect of Information Service Competence and Contextual Factors on the Effectiveness of Strategic Information Systems Planning in Hospitals. *Journal of Global Information Management*, *24*(1), 14–36. doi:10.4018/JGIM.2016010102

Ifinedo, P. (2017). Using an Extended Theory of Planned Behavior to Study Nurses' Adoption of Healthcare Information Systems in Nova Scotia. *International Journal of Technology Diffusion*, *8*(1), 1–17. doi:10.4018/IJTD.2017010101

Ilie, V., & Sneha, S. (2018). A Three Country Study for Understanding Physicians' Engagement With Electronic Information Resources Pre and Post System Implementation. *Journal of Global Information Management*, *26*(2), 48–73. doi:10.4018/JGIM.2018040103

Inoue-Smith, Y. (2017). Perceived Ease in Using Technology Predicts Teacher Candidates' Preferences for Online Resources. *International Journal of Online Pedagogy and Course Design*, *7*(3), 17–28. doi:10.4018/IJOPCD.2017070102

Islam, A. A. (2016). Development and Validation of the Technology Adoption and Gratification (TAG) Model in Higher Education: A Cross-Cultural Study Between Malaysia and China. *International Journal of Technology and Human Interaction*, *12*(3), 78–105. doi:10.4018/IJTHI.2016070106

Islam, A. Y. (2017). Technology Satisfaction in an Academic Context: Moderating Effect of Gender. In A. Mesquita (Ed.), *Research Paradigms and Contemporary Perspectives on Human-Technology Interaction* (pp. 187–211). Hershey, PA: IGI Global. doi:10.4018/978-1-5225-1868-6.ch009

Jamil, G. L., & Jamil, C. C. (2017). Information and Knowledge Management Perspective Contributions for Fashion Studies: Observing Logistics and Supply Chain Management Processes. In G. Jamil, A. Soares, & C. Pessoa (Eds.), *Handbook of Research on Information Management for Effective Logistics and Supply Chains* (pp. 199–221). Hershey, PA: IGI Global. doi:10.4018/978-1-5225-0973-8.ch011

Jamil, G. L., Jamil, L. C., Vieira, A. A., & Xavier, A. J. (2016). Challenges in Modelling Healthcare Services: A Study Case of Information Architecture Perspectives. In G. Jamil, J. Poças Rascão, F. Ribeiro, & A. Malheiro da Silva (Eds.), *Handbook of Research on Information Architecture and Management in Modern Organizations* (pp. 1–23). Hershey, PA: IGI Global. doi:10.4018/978-1-4666-8637-3.ch001

Janakova, M. (2018). Big Data and Simulations for the Solution of Controversies in Small Businesses. In M. Khosrow-Pour, D.B.A. (Ed.), Encyclopedia of Information Science and Technology, Fourth Edition (pp. 6907-6915). Hershey, PA: IGI Global. doi:10.4018/978-1-5225-2255-3.ch598

Jha, D. G. (2016). Preparing for Information Technology Driven Changes. In S. Tiwari & L. Nafees (Eds.), *Innovative Management Education Pedagogies for Preparing Next-Generation Leaders* (pp. 258–274). Hershey, PA: IGI Global. doi:10.4018/978-1-4666-9691-4.ch015

Jhawar, A., & Garg, S. K. (2018). Logistics Improvement by Investment in Information Technology Using System Dynamics. In A. Azar & S. Vaidyanathan (Eds.), *Advances in System Dynamics and Control* (pp. 528–567). Hershey, PA: IGI Global. doi:10.4018/978-1-5225-4077-9.ch017

Kalelioğlu, F., Gülbahar, Y., & Doğan, D. (2018). Teaching How to Think Like a Programmer: Emerging Insights. In H. Ozcinar, G. Wong, & H. Ozturk (Eds.), *Teaching Computational Thinking in Primary Education* (pp. 18–35). Hershey, PA: IGI Global. doi:10.4018/978-1-5225-3200-2.ch002

Kamberi, S. (2017). A Girls-Only Online Virtual World Environment and its Implications for Game-Based Learning. In A. Stricker, C. Calongne, B. Truman, & F. Arenas (Eds.), *Integrating an Awareness of Selfhood and Society into Virtual Learning* (pp. 74–95). Hershey, PA: IGI Global. doi:10.4018/978-1-5225-2182-2.ch006

Kamel, S., & Rizk, N. (2017). ICT Strategy Development: From Design to Implementation – Case of Egypt. In C. Howard & K. Hargiss (Eds.), *Strategic Information Systems and Technologies in Modern Organizations* (pp. 239–257). Hershey, PA: IGI Global. doi:10.4018/978-1-5225-1680-4.ch010

Kamel, S. H. (2018). The Potential Role of the Software Industry in Supporting Economic Development. In M. Khosrow-Pour, D.B.A. (Ed.), Encyclopedia of Information Science and Technology, Fourth Edition (pp. 7259-7269). Hershey, PA: IGI Global. doi:10.4018/978-1-5225-2255-3.ch631

Karon, R. (2016). Utilisation of Health Information Systems for Service Delivery in the Namibian Environment. In T. Iyamu & A. Tatnall (Eds.), *Maximizing Healthcare Delivery and Management through Technology Integration* (pp. 169–183). Hershey, PA: IGI Global. doi:10.4018/978-1-4666-9446-0.ch011

Kawata, S. (2018). Computer-Assisted Parallel Program Generation. In M. Khosrow-Pour, D.B.A. (Ed.), Encyclopedia of Information Science and Technology, Fourth Edition (pp. 4583-4593). Hershey, PA: IGI Global. doi:10.4018/978-1-5225-2255-3. ch398

Khanam, S., Siddiqui, J., & Talib, F. (2016). A DEMATEL Approach for Prioritizing the TQM Enablers and IT Resources in the Indian ICT Industry. *International Journal of Applied Management Sciences and Engineering, 3*(1), 11–29. doi:10.4018/IJAMSE.2016010102

Khari, M., Shrivastava, G., Gupta, S., & Gupta, R. (2017). Role of Cyber Security in Today's Scenario. In R. Kumar, P. Pattnaik, & P. Pandey (Eds.), *Detecting and Mitigating Robotic Cyber Security Risks* (pp. 177–191). Hershey, PA: IGI Global. doi:10.4018/978-1-5225-2154-9.ch013

Khouja, M., Rodriguez, I. B., Ben Halima, Y., & Moalla, S. (2018). IT Governance in Higher Education Institutions: A Systematic Literature Review. *International Journal of Human Capital and Information Technology Professionals, 9*(2), 52–67. doi:10.4018/IJHCITP.2018040104

Kim, S., Chang, M., Choi, N., Park, J., & Kim, H. (2016). The Direct and Indirect Effects of Computer Uses on Student Success in Math. *International Journal of Cyber Behavior, Psychology and Learning, 6*(3), 48–64. doi:10.4018/IJCBPL.2016070104

Kiourt, C., Pavlidis, G., Koutsoudis, A., & Kalles, D. (2017). Realistic Simulation of Cultural Heritage. *International Journal of Computational Methods in Heritage Science, 1*(1), 10–40. doi:10.4018/IJCMHS.2017010102

Korikov, A., & Krivtsov, O. (2016). System of People-Computer: On the Way of Creation of Human-Oriented Interface. In V. Mkrttchian, A. Bershadsky, A. Bozhday, M. Kataev, & S. Kataev (Eds.), *Handbook of Research on Estimation and Control Techniques in E-Learning Systems* (pp. 458–470). Hershey, PA: IGI Global. doi:10.4018/978-1-4666-9489-7.ch032

Köse, U. (2017). An Augmented-Reality-Based Intelligent Mobile Application for Open Computer Education. In G. Kurubacak & H. Altinpulluk (Eds.), *Mobile Technologies and Augmented Reality in Open Education* (pp. 154–174). Hershey, PA: IGI Global. doi:10.4018/978-1-5225-2110-5.ch008

Lahmiri, S. (2018). Information Technology Outsourcing Risk Factors and Provider Selection. In M. Gupta, R. Sharman, J. Walp, & P. Mulgund (Eds.), *Information Technology Risk Management and Compliance in Modern Organizations* (pp. 214–228). Hershey, PA: IGI Global. doi:10.4018/978-1-5225-2604-9.ch008

Landriscina, F. (2017). Computer-Supported Imagination: The Interplay Between Computer and Mental Simulation in Understanding Scientific Concepts. In I. Levin & D. Tsybulsky (Eds.), *Digital Tools and Solutions for Inquiry-Based STEM Learning* (pp. 33–60). Hershey, PA: IGI Global. doi:10.4018/978-1-5225-2525-7.ch002

Lau, S. K., Winley, G. K., Leung, N. K., Tsang, N., & Lau, S. Y. (2016). An Exploratory Study of Expectation in IT Skills in a Developing Nation: Vietnam. *Journal of Global Information Management*, *24*(1), 1–13. doi:10.4018/JGIM.2016010101

Lavranos, C., Kostagiolas, P., & Papadatos, J. (2016). Information Retrieval Technologies and the "Realities" of Music Information Seeking. In I. Deliyannis, P. Kostagiolas, & C. Banou (Eds.), *Experimental Multimedia Systems for Interactivity and Strategic Innovation* (pp. 102–121). Hershey, PA: IGI Global. doi:10.4018/978-1-4666-8659-5.ch005

Lee, W. W. (2018). Ethical Computing Continues From Problem to Solution. In M. Khosrow-Pour, D.B.A. (Ed.), Encyclopedia of Information Science and Technology, Fourth Edition (pp. 4884-4897). Hershey, PA: IGI Global. doi:10.4018/978-1-5225-2255-3.ch423

Lehto, M. (2016). Cyber Security Education and Research in the Finland's Universities and Universities of Applied Sciences. *International Journal of Cyber Warfare & Terrorism*, *6*(2), 15–31. doi:10.4018/IJCWT.2016040102

Lin, C., Jalleh, G., & Huang, Y. (2016). Evaluating and Managing Electronic Commerce and Outsourcing Projects in Hospitals. In A. Dwivedi (Ed.), *Reshaping Medical Practice and Care with Health Information Systems* (pp. 132–172). Hershey, PA: IGI Global. doi:10.4018/978-1-4666-9870-3.ch005

Lin, S., Chen, S., & Chuang, S. (2017). Perceived Innovation and Quick Response Codes in an Online-to-Offline E-Commerce Service Model. *International Journal of E-Adoption*, *9*(2), 1–16. doi:10.4018/IJEA.2017070101

Liu, M., Wang, Y., Xu, W., & Liu, L. (2017). Automated Scoring of Chinese Engineering Students' English Essays. *International Journal of Distance Education Technologies*, *15*(1), 52–68. doi:10.4018/IJDET.2017010104

Luciano, E. M., Wiedenhöft, G. C., Macadar, M. A., & Pinheiro dos Santos, F. (2016). Information Technology Governance Adoption: Understanding its Expectations Through the Lens of Organizational Citizenship. *International Journal of IT/Business Alignment and Governance,* *7*(2), 22-32. doi:10.4018/IJITBAG.2016070102

Mabe, L. K., & Oladele, O. I. (2017). Application of Information Communication Technologies for Agricultural Development through Extension Services: A Review. In T. Tossy (Ed.), *Information Technology Integration for Socio-Economic Development* (pp. 52–101). Hershey, PA: IGI Global. doi:10.4018/978-1-5225-0539-6.ch003

Manogaran, G., Thota, C., & Lopez, D. (2018). Human-Computer Interaction With Big Data Analytics. In D. Lopez & M. Durai (Eds.), *HCI Challenges and Privacy Preservation in Big Data Security* (pp. 1–22). Hershey, PA: IGI Global. doi:10.4018/978-1-5225-2863-0.ch001

Margolis, J., Goode, J., & Flapan, J. (2017). A Critical Crossroads for Computer Science for All: "Identifying Talent" or "Building Talent," and What Difference Does It Make? In Y. Rankin & J. Thomas (Eds.), *Moving Students of Color from Consumers to Producers of Technology* (pp. 1–23). Hershey, PA: IGI Global. doi:10.4018/978-1-5225-2005-4.ch001

Mbale, J. (2018). Computer Centres Resource Cloud Elasticity-Scalability (CRECES): Copperbelt University Case Study. In S. Aljawarneh & M. Malhotra (Eds.), *Critical Research on Scalability and Security Issues in Virtual Cloud Environments* (pp. 48–70). Hershey, PA: IGI Global. doi:10.4018/978-1-5225-3029-9.ch003

McKee, J. (2018). The Right Information: The Key to Effective Business Planning. In *Business Architectures for Risk Assessment and Strategic Planning: Emerging Research and Opportunities* (pp. 38–52). Hershey, PA: IGI Global. doi:10.4018/978-1-5225-3392-4.ch003

Mensah, I. K., & Mi, J. (2018). Determinants of Intention to Use Local E-Government Services in Ghana: The Perspective of Local Government Workers. *International Journal of Technology Diffusion*, 9(2), 41–60. doi:10.4018/IJTD.2018040103

Mohamed, J. H. (2018). Scientograph-Based Visualization of Computer Forensics Research Literature. In J. Jeyasekar & P. Saravanan (Eds.), *Innovations in Measuring and Evaluating Scientific Information* (pp. 148–162). Hershey, PA: IGI Global. doi:10.4018/978-1-5225-3457-0.ch010

Moore, R. L., & Johnson, N. (2017). Earning a Seat at the Table: How IT Departments Can Partner in Organizational Change and Innovation. *International Journal of Knowledge-Based Organizations*, 7(2), 1–12. doi:10.4018/IJKBO.2017040101

Mtebe, J. S., & Kissaka, M. M. (2016). Enhancing the Quality of Computer Science Education with MOOCs in Sub-Saharan Africa. In J. Keengwe & G. Onchwari (Eds.), *Handbook of Research on Active Learning and the Flipped Classroom Model in the Digital Age* (pp. 366–377). Hershey, PA: IGI Global. doi:10.4018/978-1-4666-9680-8.ch019

Mukul, M. K., & Bhattaharyya, S. (2017). Brain-Machine Interface: Human-Computer Interaction. In E. Noughabi, B. Raahemi, A. Albadvi, & B. Far (Eds.), *Handbook of Research on Data Science for Effective Healthcare Practice and Administration* (pp. 417–443). Hershey, PA: IGI Global. doi:10.4018/978-1-5225-2515-8.ch018

Na, L. (2017). Library and Information Science Education and Graduate Programs in Academic Libraries. In L. Ruan, Q. Zhu, & Y. Ye (Eds.), *Academic Library Development and Administration in China* (pp. 218–229). Hershey, PA: IGI Global. doi:10.4018/978-1-5225-0550-1.ch013

Nabavi, A., Taghavi-Fard, M. T., Hanafizadeh, P., & Taghva, M. R. (2016). Information Technology Continuance Intention: A Systematic Literature Review. *International Journal of E-Business Research*, *12*(1), 58–95. doi:10.4018/IJEBR.2016010104

Nath, R., & Murthy, V. N. (2018). What Accounts for the Differences in Internet Diffusion Rates Around the World? In M. Khosrow-Pour, D.B.A. (Ed.), Encyclopedia of Information Science and Technology, Fourth Edition (pp. 8095-8104). Hershey, PA: IGI Global. doi:10.4018/978-1-5225-2255-3.ch705

Nedelko, Z., & Potocan, V. (2018). The Role of Emerging Information Technologies for Supporting Supply Chain Management. In M. Khosrow-Pour, D.B.A. (Ed.), Encyclopedia of Information Science and Technology, Fourth Edition (pp. 5559-5569). Hershey, PA: IGI Global. doi:10.4018/978-1-5225-2255-3.ch483

Ngafeeson, M. N. (2018). User Resistance to Health Information Technology. In M. Khosrow-Pour, D.B.A. (Ed.), Encyclopedia of Information Science and Technology, Fourth Edition (pp. 3816-3825). Hershey, PA: IGI Global. doi:10.4018/978-1-5225-2255-3.ch331

Nozari, H., Najafi, S. E., Jafari-Eskandari, M., & Aliahmadi, A. (2016). Providing a Model for Virtual Project Management with an Emphasis on IT Projects. In C. Graham (Ed.), *Strategic Management and Leadership for Systems Development in Virtual Spaces* (pp. 43–63). Hershey, PA: IGI Global. doi:10.4018/978-1-4666-9688-4.ch003

Nurdin, N., Stockdale, R., & Scheepers, H. (2016). Influence of Organizational Factors in the Sustainability of E-Government: A Case Study of Local E-Government in Indonesia. In I. Sodhi (Ed.), *Trends, Prospects, and Challenges in Asian E-Governance* (pp. 281–323). Hershey, PA: IGI Global. doi:10.4018/978-1-4666-9536-8.ch014

Odagiri, K. (2017). Introduction of Individual Technology to Constitute the Current Internet. In *Strategic Policy-Based Network Management in Contemporary Organizations* (pp. 20–96). Hershey, PA: IGI Global. doi:10.4018/978-1-68318-003-6.ch003

Okike, E. U. (2018). Computer Science and Prison Education. In I. Biao (Ed.), *Strategic Learning Ideologies in Prison Education Programs* (pp. 246–264). Hershey, PA: IGI Global. doi:10.4018/978-1-5225-2909-5.ch012

Olelewe, C. J., & Nwafor, I. P. (2017). Level of Computer Appreciation Skills Acquired for Sustainable Development by Secondary School Students in Nsukka LGA of Enugu State, Nigeria. In C. Ayo & V. Mbarika (Eds.), *Sustainable ICT Adoption and Integration for Socio-Economic Development* (pp. 214–233). Hershey, PA: IGI Global. doi:10.4018/978-1-5225-2565-3.ch010

Oliveira, M., Maçada, A. C., Curado, C., & Nodari, F. (2017). Infrastructure Profiles and Knowledge Sharing. *International Journal of Technology and Human Interaction*, *13*(3), 1–12. doi:10.4018/IJTHI.2017070101

Otarkhani, A., Shokouhyar, S., & Pour, S. S. (2017). Analyzing the Impact of Governance of Enterprise IT on Hospital Performance: Tehran's (Iran) Hospitals – A Case Study. *International Journal of Healthcare Information Systems and Informatics*, *12*(3), 1–20. doi:10.4018/IJHISI.2017070101

Otunla, A. O., & Amuda, C. O. (2018). Nigerian Undergraduate Students' Computer Competencies and Use of Information Technology Tools and Resources for Study Skills and Habits' Enhancement. In M. Khosrow-Pour, D.B.A. (Ed.), Encyclopedia of Information Science and Technology, Fourth Edition (pp. 2303-2313). Hershey, PA: IGI Global. doi:10.4018/978-1-5225-2255-3.ch200

Özçınar, H. (2018). A Brief Discussion on Incentives and Barriers to Computational Thinking Education. In H. Ozcinar, G. Wong, & H. Ozturk (Eds.), *Teaching Computational Thinking in Primary Education* (pp. 1–17). Hershey, PA: IGI Global. doi:10.4018/978-1-5225-3200-2.ch001

Pandey, J. M., Garg, S., Mishra, P., & Mishra, B. P. (2017). Computer Based Psychological Interventions: Subject to the Efficacy of Psychological Services. *International Journal of Computers in Clinical Practice*, *2*(1), 25–33. doi:10.4018/IJCCP.2017010102

Parry, V. K., & Lind, M. L. (2016). Alignment of Business Strategy and Information Technology Considering Information Technology Governance, Project Portfolio Control, and Risk Management. *International Journal of Information Technology Project Management*, *7*(4), 21–37. doi:10.4018/IJITPM.2016100102

Patro, C. (2017). Impulsion of Information Technology on Human Resource Practices. In P. Ordóñez de Pablos (Ed.), *Managerial Strategies and Solutions for Business Success in Asia* (pp. 231–254). Hershey, PA: IGI Global. doi:10.4018/978-1-5225-1886-0.ch013

Patro, C. S., & Raghunath, K. M. (2017). Information Technology Paraphernalia for Supply Chain Management Decisions. In M. Tavana (Ed.), *Enterprise Information Systems and the Digitalization of Business Functions* (pp. 294–320). Hershey, PA: IGI Global. doi:10.4018/978-1-5225-2382-6.ch014

Paul, P. K. (2016). Cloud Computing: An Agent of Promoting Interdisciplinary Sciences, Especially Information Science and I-Schools – Emerging Techno-Educational Scenario. In L. Chao (Ed.), *Handbook of Research on Cloud-Based STEM Education for Improved Learning Outcomes* (pp. 247–258). Hershey, PA: IGI Global. doi:10.4018/978-1-4666-9924-3.ch016

Paul, P. K. (2018). The Context of IST for Solid Information Retrieval and Infrastructure Building: Study of Developing Country. *International Journal of Information Retrieval Research*, 8(1), 86–100. doi:10.4018/IJIRR.2018010106

Paul, P. K., & Chatterjee, D. (2018). iSchools Promoting "Information Science and Technology" (IST) Domain Towards Community, Business, and Society With Contemporary Worldwide Trend and Emerging Potentialities in India. In M. Khosrow-Pour, D.B.A. (Ed.), Encyclopedia of Information Science and Technology, Fourth Edition (pp. 4723-4735). Hershey, PA: IGI Global. doi:10.4018/978-1-5225-2255-3.ch410

Pessoa, C. R., & Marques, M. E. (2017). Information Technology and Communication Management in Supply Chain Management. In G. Jamil, A. Soares, & C. Pessoa (Eds.), *Handbook of Research on Information Management for Effective Logistics and Supply Chains* (pp. 23–33). Hershey, PA: IGI Global. doi:10.4018/978-1-5225-0973-8.ch002

Pineda, R. G. (2016). Where the Interaction Is Not: Reflections on the Philosophy of Human-Computer Interaction. *International Journal of Art, Culture and Design Technologies*, 5(1), 1–12. doi:10.4018/IJACDT.2016010101

Pineda, R. G. (2018). Remediating Interaction: Towards a Philosophy of Human-Computer Relationship. In M. Khosrow-Pour (Ed.), *Enhancing Art, Culture, and Design With Technological Integration* (pp. 75–98). Hershey, PA: IGI Global. doi:10.4018/978-1-5225-5023-5.ch004

Poikela, P., & Vuojärvi, H. (2016). Learning ICT-Mediated Communication through Computer-Based Simulations. In M. Cruz-Cunha, I. Miranda, R. Martinho, & R. Rijo (Eds.), *Encyclopedia of E-Health and Telemedicine* (pp. 674–687). Hershey, PA: IGI Global. doi:10.4018/978-1-4666-9978-6.ch052

Qian, Y. (2017). Computer Simulation in Higher Education: Affordances, Opportunities, and Outcomes. In P. Vu, S. Fredrickson, & C. Moore (Eds.), *Handbook of Research on Innovative Pedagogies and Technologies for Online Learning in Higher Education* (pp. 236–262). Hershey, PA: IGI Global. doi:10.4018/978-1-5225-1851-8.ch011

Radant, O., Colomo-Palacios, R., & Stantchev, V. (2016). Factors for the Management of Scarce Human Resources and Highly Skilled Employees in IT-Departments: A Systematic Review. *Journal of Information Technology Research*, *9*(1), 65–82. doi:10.4018/JITR.2016010105

Rahman, N. (2016). Toward Achieving Environmental Sustainability in the Computer Industry. *International Journal of Green Computing*, *7*(1), 37–54. doi:10.4018/IJGC.2016010103

Rahman, N. (2017). Lessons from a Successful Data Warehousing Project Management. *International Journal of Information Technology Project Management*, *8*(4), 30–45. doi:10.4018/IJITPM.2017100103

Rahman, N. (2018). Environmental Sustainability in the Computer Industry for Competitive Advantage. In M. Khosrow-Pour (Ed.), *Green Computing Strategies for Competitive Advantage and Business Sustainability* (pp. 110–130). Hershey, PA: IGI Global. doi:10.4018/978-1-5225-5017-4.ch006

Rajh, A., & Pavetic, T. (2017). Computer Generated Description as the Required Digital Competence in Archival Profession. *International Journal of Digital Literacy and Digital Competence*, *8*(1), 36–49. doi:10.4018/IJDLDC.2017010103

Raman, A., & Goyal, D. P. (2017). Extending IMPLEMENT Framework for Enterprise Information Systems Implementation to Information System Innovation. In M. Tavana (Ed.), *Enterprise Information Systems and the Digitalization of Business Functions* (pp. 137–177). Hershey, PA: IGI Global. doi:10.4018/978-1-5225-2382-6.ch007

Rao, Y. S., Rauta, A. K., Saini, H., & Panda, T. C. (2017). Mathematical Model for Cyber Attack in Computer Network. *International Journal of Business Data Communications and Networking*, *13*(1), 58–65. doi:10.4018/IJBDCN.2017010105

Rapaport, W. J. (2018). Syntactic Semantics and the Proper Treatment of Computationalism. In M. Danesi (Ed.), *Empirical Research on Semiotics and Visual Rhetoric* (pp. 128–176). Hershey, PA: IGI Global. doi:10.4018/978-1-5225-5622-0.ch007

Raut, R., Priyadarshinee, P., & Jha, M. (2017). Understanding the Mediation Effect of Cloud Computing Adoption in Indian Organization: Integrating TAM-TOE- Risk Model. *International Journal of Service Science, Management, Engineering, and Technology*, *8*(3), 40–59. doi:10.4018/IJSSMET.2017070103

Regan, E. A., & Wang, J. (2016). Realizing the Value of EHR Systems Critical Success Factors. *International Journal of Healthcare Information Systems and Informatics*, *11*(3), 1–18. doi:10.4018/IJHISI.2016070101

Rezaie, S., Mirabedini, S. J., & Abtahi, A. (2018). Designing a Model for Implementation of Business Intelligence in the Banking Industry. *International Journal of Enterprise Information Systems*, *14*(1), 77–103. doi:10.4018/IJEIS.2018010105

Rezende, D. A. (2016). Digital City Projects: Information and Public Services Offered by Chicago (USA) and Curitiba (Brazil). *International Journal of Knowledge Society Research*, *7*(3), 16–30. doi:10.4018/IJKSR.2016070102

Rezende, D. A. (2018). Strategic Digital City Projects: Innovative Information and Public Services Offered by Chicago (USA) and Curitiba (Brazil). In M. Lytras, L. Daniela, & A. Visvizi (Eds.), *Enhancing Knowledge Discovery and Innovation in the Digital Era* (pp. 204–223). Hershey, PA: IGI Global. doi:10.4018/978-1-5225-4191-2.ch012

Riabov, V. V. (2016). Teaching Online Computer-Science Courses in LMS and Cloud Environment. *International Journal of Quality Assurance in Engineering and Technology Education*, *5*(4), 12–41. doi:10.4018/IJQAETE.2016100102

Ricordel, V., Wang, J., Da Silva, M. P., & Le Callet, P. (2016). 2D and 3D Visual Attention for Computer Vision: Concepts, Measurement, and Modeling. In R. Pal (Ed.), *Innovative Research in Attention Modeling and Computer Vision Applications* (pp. 1–44). Hershey, PA: IGI Global. doi:10.4018/978-1-4666-8723-3.ch001

Rodriguez, A., Rico-Diaz, A. J., Rabuñal, J. R., & Gestal, M. (2017). Fish Tracking with Computer Vision Techniques: An Application to Vertical Slot Fishways. In M. S., & V. V. (Eds.), Multi-Core Computer Vision and Image Processing for Intelligent Applications (pp. 74-104). Hershey, PA: IGI Global. doi:10.4018/978-1-5225-0889-2.ch003

Romero, J. A. (2018). Sustainable Advantages of Business Value of Information Technology. In M. Khosrow-Pour, D.B.A. (Ed.), Encyclopedia of Information Science and Technology, Fourth Edition (pp. 923-929). Hershey, PA: IGI Global. doi:10.4018/978-1-5225-2255-3.ch079

Romero, J. A. (2018). The Always-On Business Model and Competitive Advantage. In N. Bajgoric (Ed.), *Always-On Enterprise Information Systems for Modern Organizations* (pp. 23–40). Hershey, PA: IGI Global. doi:10.4018/978-1-5225-3704-5.ch002

Rosen, Y. (2018). Computer Agent Technologies in Collaborative Learning and Assessment. In M. Khosrow-Pour, D.B.A. (Ed.), Encyclopedia of Information Science and Technology, Fourth Edition (pp. 2402-2410). Hershey, PA: IGI Global. doi:10.4018/978-1-5225-2255-3.ch209

Rosen, Y., & Mosharraf, M. (2016). Computer Agent Technologies in Collaborative Assessments. In Y. Rosen, S. Ferrara, & M. Mosharraf (Eds.), *Handbook of Research on Technology Tools for Real-World Skill Development* (pp. 319–343). Hershey, PA: IGI Global. doi:10.4018/978-1-4666-9441-5.ch012

Roy, D. (2018). Success Factors of Adoption of Mobile Applications in Rural India: Effect of Service Characteristics on Conceptual Model. In M. Khosrow-Pour (Ed.), *Green Computing Strategies for Competitive Advantage and Business Sustainability* (pp. 211–238). Hershey, PA: IGI Global. doi:10.4018/978-1-5225-5017-4.ch010

Ruffin, T. R. (2016). Health Information Technology and Change. In V. Wang (Ed.), *Handbook of Research on Advancing Health Education through Technology* (pp. 259–285). Hershey, PA: IGI Global. doi:10.4018/978-1-4666-9494-1.ch012

Ruffin, T. R. (2016). Health Information Technology and Quality Management. *International Journal of Information Communication Technologies and Human Development*, 8(4), 56–72. doi:10.4018/IJICTHD.2016100105

Ruffin, T. R., & Hawkins, D. P. (2018). Trends in Health Care Information Technology and Informatics. In M. Khosrow-Pour, D.B.A. (Ed.), Encyclopedia of Information Science and Technology, Fourth Edition (pp. 3805-3815). Hershey, PA: IGI Global. doi:10.4018/978-1-5225-2255-3.ch330

Safari, M. R., & Jiang, Q. (2018). The Theory and Practice of IT Governance Maturity and Strategies Alignment: Evidence From Banking Industry. *Journal of Global Information Management*, 26(2), 127–146. doi:10.4018/JGIM.2018040106

Sahin, H. B., & Anagun, S. S. (2018). Educational Computer Games in Math Teaching: A Learning Culture. In E. Toprak & E. Kumtepe (Eds.), *Supporting Multiculturalism in Open and Distance Learning Spaces* (pp. 249–280). Hershey, PA: IGI Global. doi:10.4018/978-1-5225-3076-3.ch013

Sanna, A., & Valpreda, F. (2017). An Assessment of the Impact of a Collaborative Didactic Approach and Students' Background in Teaching Computer Animation. *International Journal of Information and Communication Technology Education*, *13*(4), 1–16. doi:10.4018/IJICTE.2017100101

Savita, K., Dominic, P., & Ramayah, T. (2016). The Drivers, Practices and Outcomes of Green Supply Chain Management: Insights from ISO14001 Manufacturing Firms in Malaysia. *International Journal of Information Systems and Supply Chain Management*, *9*(2), 35–60. doi:10.4018/IJISSCM.2016040103

Scott, A., Martin, A., & McAlear, F. (2017). Enhancing Participation in Computer Science among Girls of Color: An Examination of a Preparatory AP Computer Science Intervention. In Y. Rankin & J. Thomas (Eds.), *Moving Students of Color from Consumers to Producers of Technology* (pp. 62–84). Hershey, PA: IGI Global. doi:10.4018/978-1-5225-2005-4.ch004

Shahsavandi, E., Mayah, G., & Rahbari, H. (2016). Impact of E-Government on Transparency and Corruption in Iran. In I. Sodhi (Ed.), *Trends, Prospects, and Challenges in Asian E-Governance* (pp. 75–94). Hershey, PA: IGI Global. doi:10.4018/978-1-4666-9536-8.ch004

Siddoo, V., & Wongsai, N. (2017). Factors Influencing the Adoption of ISO/IEC 29110 in Thai Government Projects: A Case Study. *International Journal of Information Technologies and Systems Approach*, *10*(1), 22–44. doi:10.4018/IJITSA.2017010102

Sidorkina, I., & Rybakov, A. (2016). Computer-Aided Design as Carrier of Set Development Changes System in E-Course Engineering. In V. Mkrttchian, A. Bershadsky, A. Bozhday, M. Kataev, & S. Kataev (Eds.), *Handbook of Research on Estimation and Control Techniques in E-Learning Systems* (pp. 500–515). Hershey, PA: IGI Global. doi:10.4018/978-1-4666-9489-7.ch035

Sidorkina, I., & Rybakov, A. (2016). Creating Model of E-Course: As an Object of Computer-Aided Design. In V. Mkrttchian, A. Bershadsky, A. Bozhday, M. Kataev, & S. Kataev (Eds.), *Handbook of Research on Estimation and Control Techniques in E-Learning Systems* (pp. 286–297). Hershey, PA: IGI Global. doi:10.4018/978-1-4666-9489-7.ch019

Simões, A. (2017). Using Game Frameworks to Teach Computer Programming. In R. Alexandre Peixoto de Queirós & M. Pinto (Eds.), *Gamification-Based E-Learning Strategies for Computer Programming Education* (pp. 221–236). Hershey, PA: IGI Global. doi:10.4018/978-1-5225-1034-5.ch010

Sllame, A. M. (2017). Integrating LAB Work With Classes in Computer Network Courses. In H. Alphin Jr, R. Chan, & J. Lavine (Eds.), *The Future of Accessibility in International Higher Education* (pp. 253–275). Hershey, PA: IGI Global. doi:10.4018/978-1-5225-2560-8.ch015

Smirnov, A., Ponomarev, A., Shilov, N., Kashevnik, A., & Teslya, N. (2018). Ontology-Based Human-Computer Cloud for Decision Support: Architecture and Applications in Tourism. *International Journal of Embedded and Real-Time Communication Systems*, *9*(1), 1–19. doi:10.4018/IJERTCS.2018010101

Smith-Ditizio, A. A., & Smith, A. D. (2018). Computer Fraud Challenges and Its Legal Implications. In M. Khosrow-Pour, D.B.A. (Ed.), Encyclopedia of Information Science and Technology, Fourth Edition (pp. 4837-4848). Hershey, PA: IGI Global. doi:10.4018/978-1-5225-2255-3.ch419

Sohani, S. S. (2016). Job Shadowing in Information Technology Projects: A Source of Competitive Advantage. *International Journal of Information Technology Project Management*, *7*(1), 47–57. doi:10.4018/IJITPM.2016010104

Sosnin, P. (2018). Figuratively Semantic Support of Human-Computer Interactions. In *Experience-Based Human-Computer Interactions: Emerging Research and Opportunities* (pp. 244–272). Hershey, PA: IGI Global. doi:10.4018/978-1-5225-2987-3.ch008

Spinelli, R., & Benevolo, C. (2016). From Healthcare Services to E-Health Applications: A Delivery System-Based Taxonomy. In A. Dwivedi (Ed.), *Reshaping Medical Practice and Care with Health Information Systems* (pp. 205–245). Hershey, PA: IGI Global. doi:10.4018/978-1-4666-9870-3.ch007

Srinivasan, S. (2016). Overview of Clinical Trial and Pharmacovigilance Process and Areas of Application of Computer System. In P. Chakraborty & A. Nagal (Eds.), *Software Innovations in Clinical Drug Development and Safety* (pp. 1–13). Hershey, PA: IGI Global. doi:10.4018/978-1-4666-8726-4.ch001

Srisawasdi, N. (2016). Motivating Inquiry-Based Learning Through a Combination of Physical and Virtual Computer-Based Laboratory Experiments in High School Science. In M. Urban & D. Falvo (Eds.), *Improving K-12 STEM Education Outcomes through Technological Integration* (pp. 108–134). Hershey, PA: IGI Global. doi:10.4018/978-1-4666-9616-7.ch006

Stavridi, S. V., & Hamada, D. R. (2016). Children and Youth Librarians: Competencies Required in Technology-Based Environment. In J. Yap, M. Perez, M. Ayson, & G. Entico (Eds.), *Special Library Administration, Standardization and Technological Integration* (pp. 25–50). Hershey, PA: IGI Global. doi:10.4018/978-1-4666-9542-9.ch002

Sung, W., Ahn, J., Kai, S. M., Choi, A., & Black, J. B. (2016). Incorporating Touch-Based Tablets into Classroom Activities: Fostering Children's Computational Thinking through iPad Integrated Instruction. In D. Mentor (Ed.), *Handbook of Research on Mobile Learning in Contemporary Classrooms* (pp. 378–406). Hershey, PA: IGI Global. doi:10.4018/978-1-5225-0251-7.ch019

Syväjärvi, A., Leinonen, J., Kivivirta, V., & Kesti, M. (2017). The Latitude of Information Management in Local Government: Views of Local Government Managers. *International Journal of Electronic Government Research*, *13*(1), 69–85. doi:10.4018/IJEGR.2017010105

Tanque, M., & Foxwell, H. J. (2018). Big Data and Cloud Computing: A Review of Supply Chain Capabilities and Challenges. In A. Prasad (Ed.), *Exploring the Convergence of Big Data and the Internet of Things* (pp. 1–28). Hershey, PA: IGI Global. doi:10.4018/978-1-5225-2947-7.ch001

Teixeira, A., Gomes, A., & Orvalho, J. G. (2017). Auditory Feedback in a Computer Game for Blind People. In T. Issa, P. Kommers, T. Issa, P. Isaías, & T. Issa (Eds.), *Smart Technology Applications in Business Environments* (pp. 134–158). Hershey, PA: IGI Global. doi:10.4018/978-1-5225-2492-2.ch007

Thompson, N., McGill, T., & Murray, D. (2018). Affect-Sensitive Computer Systems. In M. Khosrow-Pour, D.B.A. (Ed.), Encyclopedia of Information Science and Technology, Fourth Edition (pp. 4124-4135). Hershey, PA: IGI Global. doi:10.4018/978-1-5225-2255-3.ch357

Trad, A., & Kalpić, D. (2016). The E-Business Transformation Framework for E-Commerce Control and Monitoring Pattern. In I. Lee (Ed.), *Encyclopedia of E-Commerce Development, Implementation, and Management* (pp. 754–777). Hershey, PA: IGI Global. doi:10.4018/978-1-4666-9787-4.ch053

Triberti, S., Brivio, E., & Galimberti, C. (2018). On Social Presence: Theories, Methodologies, and Guidelines for the Innovative Contexts of Computer-Mediated Learning. In M. Marmon (Ed.), *Enhancing Social Presence in Online Learning Environments* (pp. 20–41). Hershey, PA: IGI Global. doi:10.4018/978-1-5225-3229-3.ch002

Tripathy, B. K. T. R., S., & Mohanty, R. K. (2018). Memetic Algorithms and Their Applications in Computer Science. In S. Dash, B. Tripathy, & A. Rahman (Eds.), Handbook of Research on Modeling, Analysis, and Application of Nature-Inspired Metaheuristic Algorithms (pp. 73-93). Hershey, PA: IGI Global. doi:10.4018/978-1-5225-2857-9.ch004

Turulja, L., & Bajgoric, N. (2017). Human Resource Management IT and Global Economy Perspective: Global Human Resource Information Systems. In M. Khosrow-Pour (Ed.), *Handbook of Research on Technology Adoption, Social Policy, and Global Integration* (pp. 377–394). Hershey, PA: IGI Global. doi:10.4018/978-1-5225-2668-1.ch018

Unwin, D. W., Sanzogni, L., & Sandhu, K. (2017). Developing and Measuring the Business Case for Health Information Technology. In K. Moahi, K. Bwalya, & P. Sebina (Eds.), *Health Information Systems and the Advancement of Medical Practice in Developing Countries* (pp. 262–290). Hershey, PA: IGI Global. doi:10.4018/978-1-5225-2262-1.ch015

Vadhanam, B. R. S., M., Sugumaran, V., V., V., & Ramalingam, V. V. (2017). Computer Vision Based Classification on Commercial Videos. In M. S., & V. V. (Eds.), Multi-Core Computer Vision and Image Processing for Intelligent Applications (pp. 105-135). Hershey, PA: IGI Global. doi:10.4018/978-1-5225-0889-2.ch004

Valverde, R., Torres, B., & Motaghi, H. (2018). A Quantum NeuroIS Data Analytics Architecture for the Usability Evaluation of Learning Management Systems. In S. Bhattacharyya (Ed.), *Quantum-Inspired Intelligent Systems for Multimedia Data Analysis* (pp. 277–299). Hershey, PA: IGI Global. doi:10.4018/978-1-5225-5219-2.ch009

Vassilis, E. (2018). Learning and Teaching Methodology: "1:1 Educational Computing. In K. Koutsopoulos, K. Doukas, & Y. Kotsanis (Eds.), *Handbook of Research on Educational Design and Cloud Computing in Modern Classroom Settings* (pp. 122–155). Hershey, PA: IGI Global. doi:10.4018/978-1-5225-3053-4.ch007

Wadhwani, A. K., Wadhwani, S., & Singh, T. (2016). Computer Aided Diagnosis System for Breast Cancer Detection. In Y. Morsi, A. Shukla, & C. Rathore (Eds.), *Optimizing Assistive Technologies for Aging Populations* (pp. 378–395). Hershey, PA: IGI Global. doi:10.4018/978-1-4666-9530-6.ch015

Wang, L., Wu, Y., & Hu, C. (2016). English Teachers' Practice and Perspectives on Using Educational Computer Games in EIL Context. *International Journal of Technology and Human Interaction*, *12*(3), 33–46. doi:10.4018/IJTHI.2016070103

Watfa, M. K., Majeed, H., & Salahuddin, T. (2016). Computer Based E-Healthcare Clinical Systems: A Comprehensive Survey. *International Journal of Privacy and Health Information Management, 4*(1), 50–69. doi:10.4018/IJPHIM.2016010104

Weeger, A., & Haase, U. (2016). Taking up Three Challenges to Business-IT Alignment Research by the Use of Activity Theory. *International Journal of IT/ Business Alignment and Governance, 7*(2), 1-21. doi:10.4018/IJITBAG.2016070101

Wexler, B. E. (2017). Computer-Presented and Physical Brain-Training Exercises for School Children: Improving Executive Functions and Learning. In B. Dubbels (Ed.), *Transforming Gaming and Computer Simulation Technologies across Industries* (pp. 206–224). Hershey, PA: IGI Global. doi:10.4018/978-1-5225-1817-4.ch012

Williams, D. M., Gani, M. O., Addo, I. D., Majumder, A. J., Tamma, C. P., Wang, M., ... Chu, C. (2016). Challenges in Developing Applications for Aging Populations. In Y. Morsi, A. Shukla, & C. Rathore (Eds.), *Optimizing Assistive Technologies for Aging Populations* (pp. 1–21). Hershey, PA: IGI Global. doi:10.4018/978-1-4666-9530-6.ch001

Wimble, M., Singh, H., & Phillips, B. (2018). Understanding Cross-Level Interactions of Firm-Level Information Technology and Industry Environment: A Multilevel Model of Business Value. *Information Resources Management Journal, 31*(1), 1–20. doi:10.4018/IRMJ.2018010101

Wimmer, H., Powell, L., Kilgus, L., & Force, C. (2017). Improving Course Assessment via Web-based Homework. *International Journal of Online Pedagogy and Course Design, 7*(2), 1–19. doi:10.4018/IJOPCD.2017040101

Wong, Y. L., & Siu, K. W. (2018). Assessing Computer-Aided Design Skills. In M. Khosrow-Pour, D.B.A. (Ed.), Encyclopedia of Information Science and Technology, Fourth Edition (pp. 7382-7391). Hershey, PA: IGI Global. doi:10.4018/978-1-5225-2255-3.ch642

Wongsurawat, W., & Shrestha, V. (2018). Information Technology, Globalization, and Local Conditions: Implications for Entrepreneurs in Southeast Asia. In P. Ordóñez de Pablos (Ed.), *Management Strategies and Technology Fluidity in the Asian Business Sector* (pp. 163–176). Hershey, PA: IGI Global. doi:10.4018/978-1-5225-4056-4.ch010

Yang, Y., Zhu, X., Jin, C., & Li, J. J. (2018). Reforming Classroom Education Through a QQ Group: A Pilot Experiment at a Primary School in Shanghai. In H. Spires (Ed.), *Digital Transformation and Innovation in Chinese Education* (pp. 211–231). Hershey, PA: IGI Global. doi:10.4018/978-1-5225-2924-8.ch012

Yilmaz, R., Sezgin, A., Kurnaz, S., & Arslan, Y. Z. (2018). Object-Oriented Programming in Computer Science. In M. Khosrow-Pour, D.B.A. (Ed.), Encyclopedia of Information Science and Technology, Fourth Edition (pp. 7470-7480). Hershey, PA: IGI Global. doi:10.4018/978-1-5225-2255-3.ch650

Yu, L. (2018). From Teaching Software Engineering Locally and Globally to Devising an Internationalized Computer Science Curriculum. In S. Dikli, B. Etheridge, & R. Rawls (Eds.), *Curriculum Internationalization and the Future of Education* (pp. 293–320). Hershey, PA: IGI Global. doi:10.4018/978-1-5225-2791-6.ch016

Yuhua, F. (2018). Computer Information Library Clusters. In M. Khosrow-Pour, D.B.A. (Ed.), Encyclopedia of Information Science and Technology, Fourth Edition (pp. 4399-4403). Hershey, PA: IGI Global. doi:10.4018/978-1-5225-2255-3.ch382

Zare, M. A., Taghavi Fard, M. T., & Hanafizadeh, P. (2016). The Assessment of Outsourcing IT Services using DEA Technique: A Study of Application Outsourcing in Research Centers. *International Journal of Operations Research and Information Systems*, 7(1), 45–57. doi:10.4018/IJORIS.2016010104

Zhao, J., Wang, Q., Guo, J., Gao, L., & Yang, F. (2016). An Overview on Passive Image Forensics Technology for Automatic Computer Forgery. *International Journal of Digital Crime and Forensics*, 8(4), 14–25. doi:10.4018/IJDCF.2016100102

Zimeras, S. (2016). Computer Virus Models and Analysis in M-Health IT Systems: Computer Virus Models. In A. Moumtzoglou (Ed.), *M-Health Innovations for Patient-Centered Care* (pp. 284–297). Hershey, PA: IGI Global. doi:10.4018/978-1-4666-9861-1.ch014

Zlatanovska, K. (2016). Hacking and Hacktivism as an Information Communication System Threat. In M. Hadji-Janev & M. Bogdanoski (Eds.), *Handbook of Research on Civil Society and National Security in the Era of Cyber Warfare* (pp. 68–101). Hershey, PA: IGI Global. doi:10.4018/978-1-4666-8793-6.ch004

About the Contributors

Luisa Dall'Acqua is a senior cognitive scientist. She is an author, reviewer, and editor for several international scientific journals and book editions, and was a committee member for international Workshops/Conferences. Since 1990 she performed teaching activities, training students, teachers in service, headmasters and professionals; and since 2003 she was a member of international projects and research teams (USA, Europe, Asia). After an MSc in Philosophy, Luisa received a Ph.D. in Sociology of Legal Institutions and Policies, and a second Ph.D. in Psychological and Social Sciences. The main field of research is an engineering and social-cognitive approach to the intelligence and problem solving, and in particular to the decision-making risk under stress, conflict, and unpredictability, ranging from individual, collective, institutional intelligence applications to computational intelligence. The new risk scenarios, which she is working on, are Cyber-Intelligence in safety and security sectors of analysis. Furthermore, she is an expert Instructional Technologist and a digital communication professional. Currently, she is a permanent teacher at the TCO Scientific Lyceum (Italy) and an adjunct professor at the University of Bologna.

* * *

Amitabh Anand is a Professor at SKEMA Business School, Universite Cote d'Azur, France. He has won several awards in research viz., "Excellence in Peer Review Award" from South Asian Journal of Human Resources Australia, (ABDC Rank-C), "Emerging Scholar Award" from organization studies research network in Germany in 2018, KM and IC Excellence Award nomination for a Best Case study on ShaRP in Padova, Italy. In terms of innovative teaching, he is the only one from Europe to make it to the prestigious 2018 list of "Top 50 Worlds Best UG Professors" by Poets and Quants USA. He is a member of the European Academy of Management, and a visiting faculty to many institutes in India and abroad. He is also part of the editorial board of SAJHRM Journal (ABDC-C) and Journal of

Entrepreneurship in Emerging Economies (ABS-C) and Guest Editor of Sustainability Journal and Frontiers Journal.

Jirapun Daengdej received his Ph.D. in Computer Science from University of New England, Australia in 1999. In addition to being a lecturer at a university, he has been working on more than 30 large ICT projects in both Thailand and within ASEAN. He used to also served as an Executive Technical Director of No Magic Asia Co., Ltd. He is a president of community called Thailand Software Process Improvement Network, an international community founded by Carnegie Mellon University, USA. He is currently working as a CTO of Merlin's Solution International, a company specializes in providing consultant on Digital Transformation and Design and Development of airport systems. He is also founder of Innocorp Co., Ltd, a company that focuses mainly on designing and developing AI solutions for various companies such as financial institutes and energy companies. He has recently been serving as a member of MIT's Global Panel for Technology Review.

Irene M. Gironacci is a Software Engineer and she is currently working as Project Manager at the Swinburne University of Technology - Centre for Transformative Media Technologies (Melbourne, Australia). She is also concluding a PhD at the same university. Her research interests include Extended Reality, Artificial Intelligence, Game Design and Management. Previously, she worked as a Mixed Reality Engineer at Luxembourg Institute of Science and Technology (Luxembourg, Europe). She received both MSc and BSc in Software Engineering at the University of Parma (Italy).

Idahosa Igbinakhase received his MSc in Management from The Robert Gordon University, Aberdeen (United Kingdom) and received his BSc in Technical Education (Mechanical Technology Option) from Rivers State university of Science and Technology, Port Harcourt (Nigeria) in 2004. In 2011 he was hired by the Federal Ministry of Education Nigeria to teach Technical Subjects in Federal Unity Colleges in Nigeria.He completed a PHD Doctoral study at the University of KwaZulu- Natal. His other research interests include family entrepreneurship, technology management, strategic management, resource management and sustainable development. He is very passionate about management research and strongly believes that sound management practices holds the key to a sustainable society.

Maria Antonietta Impedovo, Ph.D., is Associate Professor at ADEF Laboratory, Aix-Marseille University, France. She teaches at School of Education at Aix-Marseille University, France. Her main research interests are collaborative learning; identity; and sociocultural psychology.

Giulia Mantovani graduated in 2017 in Political Science and International Relations at the University of Pavia (Italy). Then, she attended a master's degree in International and Diplomatic Sciences at the University of Bologna (Italy) where she graduated with a thesis in "Intelligence and Political Decision Making".

Aldo Montanari is a researcher skilled in intelligence and investments with regularly upgraded security and real estate competences. Montanari attended the Italian Military Academy, the Infantry School and held different small units commanding roles. Montanari graduated from Turin University with a master's degree in Military Strategic Studies and he graduated from Bologna University with a master's degree in International Relations and Diplomatic Affairs. He is part of the Power, Information and Intelligence in International Policy board of Bologna University. Specialties: Intel, Real Estate, PR, GIS, Diving, AFF, First Aid.

Vannie Naidoo is an Associate Professor academic in the School of Management, Information Technology and Governance at University of KwaZulu-Natal, South Africa. She teachers both undergrad and post graduate students in Management Research Methodology and Entrepreneurship. Prof.Vannie Naidoo's focus areas in research are in the fields of business, marketing, education, ICT's, SMME's and strategy. She is a seasoned researcher who has presented papers at numerous international and local conferences. In November 2017 she was Keynote speaker at the ETAR conference held in Bali. Dr Naidoo has published various international journal articles and book chapter on various areas of business, ethics, education, marketing and workplace dynamics.

Maria Luisa Nardi is a Historian of Political and Economic Institutions. She performed as a high school teacher for more than 30 years, and during this time she was awarded for innovation and experimentation in teaching methods and forefront technology. She conducted research in Economic History, starting from Greek and Roman times to the current context. Her work offers valuable empirical and theoretical insights into the development of market-supporting institutions, their long-term consequences, and their relationship to state-building. Her historical review discusses recent advances in understanding the precise Mechanisms responsible for the persistent effects of institutions on economic development.

J. Tom Riley holds a degree in Electrical Engineering and another one in Management Engineering, Tom holds 40 years' experience in aerospace at NASA (the Goddard Space Flight Center in Maryland - USA). He worked on teams of engineers and scientists that build and flew scientific instruments in space. I worked on many projects including: Mercury Laser Altimeter (MLA); SeaWiFS an ocean color satellite; several TOMS missions monitoring the Earth's ozone, SBUV in the Shuttle bay for multiple flights, and two Hubble repair missions. Now retired, he proposed a grassroots space concept (the Big Moon Dig) which has now morphed into tales writing focused on Our Climate Crisis. He chose to mix scientific contents with some of his scientific tales (science fiction), describing the relationship among technology, safety, security, and topical political issues.

Thea Van der Westhuizen is a multi-award-winning academic professional, acting as Deputy Convener for Department of Higher Education and Training in South Africa to develop academic entrepreneurship in South-Africa. Founder of SHAPE (Shifting Hope, Activating Potential Entrepreneurship) which was awarded as Best Youth Development Organization in KZN. She acts as International Director of Paddle for the Planet. Dr van der Westhuizen has over 20 years of international work experience in the corporate and academic sectors. High profile collaborations with Ambassadors, Municipality Managers, Sheikhs as well as CEOs of multi-national companies all forms part of her portfolio. She resides in the School of Management information Technology and Governance, Discipline of Management and Entrepreneurship at the University of KwaZulu-Natal, South Africa.

Index

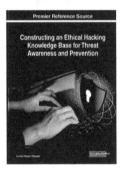

Ensure Quality Research is Introduced to the Academic Community

Become an IGI Global Reviewer for Authored Book Projects

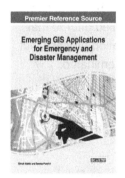
Premier Reference Source

Emerging GIS Applications for Emergency and Disaster Management

Premier Reference Source

Managerial Strategies and Green Solutions for Project Sustainability

Premier Reference Source

Comparative Approaches to Using R and Python for Statistical Data Analysis

Premier Reference Source

Solutions for High-Touch Communications in a High-Tech World

The overall success of an authored book project is dependent on quality and timely reviews.

In this competitive age of scholarly publishing, constructive and timely feedback significantly expedites the turnaround time of manuscripts from submission to acceptance, allowing the publication and discovery of forward-thinking research at a much more expeditious rate. Several IGI Global authored book projects are currently seeking highly-qualified experts in the field to fill vacancies on their respective editorial review boards:

Applications and Inquiries may be sent to:
development@igi-global.com

Applicants must have a doctorate (or an equivalent degree) as well as publishing and reviewing experience. Reviewers are asked to complete the open-ended evaluation questions with as much detail as possible in a timely, collegial, and constructive manner. All reviewers' tenures run for one-year terms on the editorial review boards and are expected to complete at least three reviews per term. Upon successful completion of this term, reviewers can be considered for an additional term.

If you have a colleague that may be interested in this opportunity, we encourage you to share this information with them.